POVERTY IN NEW YORK, 1783-1825

THE URBAN LIFE IN AMERICA SERIES

RICHARD C. WADE, GENERAL EDITOR

STANLEY BUDER
PULLMAN: An Experiment in Industrial Order
and Community Planning, 1880–1930

ALLEN F. DAVIS
SPEARHEADS FOR REFORM: The Social Settlements
and the Progressive Movement, 1890–1914

LYLE W. DORSETT
THE PENDERGAST MACHINE

JOSEPH M. HAWES
SOCIETY AGAINST ITS CHILDREN: Juvenile Delinquency in
Nineteenth-Century America

MELVIN G. HOLLI
REFORM IN DETROIT: Hazen S. Pingree and Urban Politics

KENNETH T. JACKSON
THE KU KLUX KLAN IN THE CITY, 1915–1930

ZANE L. MILLER
BOSS COX'S CINCINNATI: Urban Politics in the Progressive Era

JAMES F. RICHARDSON
THE NEW YORK POLICE: Colonial Times to 1901

PETER SCHMITT
BACK TO NATURE: The Arcadian Myth in Urban America

HUMBERT S. NELLI
ITALIANS IN CHICAGO, 1890–1930: A Study in Ethnic Mobility

RAYMOND A. MOHL
POVERTY IN NEW YORK, 1783–1825

POVERTY IN NEW YORK
1783-1825

RAYMOND A. MOHL

NEW YORK
OXFORD UNIVERSITY PRESS
1971

To Penny, Raymond, and Nancy

Foreword

In the 1960's the American people suddenly "discovered" poverty. Perhaps that national awareness began in the spring of 1960 when John F. Kennedy took his campaign for the presidency into West Virginia. Following the candidate's schedule, the television cameras began to scan the faces and shacks of the poor; Kennedy started to speak of "millions" of people going to bed hungry every night. A little later Michael Harrington provided a national framework for the problem in *The Other America*. Soon a nation described as the "affluent society" in the 1950's declared a "war on poverty." Public and private agencies quickly devised new programs, and Congress appropriated unprecedented funds for the effort. Yet after ten years, the question was still unsolved. Although a million moved out of poverty each year, the residual numbers of poor remained unacceptably high.

American opinion was unprepared for the nature and extent of modern poverty. The old thought that the problem had been ended with the New Deal; the young knew only prosperity and plenty. The initial response was disbelief and even shame. When the problem failed to yield to new programs and more money, serious public leaders started to search for the deeper causes of poverty and the source of this intractability. The result has been a spate of books dealing with the present poor and usually designed to find a way out of the crisis.

In this examination of contemporary poverty historians have been increasingly active. As early as 1956 Robert Bremner provided a broad framework in *From the Depths,* significantly subtitled *The Discovery of Poverty in the United States.* Others probed the development of private philanthropy and the growth of public welfare. Yet most of the emphasis remained on the nineteenth and especially twentieth centuries. This volume establishes the centrality of the question at an even earlier period; indeed, it demonstrates that poverty is co-terminus with American history.

Raymond Mohl's study focuses on New York City in the half-century before 1830. It was a crucial moment in the history of the Empire City, the time when it surpassed Philadelphia in population, when it reached out with the Erie Canal to corral the growing market of the West, and when it secured its unique foothold in the Atlantic trade. This expansion, however, was sporadic rather than continuous; the upward curve was pocked with depressions, wars, embargoes, boycotts, and significant seasonal variations. Every decade knew want as well as plenty, unemployment as well as prosperity.

"How many are there this day and this evening," the editor of the *New-York Evening Post* asked wearily in 1805, "to be found sitting disconsolate—shivering—naked—hungry—steeped in tears —or nearly frantic at their situations?" Nor was this a special lament. Mr. Mohl's extensive research into private sources and public records indicates that for fifty years sensitive citizens and official bodies worried about the increasing incidence of poverty. No doubt rural distress was at least as widespread, but the large (in nineteenth-century terms) urban concentrations made the problem more visible, the impact on the successful more telling. So long as the poor were spread indifferently across the landscape, the fact was resolved by the historic fatalism of "the poor are always with us." But when seen in numbers on the streets, huddled in tenements near the well-to-do, as crowding jails and almshouses, the poor seemed more disturbing.

It is the conjunction of urbanization and poverty which gives this book added importance. Mr. Mohl describes the connection between this early "urban explosion" and the fallout of joblessness, want, misery, and despair of a large number of early New Yorkers. His discussion begins with the revolutionary period when the city was small, compact, and manageable. It ends after the building of the Erie Canal when newcomers, both from the countryside and Europe, had swollen the population, increased densities, and created a wide range of new problems.

Indeed, the modern reader will find this a very contemporary volume. The problem of poverty was at once intolerable for a free republic but also intractable when approached. Early American society responded by creating both private and public programs. Awareness of widespread want brought almost a hundred citizens associations into being. Public bodies, too, began to seek for proper institutional arrangements to meet the growing numbers of poor. And both, though acting from genuine concern and benevolence, also worried about the consequences to the social fabric if nothing at all were done.

Moderns will also find much of the vocabulary and speculation familiar. Were people poor because of their own inadequacies or because the social system would find no useful place for them? Did the primitive welfare system produce a debilitating dependency rather than encourage self-help and independence? Could poverty be explained by intemperance (read large families, narcotics, etc.) and cured by education? Was not, after all, the long-range solution to be found in self-sufficient citizens adequately educated by the State and provided with a useful job or trade? Mr. Mohl's study adds a new dimension to our understanding of the past while it informs us about an urgent and persistent problem of our time.

RICHARD C. WADE

GENERAL EDITOR

URBAN LIFE IN AMERICA SERIES

Chicago, Ill.
November 1970

Preface

Americans view entrenched economic dependency in urban ghettoes as a relatively new development. For most, the "welfare mess" stems from the recent past. One well-established, well-revered myth holds that America throughout its history has been a land of opportunity, a place where hard-working, industrious men and women—even those without skills—could labor, earn, save, and get ahead. Reality for most Americans, past and present, has been something far different, far less visionary. Most immigrants came poor and stayed poor, although measurable mobility might be achieved over generations. Given such circumstances, economic dependency early became a serious problem, especially in urban centers with relatively large numbers of unskilled, unemployed workers and immigrants. Thus state and city governments, borrowing largely from the English experience, passed poor laws and enacted welfare programs. Urban relief, and the private charity which accompanied it, stemmed partially from humanitarian motives, but it often seemed designed to achieve social control and maintain urban order as well.

This book is a case study in the social-welfare history of a single, but important, city during a period of economic and social transition. It argues that concern for economic security antedates the twentieth century, that poverty and welfare are old problems. The book is primarily an effort to illuminate an unexplored area of urban development in early America, but it is also intended to add a measure of badly needed perspective to current attempts to grapple with poverty. Modern welfare approaches, to be effective, must be based upon sound historical understanding.

This study began as a doctoral dissertation in the history department at New York University. I am deeply indebted to Professor Bayrd Still, who guided that original effort, for many helpful suggestions, kind but firm criticisms, and continual inspiration. I am also grateful to two former colleagues, Frank Merli of Queens College and David Fahey of Miami University, for critical readings of portions of earlier drafts. Another former colleague, Neil Betten of Florida State University, read the entire manuscript and improved it in many ways. At every stage the research was eased by the generous aid of librarians and manuscript curators at the New-York Historical Society, the New York Public Library, the New York City Municipal Archives and Records Center, the New York University Library, the Columbia University Library, the American Bible Society, the New York City Mission Society, the General Society of Mechanics and Tradesmen, the Haviland Records Room of the Society of Friends, and the Indiana University libraries at Gary and Bloomington. I especially appreciate the assistance of Tom Dunnings and Arthur Breton of the New-York Historical Society. I am grateful for the financial aid of the New York University Graduate School, the New York State Education Department, the Samuel S. Fels Fund, the Indiana University Foundation, and the American Philosophical Society. Some chapters are revisions of articles published in *New York History*, the *New-York Historical Society Quarterly*, *Labor History*, and the *Journal of American History*, and appear here by permission of the editors. I would also like to thank my typists, Mrs. Rosalie Zak, who prepared early drafts with good cheer, and Mrs. Virginia

Burnham, who typed the final manuscript with care and compe-
tence. My wife, Penny, aided, encouraged, and sustained this
project from its beginnings, improved style and meaning, and put
up with the unusual hours of a working historian.

R.A.M.

Boca Raton, Fla.
November 1970

Contents

Tables

Maps

I

THE URBAN ENVIRONMENT

1

New York in Transition

When New Yorkers celebrated the completion of the Erie Canal in 1825, they did so in ebullient and grandiose style. The new waterway which linked the metropolis with a vast western hinterland had opened on October 26 when the canal-boat *Seneca Chief* left Buffalo for New York with a group of passengers headed by Governor De Witt Clinton. The governor and his party arrived in New York Bay on November 4 to the sound of cannons and church bells, while city officials prepared a majestic reception. With distinguished guests looking on and a grand fleet of steamboats and sailing vessels standing by, Governor Clinton symbolically emptied a keg of Lake Erie water into the Atlantic, a testament to man's triumph over nature. Following the harbor ceremonies, a long parade wound through the narrow, crooked streets of lower Manhattan from the Battery to City Hall. Banners, flags, uniforms, and brightly painted wagons and carriages added to the excitement and gaiety of the occasion, as thousands of New Yorkers turned out to cheer the marchers. Illuminated transparencies and murals depicting canal scenes and historical allegories decorated the façades of theaters, museums, and public buildings. A fireworks display lit up the city during the evening and entertained some ten thousand spectators in City Hall Park. A sumptuous banquet and a magnificent ball attended by leading citizens of city and state brought the canal festivities to an end three days later.[1]

The completion of the Erie route and the energetic character of the canal celebration which followed typified the dynamism of New York City in transition. Between the Revolution and the mid-1820's the Hudson River port passed beyond the preindustrial period. The pattern and problems of colonial urbanism remained and intensified, yet the city stood poised at the threshold of the industrial era. Commerce continued to sustain economic development, but shifts in occupation and the social organization of work revealed the growing importance of manufacturing. The traditional, orderly society of the eighteenth century wavered under the combined impact of immigration, industrial beginnings, and unplanned city growth. The sense of community which characterized the colonial city fell before the pressure of these new forces of social and economic change. Established institutions of family and faction, church and government no longer served the purposes of community integration and social control. Urban chaos and social confusion resulted, while a new generation of civic, commercial, and political leaders struggled to impose order upon their city. The opening of the Erie Canal reflected a degree of urban accomplishment; it indicated that New York's mercantile community had come to terms with the transitional city.

Throughout the transition period, commerce provided the measure of urban importance. Tory-patriot dissension had split the business community during the Revolution, and fire had ravaged much of the commercial section of the city. Restrictions on American trade in the British West Indies and lack of capital and credit slowed economic development in the Confederation period. But after a few years of post-Revolutionary readjustment, New York merchants quickly displayed the aggressiveness and initiative which typified the city's commercial activity for the next half-century. They rebuilt the business district, healed internal squabbles, and uniformly supported the Constitution; they enlarged harbor facilities, reclaimed acres of waterfront with a landfill program, and built new docks, wharves, and warehouses; and they developed new and profitable trade routes to England, Europe, and the non-British West Indies. By 1797 New York City had asserted commercial primacy and surpassed rival Philadelphia in both imports and exports.[2]

With a series of imaginative mercantile innovations in the early nineteenth century, particularly in the years following the War of 1812, New York City firmly secured its place as the nation's metropolis. Specialization of business functions and the rise of banking and insurance companies facilitated commercial operations. To their fine natural harbor New Yorkers added an economically efficient auction system and the first scheduled shipping service to Europe. These new techniques attracted European goods, eliminated commercial uncertainties, and permitted New York domination of the overseas trade. The city's merchants, bankers, and insurance brokers boldly won control of disposal of southern cotton and thus came to monopolize the coastal carrying trade as well. The Erie Canal successfully tapped the produce of populous upstate New York and the rising Middle West, solidified New York's commercial position, and hastened the transition to manufacturing. By 1825 New York City had become "the grand emporium of the Western world."[3]

Commercial prosperity stimulated manufacturing. Throughout the pre-canal period New York City functioned as an economic "hinge," transshipping European goods to the interior and, in turn, drawing the produce of the American hinterland for the foreign trade. Entrepreneurs capitalized on the entrepôt position of the New York port by processing both import and export commodities. The city early became an important center for flour milling, sugar refining, liquor distilling and brewing, and leather and tobacco processing. Other kinds of manufacturing supplemented the mercantile base, especially shipbuilding and numbers of shops producing barrels, sails, rope, ship fittings, and ship provisions. The domestic market supported the ready-made clothing industry, boot and shoe factories, and printing and publishing establishments.

By the mid-twenties the factory organization of work had replaced much household manufacturing and handicraft industry, a trend accompanied by occupational specialization, division of labor, and a strong but short-lived trade union movement. Although commerce remained the basis of New York prosperity, advances in manufacturing brought money into the economy, widened the domestic market, and promoted urban growth.[4]

The city grew at a tremendous pace during the four decades following the Revolution. When British forces evacuated New York in November 1783, the influx of Americans from the surrounding countryside brought the population to only about 12,000, little more than half the prewar level. However, new commercial prosperity stimulated an increase to 33,131 by 1790. Between 1790 and 1800 the number of New Yorkers rose by more than 80 per cent to 60,515, while the following ten-year period witnessed an increase of almost 60 per cent to 96,373. Although population growth slowed considerably during the decade after 1810 because of war and depression, the rate picked up again during the 1820's. In 1825, according to a state census, some 166,086 people resided in New York City. The percentage of population increase for the whole period from 1790 to 1830 amounted to 548.9 per cent, a growth rate unequaled by any other American city during the same years.[5]

The physical growth of the city matched its population increase. Patriots returned to a city devastated by eight years of war and occupation. Major fires in 1776 and 1778 destroyed at least a quarter of the settled parts of town. The breakdown of municipal controls under British rule left streets, houses, public buildings, and city services in total disarray. The energy which New Yorkers expended in mercantile and manufacturing enterprises was applied to new urban construction as well. Brick and wood houses and shops quickly replaced the fire-scarred ruins of the business district, while other commercial and residential buildings went up on the outskirts of town and along the Hudson River shore and the East River waterfront. When the municipal government selected a site in 1803 for a new city hall, they picked a spot at the northern edge of the city—the triangular-shaped park formed by the intersection of Broadway, Chambers Street, and Chatham Street. So far from the city's center was the new building that municipal officials authorized red sandstone for the rear part of the structure (in contrast to the white marble of front and sides), "inasmuch as it was not likely to attract much notice." Yet, by 1825, when dense settlement extended as far north as 14th Street, City Hall lay at the heart of the city.[6]

The northward march of the physical city reflected the process of urbanization in general. Native Americans and European travelers alike consistently noted the remarkable pace of urban life in New York. Numbers of visitors commented on the "forest of masts," the intensity of mercantile activity along the waterfront, crowded streets and wharves, and constant movement and noise. Visiting the city in 1811, President Timothy Dwight of Yale University reported "bustle in the streets; the perpetual activity of the carts; the noise and hurry at the docks . . . ; the sound of saws, axes, and hammers, at the shipyards; the continually repeated views of the numerous buildings, rising in almost every part," and "the vast number of vessels and boats continually plying on the bay and the rivers." Other travelers, impressed by the "air of industry and animation," termed the city's growth "beyond all calculation." One measure of urban progress, house construction, usually excited comment as well. Bostonian Jonathan Mason reported with amazement in 1804 that seven hundred houses had been built during the previous year; Governor De Witt Clinton, in an 1824 letter to John Jacob Astor, boasted of more than three thousand new buildings in a twelve-month span. "I myself am astonished," wrote resident merchant and civic leader John Pintard in 1826, "& this city is the wonder of every stranger."[7]

The city grew, but municipal services did not expand correspondingly. The city charter of 1731, granted by the provincial assembly and confirmed in the state constitution of 1777, entrusted governmental powers to the municipal corporation (mayor and aldermen) and established the framework for urban services. In colonial years the corporation of the city of New York assumed

NEW YORK CITY IN 1789

From James G. Wilson, *The Memorial History of the City of New-York* (New York, 1893), courtesy of Florida Atlantic University.

some important administrative functions. Fire and police protection, public wells and pumps, poor relief, building codes, public health regulations, administration of justice, construction and repair of streets and harbor facilities—all these and more occupied the attention of early city fathers. Drawing from British precedent, the municipal corporation adopted mercantilistic regulatory policies and displayed paternalistic concern for the welfare of town dwellers. The prosperity of the colonial city depended on orderly economic activity; thus the medieval doctrine of the "just price" guided municipal supervision of the market place. A small army of public officials—commissioners, superintendents, clerks, weighers, gaugers, measurers, inspectors—supervised the execution and administration of local ordinances. As the colonial period progressed, urban problems and demands were met with an increasing degree of sophistication by civic leaders. As Carl Bridenbaugh showed in his massive studies of colonial urbanism, New York and other seaport towns had developed by the time of the Revolution a distinct social consciousness and a deep sense of civic responsibility.[8]

The rapid physical expansion of the city and the high rate of population increase in post-Revolutionary years did impose a number of new administrative burdens upon a municipal government ill-prepared and indisposed to accept additional responsibilities. The essentially negative controls and restrictive regulatory policies of the colonial era no longer sufficed in the larger, more diverse city of the early nineteenth century. The city corporation which served the compact, stable community of the eighteenth century no longer met the needs of many thousands of immigrant and native newcomers spread over a more expansive urban community. The city required positive government, but mayors and aldermen failed to provide it. As the sense of community broke down, so also did municipal government.

Municipal lapses contributed to the disorder of the transitional city. For example, the city corporation failed to deal effectively with the problem of street sanitation and refuse disposal. In the colonial town local ordinances required property owners to keep adjacent streets clean and free of garbage and sewage. After the

Revolution public scavengers collected refuse piled in the streets by householders and dumped it in the rivers. But judging by numerous complaints in the newspapers and at common council meetings, the municipality rarely enforced its regulations and scavengers worked irregularly.

As the metropolis expanded rapidly in size and population, these unsanitary conditions worsened. By the nineteenth century foreign travelers and native New Yorkers alike complained about filthy, stinking streets filled with garbage, the excrement of man and beast, and pools of stagnant, scum-covered water. Shoppers in the public markets passed among carts of putrid vegetables and week-old fish and stepped carefully around "the heads of sheep, lambs, &c. the hoofs of Cattle, blood, and offals strewed in the gutters, and sometimes on the pavement dead dogs, cats, rats and hogs." Numerous stables, shambles, tanneries, and overflowing backyard privies gave off a "noisome effluvia" and foul-smelling "miasmas." Offensive odors permeated the waterfront as well, for the tides sloshed sewage, the carcasses of slaughtered cattle, and all manner of refuse among the slips and quays. By the 1830's New York diarist George Templeton Strong could write that New York had become "one huge pigstye." Indeed, in the absence of real public responsibility, roving pigs rivaled the scavengers in efficiency— a sure indication, wrote British traveler William Dalton, of "something wrong" with municipal administration.[9]

The unsanitary conditions intensified other municipal problems. Water supply, never quite adequate to begin with, became increasingly foul and polluted as sewage seeped into public and private wells. Similarly, the Collect, a fresh water pond just north of the city, became a "shocking hole" filled with garbage and filth. The Manhattan Company, whose legislative petition for a charter to supply the city with "pure and wholesome water" was supported by the common council in 1799, devoted most of its energies to banking and politics. Not until 1842 was a public water supply system completed, another indication of municipal failure during the transition to the industrial city.[10]

Public health also needed more attention. Weak enforcement

generally compromised the effectiveness of city ordinances and health regulations. Municipal officials, particularly the city inspector, lacked sufficient authority to preserve a healthy city. Moderate reforms usually came only after an epidemic or some other crisis generated public demand, but even these were poorly implemented. The long-standing controversy between the sanitationists (those who considered disease a result of the dirt and filth of the city) and the advocates of quarantine (those who believed disease was imported) produced inadequate compromise solutions. Shortsighted municipal policies, inefficient and occasionally dishonest administration, bickering among medical officers, and partisan priorities at public expense resulted in ineffective municipal health measures. Not surprisingly, epidemics of yellow fever and cholera periodically ravaged the city.[11]

In 1955 historian and social scientist R. Richard Wohl suggested that American cities have passed through a continuous series of "cycles of obsolescence." In other words, urban growth in the United States has been characterized, and urban institutions shaped, by a haphazard succession of expedients and temporary solutions to pressing municipal problems. Clearly, New York City experienced this kind of growth—unplanned, uncontrolled, unhealthy—in the early nineteenth century.[12]

New York City, then, reflected the achievements and the failures of urban America in the transition to an industrialized society. The new economic and social forces unleashed by altered work patterns, population accretions from foreign and native migration, and urban expansion destroyed the well-ordered community of the eighteenth-century town. The closely knit social fabric of the preindustrial city became torn and tattered; as class barriers grew, group tensions heightened and occasionally boiled over in mob riots and street violence. Municipal authority broke down at a time when only more positive government could cope with rising urban social problems. Only the merchant group survived the transition intact. Yet with the exception of a small group of civic leaders, the mercantile community—aggressive, creative, innovative—literally abandoned the city in the quest for private profit. They

successfully surmounted problems related to commerce, manufacturing, and transportation but ignored until too late the human
needs of the city. In this new urban environment poverty grew
alongside private wealth. Indeed, the prevalence of squalid poverty, even destitution and dependency, for the many, as opposed
to economic prosperity for the few, symbolized perhaps better
than did the Erie Canal celebration the character of New York
City's passage to industrial urbanism.

2

Poverty in the Urban Community

Early America often has been described as a land of opportunity, an open and mobile society composed largely of the "middling sort." Land was cheap, labor scarce, and wages high, the argument runs. The nation had no beggars, no poor, not even a genuine lower class. Unlimited economic opportunity created political democracy, and both together made America the "ideal spot for the common man." Until recently these views have dominated American historical writing. Historians remarked on poverty in early America only to deny that it existed, or to assert it to be an exception rather than the rule.[1]

This middle-class interpretation of early American social structure depended on impressionistic evidence provided by the writings of selected European travelers and native boosters. Often-quoted J. P. Brissot de Warville noted in 1788 that Americans were "not sufficiently rich to give themselves up to those debaucheries which kill so many in Europe; and there are no poor, provisions being so cheap." Writing at the beginning of the nineteenth century, Felix de Beaujour asserted that "very few Americans are seen begging, and every one who is capable of working for his livelihood would be ashamed to live at the expense of another."

Charles W. Janson, British author of *The Stranger in America,* saw few beggars in the United States in 1805; "there is indeed," Janson wrote, "no pretext for begging in a country where every individual can find employment." In 1813 Hezekiah Niles, the editor of *Niles' Weekly Register,* estimated the number of beggars in the United States at less than one thousand and claimed that "a person may travel for six months through this country without meeting a regular beggar." Similarly, English traveler James Boardman remarked upon "the high character and appearance" of the working classes in New York City in the late 1820's, and observed a "total absence not only of mendicants in rags and filth, but likewise of the class we designate mob or rabble." [2]

Even the writings of those who admitted the existence of poverty in the United States seemed to buttress the traditional view of American society. For example, British political expatriate William Cobbett endowed American beggars with admirable republican qualities:

> An American beggar, dressed very much like other people, walks up to you as boldly as if his pockets were crammed with money, and, with half a smile, that seems to say, he doubts the propriety of his conduct, very civilly asks you, *if you can HELP him to a quarter of a dollar.* He mostly states the precise sum; and never sinks *below silver.* In short, there is *no begging,* properly so called. There is nothing that resembles English begging even in the most distant degree.

For Cobbett, who sought to promote European emigration, only blacks and improvident foreigners comprised the real poor of New York City; a pauper "who is a white, *native American,* is a great rarity." Such reports lent authority and substance to the image of America as a land of opportunity. [3]

Yet the facts belie the legend. Although many travel accounts provide valuable historical information, many others are notoriously inaccurate, incomplete, or purposely one-sided; some are nothing more than compilations of material plagiarized from earlier writers. Many travelers to New York recorded their impressions of the city after a short stay during which they dined

with notable citizens in elegant homes and made hasty visits to
museums, theaters, churches, public buildings, and taverns on
Broadway and Wall Street. Few visited the lower-class neighborhoods of the city. In describing "a very great collection of miserable temporary buildings" in a growing slum along the East River,
Yale President Dwight noted that "most of them stand aside from
the walks of gentlemen who visit this city." Similarly, the Society
for the Prevention of Pauperism reported in 1820 that "the enterprise, the industry, and the commerce" of the city had cast "a de-
lusive glare" over social realities and concealed the extent of urban poverty.[4]

Despite the optimistic platitudes about America issued by European travelers and home-bred promoters, nineteenth-century cities
like New York began to suffer the social and economic dislocations
traditionally associated with urbanization. New forms of economic complexity and interdependence contributed to depression,
low wages, unemployment, and dependency. The best measures
of the extent of poverty in preindustrial New York City are found
not in travel accounts but in a number of more reliable sources:
state poor laws and restrictive immigration policies; poor relief
statistics and overcrowded municipal welfare institutions; the high
costs of public assistance; the rapid development of a multiplicity
of charitable organizations and mutual-benefit societies; the anti-
poverty campaigns occasionally conducted by city newspapers; and
the preventive measures enacted by government or implemented
by private groups. For municipal officials and city residents, the
reality of poverty in the metropolis could not be hidden.

When British forces evacuated New York on November 25, 1783,
the social and economic disorder of a partially destroyed city con-
fronted returning Americans. Among pressing concerns of the new
municipal government care of the indigent and unemployed assumed a high place. In February 1784 one newspaper reported
almost one thousand families on the relief rolls. Reflecting on "the
want and distress which are so prevalent at this severe Season,"
newly appointed mayor James Duane declined the accustomed
public entertainment and asked instead that aldermen distribute

donations to the poor in their wards. At the request of the common council, several clergymen made charity collections in their churches to ameliorate "the wretched condition not only of the poor but of many Householders." Mayor Duane and his successor, Richard Varick, worried about the overcrowded condition of the almshouse; at the same time, "an idle and profligate Banditti" and other "abandoned Vagrants and Prostitutes" disturbed the peace of the city and committed "shameful Enormities." "Vagrants multiply on our Hands to an amazing Degree," Varick wrote in 1788.[5]

Immigration swelled the almshouse and the poor lists during the 1790's, when an estimated three thousand newcomers poured into New York each year. The commissioners of the almshouse reported in February 1795 that of 622 paupers in the institution, some 276, or 44 per cent, came from immigrant stock. Native New Yorkers singled out the Irish for special criticism, for this group composed a large and identifiable ingredient of the urban poor. That Irish-born paupers numbered 148 out of a total of 770 institutionalized dependents early in 1796 merely confirmed the suspicions and the hostilities of anti-Irish New Yorkers. "We shall be over-run with vagabonds," complained the editor of the New York Minerva in 1797; "we shall have the refuse of all the corrupt parts of society poured in upon our country." Immigration restriction early became a major objective of the city council and municipal welfare authorities.[6]

The crisis of poverty in the city deepened decade by decade. Natural disaster and man-made catastrophe contributed to this disturbing dimension of urban life. A series of yellow fever epidemics hit the metropolis between 1795 and 1805, placing new strains on New York's welfare program. During the epidemic of 1798 the city's health committee supported more than 2,400 destitute citizens; conditions worsened during the serious epidemics of 1803 and 1805. Severe winters produced annual emergencies for the urban poor. During the cold months of 1805 Mayor De Witt Clinton feared for the survival of 10,000 impoverished, indigent New Yorkers and demanded legislative relief appropria-

NEW YORK CITY IN 1808

18

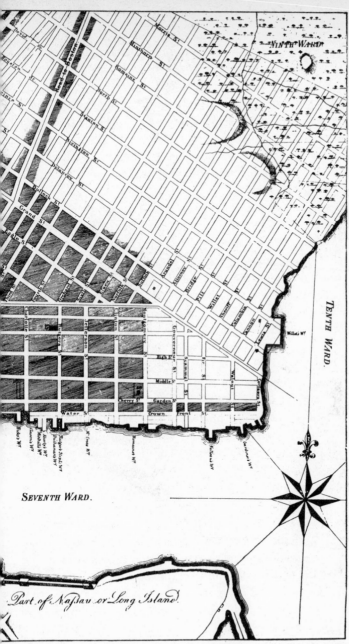

From James G. Wilson, *The Memorial History of the City of New-York* (New York, 1893), courtesy of Florida Atlantic University.

tions. Jefferson's embargo brought new demands for municipal benevolence; the city responded with large distributions of food, fuel, cash, even employment. Similar conditions prevailed at the end of the War of 1812. During twelve months after April 1814, public agencies assisted 19,078 needy persons—more than one-fifth of the city's population. Investigators in February 1817 estimated that at least 15,000 people depended on public and private charity. The magnitude of the problem is perhaps best revealed in municipal appropriations for poor relief, which annually topped all other items in the city budget.[7]

If public relief seemed excessive, the web of private benevolence saturated the city. The humanitarian spirit of the post-Revolutionary period stimulated formation of a bewildering variety of charities and relief organizations for every imaginable purpose: to aid orphans and widows, aged females and young prostitutes, immigrants, imprisoned debtors, and Negroes; to educate poor children in charity schools, Sunday schools, and free schools; to promote religion and morality among the destitute; to supply medical care to the indigent; to create and provide employment for the poor; to reform juvenile delinquents and sinful seamen; to study the causes of poverty and pauperism. Nationality groups, trade and occupational organizations, mutual-benefit societies, and patriotic, political, and fraternal groups also provided assistance to needy members. All told, more than one hundred relief organizations of various kinds had been formed by 1825. In addition, periods of special crisis—depression, disease, war, fire, severe winter—spawned *ad hoc* committees to aid the poor. One such group, during a three-week span in February 1817, distributed 103,312 quarts of soup to indigent New Yorkers. These spontaneous committees supplemented organized charity and public relief in an important way. Urban poverty, therefore, can best be measured by the extent of public assistance and private philanthropy.[8]

The poor composed an observable element in the urban community as well. While middle-class New Yorkers and prosperous merchants resided in fashionable houses on Broadway, Wall Street, and adjacent parts of lower Manhattan, poverty-striken immigrants,

native-born unskilled laborers, and free Negroes festered in the
northern wards of the city, notably the fifth, sixth, seventh, and
tenth. Reports of the superintendent of the almshouse indicate
distribution of the greatest portion of public assistance in these
four wards. By the second decade of the nineteenth century,
major slums had developed in several sections of the city. The
city's burgeoning immigrant population crowded, sometimes two
or three families to a room, into tenements, cellars, and boarding
houses on streets near the waterfront, particularly in the Corlear's
Hook area of the seventh ward. As early as 1798 observers described South Street along the East River as "generally full of poor
and dirty people." Located in the sixth ward on the low, damp
ground just north of City Hall where the Collect Pond once stood,
the "five points" eventually became one of the most notorious
slums of nineteenth-century America. In the fourth ward, Bancker
Street lay at the heart of a large black ghetto spreading between
City Hall and the East River. By the mid-twenties Irish and
German squatters populated "shanty towns" on the outskirts of
the city.[9]

Although material exists which documents the incidence of dependency in New York City and reveals emerging pockets of
poverty, evidence which would help in identifying the poor more
clearly in terms of origin, occupation, and cause of poverty is not
so available. The lower stratum of society in New York City was
characterized by a "floating" population of transients and migrants
which defies exact identification. One observer described the poor
as "constantly on the wing." Many were immigrants passing in or
out of the city; others were native Americans who drifted temporarily to the city from neighboring countryside. Even within the
urban community, the poor moved constantly from place to place.
On three different days in January 1810, for instance, the superintendent of the almshouse listed Ann Haviland, a widow on "outdoor" (home) relief, at three different addresses. Poorhouse
records show that other welfare recipients in New York City moved
regularly too, although not as often, perhaps, as the Widow Haviland.[10]

Other considerations as well make it difficult to categorize those at the bottom of the social and economic scale. The publishers of the city directories, either by choice or by necessity, omitted a large number of people—mainly the poor—from their annual listings of city residents. One account book of cash distributions to the poor for January 1810 listed 295 families or individuals on outdoor relief. Of these, only 43, or about 14 per cent, can be found in the city directory published in July 1810. Under such circumstances, exact identification of the poor is, at best, a tenuous process.[11]

In dealing with the history of the inarticulate one lacks adequate primary sources. Few day laborers, unskilled immigrants, free blacks, or almshouse residents left diaries, letters, and other material comparable to that which records the activities and attitudes of the political and economic leaders of the rising urban community. Thus, much of our knowledge of the poor comes from what others have said or written about them.

Such evidence must be used with caution since contemporary attitudes and prejudices seldom reflected social realities. For example, most nineteenth-century New Yorkers made a distinction between poverty and pauperism. Contemporary doctrines of political economy, largely derived from the writings of such "scientific" liberals as Thomas Malthus, David Ricardo, and Patrick Colquhoun, accepted poverty as the normal condition of the laboring classes. Few employers or reformers expected unskilled workingmen and immigrants to live much above a subsistence level. But pauperism meant dependence on public relief or private charity, an intolerable and unnecessary evil. Most early humanitarians really aimed at eliminating pauperism rather than poverty, which they viewed as a natural human situation.

New Yorkers also differentiated between the "deserving" and the "undeserving" poor. As early as 1736, public officials distinguished between poor persons "who have been ancient Housekeepers and lived in good Reputation and Credit and are reduced by Misfortunes" and "Other Poor who are become so by Vice and Idleness." Civic leaders recognized that for some deserving paupers public assistance provided the only alternative to starvation and death. But they also assumed that most pauperism stemmed from individual shortcomings such as idleness, intemperance, impiety, improvidence, and ignorance. Thus, moralistic humanitarians and public officials often estimated that undeserving paupers comprised as many as seven-eighths or nine-tenths of the city's poor. Few related poverty and pauperism to the social and economic conditions of the urban, industrializing, capitalistic environment.[12]

This harsh moralism on social questions obscured the extent of real poverty in the urban community in the preindustrial period. Despite the numerous handicaps, however, it is possible to gather some relevant information about New York City's lower classes, about the poor people who sought public assistance and private charity.

Helpless and destitute individuals composed a large portion of the city's poor. These included infants and dependent children, the sick poor, the aged, and those with disabilities such as blindness and crippling injuries. Most institutionalized paupers fit into one of these categories. In 1795 the commissioners of the almshouse reported the institution full of blind, lunatic, and aged paupers and many others "subject to Rheumatisms, Ulcers and Palsies and to Fits which impair their Reason and elude all the force of Medicine." The Reverend Ezra Stiles Ely, a Presbyterian clergyman who preached regularly in the almshouse, often described in his diary the "blasted, withered, dying females" and the "putrescent state" of sick paupers eagerly clamoring for salvation; on one occasion in 1812 he noted that "there was so much groaning from bodily pain that I could scarcely think of any thing else." In 1823 a special common council committee found just 46 able-bodied, healthy paupers (37 women and 9 men) among the 851 adult inmates. Other investigatory committees discovered few institutionalized dependents whose need was not real.[13]

Almshouse records reveal many of the reasons for pauperism in New York. Not unusual was the case of John Sullivan, born blind in the poorhouse in 1759 and a resident of the institution until

his death in 1819. The almshouse census of 1813 listed another
blind pauper, Susana Wilson, aged seventy-six, who first entered
the house in 1761. The same census shows that numerous other
blind, crippled, and infirm paupers of the pre-Revolutionary period
remained public pensioners well into the early national period.
Other poorhouse residents included disabled Revolutionary War
veterans admitted to the institution on condition that their government pensions be paid to welfare officials; abandoned infants
and illegitimate children placed with wet nurses in the city and
returned to the house at the age of twelve months; and violent,
emotionally disturbed individuals supported in separate rooms in
the almshouse, in the New York Hospital, and, after 1821, in the
newly constructed Bloomingdale Insane Asylum. Between 1818
and 1826 indigent immigrants consistently numbered about one-
third of the almshouse paupers, another indication of the impact of
immigration on the city's public welfare system. Dependency for
most of the institutionalized poor stemmed from real poverty
and helplessness.[14]

Much more numerous than almshouse paupers, the outdoor
poor consisted of those assisted by public agencies within their
own homes. The belief that small and well-placed donations of
cash and provisions would insure the city against the greater expense of supporting poor families in the almshouse determined
the extent of outdoor relief. Almshouse commissioners and welfare
employees regularly inspected indigent families throughout the
city and distributed firewood, grocery tickets, and cash. During
periods of crisis, the commissioners established relief stations at the
almshouse and elsewhere to service those on burgeoning welfare
rolls.

The influx of indigent immigrants, noticeable in the 1790's but
extremely heavy (averaging more than 7,000 per year) in the
1820's, accounted for a large number of the families on public
assistance. In July 1801 the *New-York Gazette* reported that 900
immigrants had entered the port during a four-week period, with
thousands of others expected shortly. They were "incumbered with
large families," wrote an observer, "without money, and without

health and strength to enable them to earn even the most scanty subsistance." Disease-ridden, lacking food and medicine, and living in hovels in the outerwards, they were *expiring from the want of sustenance.*" A medical report of 1802 pungently described recent arrivals as "vile, offensive, and pestilential"; "literally wallowing in their own filth," they debarked "besmeared and encrusted" with "pukings and purgings" and covered with "a layer of excrementitious grime from head to foot." The wretched and diseased condition of such immigrants dictated municipal assistance immediately after arrival.[15]

A variety of other causes made lower-class people dependent. Many widows with children or wives and families abandoned by husbands and fathers became pauperized. During periods of depression and unemployment men often sought work in other cities and other states, leaving families as municipal burdens. The vicissitudes of maritime employment affected the families of seamen. Other families needed relief when breadwinners suffered illness or disabling injury, received jail terms for debt or crime, and enlisted in army or militia. Remarks made by city welfare officials in a ledger of cash donations to the outdoor poor alluded to some of the reasons for dependency: "husband in prison"; "husband has broke his leg"; "they have a house full of small children"; "husband at sea"; "husband bad fellow"; "sick and distresst"; "her husband has abandoned her and she has broke her arm." [16]

The municipality not only furnished the basic needs of the outdoor poor, but often made special provisions for them as well. The 1786 request of Jacob Abrahams, an aged and sick petitioner, revealed the diversity of demands: "Your Petitioner being a Jew cannot on account of his religious principles eat the victuals served out at the Poor House and humbly begs that some other provision may be made for him." On numerous occasions the commissioners paid travel expenses for paupers or potential public charges who wished to leave the city. Welfare officials usually granted requests of this nature, "being willing," as they said in February 1792, "by Advancing a Smaller sum, to prevent the greater expence, of Supporting them here we know not how long." However, if the

NEW YORK CITY IN 1827

From James Hardie, *Description of the City of New-York* (New York,

1827), courtesy of the New-York Historical Society, New York, New York.

case of Michael Thalamis was typical, one wonders about the extent of municipal savings. In 1811 the common council granted Thalamis, a destitute wanderer from Jerusalem, the sum of $500 for a passage to Calcutta.[17]

If real need characterized most welfare families, the city's charitable associations and mutual-benefit societies confined assistance to cases of unavoidable indigence as well. During the early years of the nineteenth century the French Benevolent Society annually aided 250 to 300 dependent French immigrant families. In 1814 the Female Assistance Society relieved more than 1,500 poor women, while the Association for the Relief of Respectable, Aged, Indigent Females assisted another 150 above the age of sixty. In 1816 the Humane Society supported 1,120 imprisoned debtors. Some 254 widows and 667 children under the age of ten comprised the pension list of the Society for the Relief of Poor Widows in November 1821. During 1824 the City Dispensary treated 7,635 indigent patients and vaccinated 6,080 others. In 1824 the Free School Society provided for the education of 5,209 children from poor families. On January 1, 1826, the Orphan Society maintained 159 children in its asylum. Clearly, helpless dependents formed a substantial portion of New York City's poor.[18]

The working poor composed a second important category of indigent New Yorkers. The city was full of able-bodied men and women with low-paying jobs or without regular employment— urban workers, one observer wrote, "whose servile employments are necessary in furnishing the opulent with the conveniences and luxuries of life." Such laborers included indentured servants, free blacks, apprentices, seamstresses, washwomen, and domestic workers. Similarly, seamen worked only sporadically. The largest group consisted of unskilled common laborers—cartmen, scavengers, chimney sweeps, wood cutters, stevedores, and dock workers— men and boys who sought new jobs each day. Others dug foundations in summer and shoveled snow in winter. The steadily increasing flow of immigrants to New York City swelled the labor market and depressed the wage level for these unskilled workers.[19]

The irregular nature of employment available to unskilled workers dictated that they would rarely move above subsistence levels. The first annual report of the Society for the Relief of Distressed Debtors in 1788 acknowledged the needs of many urban workers "whose incessant application to labor, will not enable them to subsist themselves, and their families, and at the same time, secure a small provision for their support during a temporary failure of supplies." The Reverend Ezra Ely, who visited the slums as well as the poorhouse, typically found a widow seamstress in 1812 who earned twelve and one-half cents per garment—"the common price of job work"—with which she tried to support herself and ten children. A writer in the *Daily Advertiser* in 1791 noted the plight of "many of our small tradesmen, cartmen, day labourers and others, [who] dwell upon the borders of poverty and live from hand to mouth." The families of such laborers sought relief from public and private agencies in the absence of employment.[20]

The seasonal character of employment for most common laborers accounts for the large increase in relief expenditures during winter months. Most affected by winter weather were day laborers, cartmen, small tradesmen, fishermen, oystermen, and others who worked out of doors. The virtual suspension of commerce and shipping in winter also brought seasonal unemployment to laborers and craftsmen whose livelihood depended on a bustling harbor—dock workers, bargemen, river boatmen, ship carpenters, caulkers, and riggers. Similarly, building tradesmen (masons, carpenters, plasterers, bricklayers) and their laborers remained inactive during cold weather.[21]

Depression and epidemic disrupted employment patterns and forced day laborers onto the relief rolls. During the embargo crisis "thousands of mariners, mechanics, and laborers"—men who had subsisted by daily labor—could be seen "ranging the streets in search of employment, destitute of cloathing, food and a lodging." Similar conditions accompanied the depression years after 1815, when unemployment affected "all the labouring classes." When yellow fever and cholera epidemics devastated the metropolis, all business ceased; wealthy and middle-class residents abandoned the city by the thousands and left laborers and the poor to fend for themselves and succumb to disease.[22]

Those in temporary distress usually received outdoor relief in the form of cash, food, and firewood, but occasionally, as in the embargo crisis, the municipality supplied work relief as well. While most New Yorkers moralized about the poor, several discerning public officials recognized that only steady and profitable employment would permanently improve the condition of poor laborers. In 1803 Mayor Edward Livingston proposed such a plan, envisioning municipal workshops where unskilled men might be trained in useful crafts and trades. Unfortunately, the scheme aroused the ire of the city's skilled mechanics, who feared cheap competition and successfully opposed the mayor's reform.

Similar work-relief plans failed in later years, despite support from leading humanitarians. In 1823 Mayor Stephen Allen explained these failures:

> The remedy which has most often been insisted on as a preventive, is the supplying of the poor with such description of labor as their talents and abilities will permit them to perform. This, if it could be effected, would no doubt tend to reduce the number of applicants for public bounty. But the chief difficulty lies, in furnishing suitable labor for this description of persons, as those who apply for or require assistance, are principally such as have no mechanical profession, and consequently they are unable to perform any thing except the ordinary avocations of a laborer. Employment, therefore, cannot be furnished, particularly during the winter months, when assistance is the most required.

Under such conditions and without facilities for training these unskilled laborers, municipal officials and charity reformers made little progress in improving the condition of poor workingmen.[23]

A third general category of petitioners for public charity consisted of the "undeserving" or "unworthy" poor. Editors and correspondents filled the columns of the city's newspapers with complaints about throngs of beggars, peddlers, prostitutes, intemperate idlers, and others who could give "no correct account of themselves" and lived on the benevolence of the community. As early as 1776 one observer grumbled about numbers of New Yorkers on relief "able to earn their living, and not to be chargeable to the publick. They do little jobs about, which they are paid for, and they buy rum and get drunk." Another complainant suggested in 1798 that public welfare supported "a worthless scum" —"a parcel of drones" who roamed the streets "in nastiness and filth" and preyed upon "the bowels of the commonwealth." [24]

The vagrancy problem of the late eighteenth century continued into the nineteenth. "Humanitas" lamented in the *Commerical Advertiser* in 1809 "that notwithstanding much has been done to meliorate the condition of the poor, a large number of vagrants are suffered to wander about our streets, many of them in a state of drunkenness . . . and in the practice of every vice." In the years after 1810 observers variously estimated that New York City supplied employment to between 1,200 and 7,000 prostitutes, many of whom sought public aid for short periods each year. In 1821 the common council, convinced that "many persons spend the summer season in idleness and the winter in the Alms House," proposed a mandatory work program as a deterrent to public welfare.[25]

Despite local ordinances, vagrants and beggars went from door to door in search of food and alms. If newspaper allegations are any indication, the number of such "thieves in the garb of misery" increased as the nineteenth century progressed. Because of the presumed relationship between vagrancy and crime, a writer in the *Daily Advertiser* in September 1799 urged the magistrates to keep a list of every "suspicious character" in town. Others cautioned that alms-giving only increased the misery of the poor, for too frequently charity supported "the luxury of the bottle." The *Commercial Advertiser* typically complained in 1812 that a Negro beggar, "well known in Broadway," had exacted more than fifty dollars from "the charitable credulity of the Public" in a few days before being arrested by city marshals. One professional beggar, Peter Lial, petitioned the common council in 1815 for a license to practice his trade without interference from the constabulary:

The petition of Peter Lial of the City of New York setting forth
that he has a wife and two children which he is under the
necessity of Supporting by his present practice of asking Charity
of the Public and which he has done for nineteen years—that
he has always conducted himself in a Sober and orderly manner
and therefore begs of your honorable Body that you will so far
grant him the Privilege of continuing the practice that he may
still be enabled to support his family.

The council asked Lial to withdraw his petition.[26]

Observers often complained that indolent and intoxicated parents sent their children to peddle and beg in the streets. Many
such parents kept youngsters from free schools "for the purpose
of peculating upon our citizens in the guise of peddlers and hawkers of soap, brooms, ashes, oysters, &c." Some employed their
"ragged children to beg, & if this be unsuccessful, then to steal."
Numbers of other homeless children wandered the streets, fre-
quented dens of iniquity and vice in the waterfront areas, and became candidates for the almshouse and the bridewell.[27]

Periodically, the city marshals rounded up vagrants, beggars,
and prostitutes for sixty-day terms in bridewell or, for those lacking legal residence, transportation from New York. When Mayor
Clinton ordered the streets scoured of such vagrants in June 1804,
eighty were picked up and "properly disposed of" by the marshals. Almshouse records reveal the difficulty of permanently removing such dependents. Within the space of six months in 1809–
1810, for example, the marshals sent alleged prostitute Betsy
Hancock and her two daughters, aged fourteen and eighteen, to
Connecticut four times. Another woman, Patience Ames, was removed to Philadelphia in June 1809 for the third time. Notations
made by almshouse employees in a "Vessel Book" (a register of
nonresidents transported from the city) often gave reasons for
expulsion: "a Prostitute from Prison"; "an Old Offender"; "a Black
Cripple and Wicked"; "Old and Helpless"; "Sailor from Boston";
"65 Years a Vagrant"; "a Young Saucy Strumpet"; "Traveling persons, who wished to stay here all winter"; "Too well known to give
any Description." However, constant additions to New York's popu-

lation by European immigration and internal migration made enforcement of poor-law residency provisions an impossible task.[28]

Besides beggars and vagrants, the undeserving poor included
farmers and agricultural laborers from neighboring counties, allegedly "too lazy to work for a living in the country," who migrated
to the city each winter to collect relief payments. Some took advantage of lax municipal welfare administration and, without
permission or examination, entered the almshouse to partake of
the city's bounty. "It was allways the case," asserted almshouse
clerk Josiah Shippey, Jr., in 1808; "they will get in and they will
get out, and it is impossible to be otherwise, untill there are better
inclosures, better watches at the gate." Others, such as ferry boat-
man John Armstrong, imposed on the public in a different way.
In 1796 Armstrong's wife and three children entered the almshouse, while he "pretended inability and complained of a lame
leg, which however did not prevent him from following his business . . . [and] spending his money idly." These, then, typified
the undeserving poor, whose visibility and alleged proportions
shaped the humanitarian response to poverty and its urban manifestations.[29]

The idea of early America as a land of opportunity deserves
serious reconsideration, for then, as now, poverty and dependency
accompanied urbanism and urbanization. The conception of history
as the record of the ideas and activities of the articulate, of decision
makers and opinion shapers, has until recently served to mask
social and economic realities, particularly in preindustrial American
cities. The thoughts and attitudes of the inarticulate masses will
by necessity remain largely untold. But certainly the historical
record which recognizes the existence of paupers, day laborers,
and unskilled, unemployed workers—men and women, boys and
girls, blacks and immigrants—will be more nearly correct than the
one which omits them as nonexistent or irrelevant. And certainly
"history from the bottom up" adds a needed measure of accuracy to
our perspective on the past.

Those historians who find widespread economic opportunity,
who see very little poverty, who generalize about an open and

mobile society in preindustrial America have seemingly overlooked a crucial portion of the evidence. If there were no poor,
why the elaborate legislation and administrative machinery for
a problem which did not exist? If there were no poor, how does
one explain heavy relief expenditures and overcrowded almshouses? If none were in need, why the proliferation of private
charity and humanitarian organizations? If economic opportunity
was a reality for all, how does one account for large numbers of
unemployed workers and dependent immigrants on the poor lists,
for the growing slums and ghettos of the city? Certainly the class
of poor people included a much larger group than just those assisted by public and private charity, for many urban workers remained precariously perched on the nether edge of subsistence.
Slaves, free blacks, and indentured servants fall into the same
category. Jackson Turner Main has suggested in his recent study,
The Social Structure of Revolutionary America, that the poor comprised perhaps as much as one-third of the white population of
the north at the end of the eighteenth century. All evidence suggests that poverty intensified in the northern cities as the nineteenth century began. Surely the society of preindustrial America,
and especially the urban ingredient of that society, requires closer
scrutiny before the cliché of America as the land of opportunity
can be accepted at face value.

II

PUBLIC ASSISTANCE

3

English Heritage and Colonial Background

The poverty and indigence which plagued preindustrial New York City did not sprout suddenly at the end of the American Revolution. From its earliest beginnings New York has had a poverty problem of sorts. In a very real sense, all of the first American colonies, and most of the first colonists, began poor and remained so during the hard, early years of settlement. Certainly, the Dutch West India Company colony of New Amsterdam had had little financial success by the time of the English conquest in 1664. Nor did the colony prosper immediately under the Duke of York's proprietorship. As the colonial town grew into a great commercial city—as population increased through European immigration, internal geographical mobility, and natural increment—the number of unskilled laborers, helpless dependents, and "unworthy" paupers increased accordingly. Urbanization made the city a marketplace for goods and services, but the larger the marketplace grew the more interdependent it became, leaving those on the lowest rungs of the economic ladder with few protections against hard times. Strangely, as maritime profits stimulated prosperity, the more complex economy also brought business fluctuations, low

37

wages, and unemployment for those with no skills. As the city grew richer, it also grew poorer.

Nineteenth-century New Yorkers responded to urban poverty in a predictable manner, borrowing from the time-tested, yet not entirely satisfactory, welfare techniques applied in England and colonial America. English poor laws and the tradition of British humanitarianism supplied the New York attack on poverty with much of its rationale and institutional apparatus. In medieval England the Church had assumed almost exclusive responsibility for poor relief. Although guilds and private charities cared for certain kinds of distress, parish and monastery typically answered the needs of the indigent. The earliest English poor laws, enacted in the fourteenth century, when England began to pass from feudalism to a capitalistic wage economy, aimed essentially at regulating labor rather than assisting dependents. The statute of laborers of 1349, generally considered the beginning of Parliamentary involvement in welfare policy, attempted to maintain the stable labor supply which characterized feudal society by fixing maximum wages and requiring that workers remain in their place of residence. The law also prohibited the giving of alms to "sturdy" or "valiant" beggars, a practice which supposedly encouraged the movement of laborers or kept them idle. Over the next two centuries, Parliament passed a number of other prohibitory and restrictive laws, all treating vagrancy and labor supply as two aspects of the same general problem. With the Protestant Reformation, sponsored by Henry VIII in the sixteenth century, and particularly with the resulting dissolution of the monasteries, ecclesiastical poor relief broke down. Thus from Henry to Elizabeth I government gradually assumed positive responsibility for welfare policies formerly administered by the Church.

The great Elizabethan poor law of 1601 put into systematic and comprehensive form the inconsistent and erratic relief legislation of the previous half century. The new law firmly established governmental responsibility for welfare, prescribed local taxation to support paupers, and charged the parish—the unit of local government—with care of the poor. Furthermore, the law distinguished three categories of dependents and proposed institutional provisions for each: the helpless poor—those unable to work because of sickness or age—would be cared for in a poorhouse; the able-bodied unemployed would be given jobs at fixed wages in a workhouse or elsewhere; and idlers, vagabonds, and sturdy beggars—those able but unwilling to work—would be confined in a house of correction, or bridewell. The law also suggested apprenticeship as a method of training poor children in useful trades. These provisions, of course, represented an ideal formulation rarely achieved fully in practice. Overseers of the poor in each parish administered the new legislation with varying degrees of efficiency and responsibility.

The settlement act of 1662 supplemented earlier legislation and completed the English welfare structure which lasted without significant alteration until the nineteenth century. The new amendment emphasized once again the connection between poverty and mobility and sought to reduce the former by preventing the latter. Essentially, the act prohibited parish relief to any but official parish residents—those who had obtained a legal "settlement." Such status might be acquired by birth, land ownership, tax paying, or apprenticeship. Similarly, those who rented a tenement or farm for above £10 per year, lived in the parish without removal for more than one year, or placed bonds against future indigence became legal residents. Moreover, vigorous enforcement procedures made it extremely difficult for migrants to secure the legal settlement necessary for relief. Parish officials maintained the new system by removing nonresidents to their place of legal settlement. Designed to discourage internal migration and guard against excessive local poor rates, the new law had the economic effect of preventing workers in depressed areas from seeking employment elsewhere. Paradoxically, such prohibitions on mobility produced only greater dependency and higher parish taxes. Although British welfare policy retained the general principle of government responsibility for the "worthy" poor, the settlement act imposed a contradictory set of relief rules. Parishes assumed the burden of public assistance, but only those eligible could apply.

Private philanthropy complemented public relief in England and provided, by the eighteenth century, a second cluster of benevolent institutions. Individual donations and private acts of good will had characterized charity in medieval England, and even the ecclesiastical welfare structure depended upon voluntary support. In Tudor and Stuart times legislation and local officials tried to discourage private benevolence on the theory that unrestricted charity promoted idleness and wasted resources that might be expended more efficiently by parish agents. But by the eighteenth century organized charity had become a recognized part of English life. Increasingly, philanthropic associations provided institutional means for the application of British benevolence. Motivated by Puritan piety and humanitarian social concern as well as by mercantilist utilitarianism, philanthropists concentrated on establishing free schools and hospitals for the poor. "Charity schools" sponsored by the Society for Promoting Christian Knowledge sprouted rapidly throughout the British Isles; at the same time, private hospitals, almshouses, dispensaries, and specialized infirmaries found innumerable patrons and subscribers. Others in distress—orphans, debtors, seamen, victims of religious persecution, those excluded from relief under settlement laws—could secure assistance from a variety of charitable organizations. As public assistance became increasingly restrictive after the settlement law of 1662, but as poverty became more "public a phenomenon," England began to experience an age of private benevolence.[1]

Both strands of British assistance policy—public relief and private philanthropy—shaped the American response to poverty. The principles of the English poor laws formed an integral part of the cultural baggage of American settlers, and every English colony imitated the relief structure of the mother country. The associative nature of private charity which characterized eighteenth-century England also found expression in early America. In colonial New York provincial and municipal governments built the Elizabethan poor-law establishment in minuscule, and humanitarians and reformers adopted the institutional arrangements prevalent in

England. Both assistance patterns survived the Revolutionary years and lasted into the nineteenth century.

After the English conquest of New Netherland in 1664, an Elizabethan-inspired poor law replaced, but did not entirely eliminate, the combined civil-ecclesiastical relief administered in the colony by the Dutch Reformed Church. The Duke of York's agents in the new British proprietary, guided by Governor Richard Nicholls, fashioned a comprehensive legal code called the "Duke's Laws." Among other things, the new code divided the New York City area (called Yorkshire) into parishes, designated the selection of eight overseers of the poor and two church wardens in each parish, and stipulated public taxation to support the poor. Provincial legislation of 1683, passed at the meeting of New York's first assembly, extended the principle of local responsibility for the poor throughout the colony, but on a county rather than a parish basis. The law also established legal residence requirements, directed shipmasters to furnish local magistrates with lists of immigrants within twenty-four hours of arrival, and authorized the removal of potential paupers and public charges—that is, newcomers without "Visible Estate, . . . manuall craft or occupacon." Additional legislation in the eighteenth century elaborated or slightly modified these early laws but retained the basic structure.[2]

Although provincial legislation established the framework for poor-law administration, handling the relief problem became the responsibility of town or county officials. Within their jurisdictions, local overseers of the poor determined methods of relief, investigated applicants for assistance, distributed aid to the needy, and enforced the settlement clauses. In New York City the elected aldermen of each ward performed the duties of overseers until 1691, when vestrymen and church wardens assumed such functions. Despite the delegation of authority, the city magistrates (mayor and aldermen) continued to exercise relief powers concurrently.

Most municipal assistance during this early period consisted of outdoor relief. The records of the mayor's court and minutes of the meetings of vestrymen and church wardens reveal that this relief took many forms: money, firewood, food and provisions, shoes and clothing, funeral expenses, and nursing or medical care for the "sick poor" (a physician was maintained as "Doctor of the Poor"). The municipality even supplied funds to finance return trips to Europe or to some other American colony. Church wardens and aldermen also apprenticed poor children as a method of poor relief; occasionally adult paupers, too, were bound out as indentured servants. Local officials required paupers to wear badges of blue or red cloth with the large letters "N:Y" sewn on their clothing, without which no assistance would be granted. Such symbols, designating dependent status, indicated the social stigma attached to early welfare recipients.[3]

By present standards, the number of public charges seems small. According to records of January 1700, when New York's population totaled about five thousand, the permanent poor list of the church wardens numbered thirty-five; by 1725 the list included forty-two adults and numerous children; in 1735, when the city still had less than ten thousand inhabitants, the overseers recorded at least fifty-eight adult paupers and an indeterminate number of children. These records are incomplete, however, because they fail to include grants of temporary assistance always necessary during winter months. Nor do the records indicate ineligible dependents and the large numbers of city residents who received no relief but lived on a subsistence level.[4]

Even in the early eighteenth century, despite the parsimonious character of municipal welfare, poor relief costs were surprisingly high. Occasionally the church wardens dispensed more money in relief than authorities appropriated from municipal taxes. The poor tax for the period November 1697 to July 1698 totaled £250; by 1714 the annual levy for the poor had increased to £438. A complete set of church wardens accounts for the years 1723–1735 reveals average annual relief expenditures of £523. In an era of limited municipal services, the city's welfare program represented positive, although reluctant, governmental responsibility for society's dependents.[5]

Yet welfare appropriations hardly sufficed, and church wardens continuously pleaded with the common council for additional support. In September 1700, for example, they requested supplementary funds because "the Crys of the poor & Impotent for want of Reliefe are Extreamly Grevious." During the winter of 1713 they reported the poor of the city to be "in great Want & a Miserable Condition & must inevitably perish unless some speedy Method be taken for their support." Faced with such pressures, the common council occasionally took action. When the council petitioned the provincial assembly in 1702 for permission to levy additional taxes for the poor "soe often as their shall be Occasion," the assembly complied by raising the ceiling on the city's poor rates. The aldermen frequently borrowed against future tax revenues to maintain the poor-relief program, or sold municipal land to increase relief funds, and occasionally they resorted to general public subscriptions. Fines of various kinds supplied additional financial support. Provincial settlement laws failed to prevent the arrival of pauper immigrants, so the common council adopted more rigid regulations of its own, requiring not only immigrants but visitors and other "strangers" as well to register with the mayor upon entering the city.[6]

The municipal government also provided some institutional care for the poor in this early period. As early as 1696 the common council rented a small house as a hospital for sick paupers; by 1700 it also served as a house of correction "for the punishing of Vagabonds & Idle Persons that are a Nuisance & Common Grievance of the Inhabitants." A committee of aldermen considered the possibility of a general poorhouse in 1714, but without result. In February 1734 the *New-York Gazette* printed the complaint of a citizen about rising poor taxes and the "many Beggarly people daily suffered to wander about the Streets." The only solution to these undesirable conditions, the anonymous correspondent suggested, lay in the construction of public buildings for the helpless poor, for the unemployed, and for "Sloathful . . . disobedient, and Stragling Vagabonds"—the fulfillment, in other words, of the Elizabethan poor-law structure. By the 1730's the need for permanent institutional facilities for the urban poor had become clear.[7]

That governmental officials thought along the same lines is apparent from the new city charter, granted by the assembly in 1731, which authorized a municipal poorhouse. The common council studied the proposal once again and in December 1734 decided to go ahead with the building project. The council's report on the subject described the condition of the poor in the city and revealed an awareness of the social problems created by poverty:

> Whereas the Necessity, Number and Continual Increase of the Poor within this City is very great and Exceeding burthensome to the Inhabitants thereof for want of a Workhouse and House of Correction AND WHEREAS there is not as yet any Provision made for the Relief and setting on Work of Poor Needy Persons and Idle Wandering Vagabonds, Sturdy Beggars and Others, who frequently Committ divers misdemeanors within the Said City, who living Idly and unimployed, become debauched and Instructed in the Practice of Thievery and Debauchery. For Remedy Whereof . . . Resolved that there be forthwith built . . . A good, Strong and Convenient House and Tenement.

The two-story brick structure completed in 1736 received the all-inclusive title of "Poor House, Work House, and House of Correction." [8]

Insufficient funds obviously prevented separate facilities at this early date. But the several compartments or divisions of the institution did suggest some differentiation among the inmates: an infirmary for the sick poor; a cellar for the "unruly and obstinate"; and a workroom for spinning, weaving, and shoemaking "that such Poor as are able to work, may not Eat the Bread of Sloth & Idleness, and be a Burthen to the Publick." Those found "to be Lousey or to have the Itch" were placed in special wards "til perfectly Clean." A large garden laid out around the house supplied employment for some and fresh vegetables for all. Poor children acquired the elements of education and preliminary training in trades to qualify them as apprentices. Unruly slaves or servants could be sent to the house by their masters upon payment of fees for entrance, support, and whipping. An elaborate set of rules adopted by the common council required paupers to attend regular prayer readings, prohibited smoking in bed and begging in the streets, and even set forth the weekly menu for poorhouse residents—an unappetizing diet of bread and cheese, beef broth, and milk or "pease porridge." A keeper appointed by the aldermen at an annual salary of £30 maintained order within the institution, enforced regulations, and set the poor to work. Welfare recipients, whether inside or outside of the poorhouse, who refused to submit to the keeper's orders became ineligible for relief.[9]

The poorhouse rapidly became an important and indispensable public institution. When the facility opened in the spring of 1736, a total of twelve adults and at least seven children found immediate refuge; others soon followed, and by March 1772 the house contained some 425 paupers. Because the building had been designed only for the most extreme cases of indigence and sickness, the church wardens continued to assist large numbers of outdoor poor each year. Expanded and enlarged on several occasions, the almshouse with its threefold function remained the central public welfare agency in New York City throughout the eighteenth century and into the nineteenth.[10]

Despite these institutional facilities, municipal relief seemed insufficient. The problem of poverty became more serious in the four decades between the construction of the poorhouse and the outbreak of the American Revolution. A writer in the *New-York Weekly Journal*, for example, complained in February 1737 about the increasing number of young beggars in the streets and saw a solution in "a more regular Education," which would improve the morals of indigent children and "fit them to serve the Public." Economic depression in 1737 caused a decline in trade and commerce, "whereby the honest and industrious tradesmen [were] reduced to poverty for want of employ." During the winter of 1741 a private subscription raised more than £500 to supplement inadequate public funds. On several different occasions smallpox epidemics brought calls for increased aid for sick dependents.[11]

The demands of war intensified the relief problem in New York.

Military service imposed burdens upon the laboring people of the city, while wartime disruption of colonial trade brought added poverty in its wake. Municipal relief expenditures rose during the French and Indian War, amounting in 1759 to £1,200, considerably above the prewar average. In January 1760 the church wardens made special collections in each ward to supplement tax funds for the poor, and in 1762 the editor of the *Weekly Post-Boy* complained about the growing "Number of Beggers and wandering Poor" in the streets of New York. Postwar depressions had observable results as well. "A Citizen" who described the city in 1749, at the close of King George's War, adopted a pessimistic tone: "We already begin to experience the Effects of idle Hands; some of the Inhabitants have been robbed, others knocked down; many Beggars troubling our doors, and our Poor-House full; our Taxes high, our Provisions dear, and all Trade at a Stand at present. . . ." [12]

Between 1720 and 1775 New York City grew rapidly in population from 7,000 to more than 25,000. To meet the problems created by pauper immigrants, the city fathers passed numerous provincial laws and municipal regulations setting forth requirements for legal residence. Legislation and enforcement, however, are two different things. William Livingston, editor of New York's *Independent Reflector*, criticized municipal officials in 1752 for failing to guard the city against "foreign Invasions of Beggary and Idleness." Under pretext of increasing the industry and productivity of the colony, promoters had imported large numbers of Germans. But the *Independent Reflector* characterized these immigrants as "useless and insignificant Drones"—a group of poverty-stricken beggars and paupers lacking in skills and trades who taxed the benevolence of the community and drained the municipal treasury. On another occasion editor Livingston attacked the transportation of British felons to the colonies on the same grounds.[13]

Urban poverty became especially apparent during the 1760's and, indeed, as one historian has suggested, may have contributed to the growing radicalism of New York's lower classes. Postwar depression, followed by a series of boycotts of British goods, disrupted the city's commerce and produced a decade of crisis for the poor. The newspapers of the period, usually during the winter months, filled their columns with editorials and letters detailing the hardships of unemployed laborers and low-income people. Petitions for benevolence and relief demanded the attention of municipal officials and the community at large. In January 1765 the common council resorted once again to borrowing, for "the distresses of the Poor being at Present so Extremely Great that unless some Expedient Can Be fallen on for their Relief many . . . must unavoidably perish." Throughout the decade and into the 1770's New Yorkers made extra collections of taxes and charity for the poor, and in 1774 the provincial assembly made a half-hearted effort to increase relief funds by authorizing church wardens to tax dogs at the rate of one shilling each. But this additional humanitarian assistance seemed "insufficient for the numerous Objects that Stand in need of it." By February 1771 the poorhouse supported 339 paupers; during the following year the church wardens admitted 372 new public charges. Substantial outdoor relief payments continued simultaneously, amounting to as much as £67 per month. In the years just prior to the Revolution, overall welfare expenditures averaged £5,000 annually.[14]

Growing poor lists and rising relief costs forced New Yorkers to devise new solutions to deal with the welfare problem. The municipal government adopted a partially negative approach, emphasizing reduction of public expenses rather than attacking the causes of dependency. Thus the common council tried to shorten the poor list by renewing efforts to apprentice pauper children and by rounding up vagrants and "Ladies of Pleasure" for transportation from the city. A new provincial poor law of 1773 revamped the settlement clauses and set forth detailed procedures for removing paupers without legal residence. On the positive side the council ordered construction of a bridewell, completed in 1775, to separate vagrants and disorderly "abandoned

Miscreants" from the almshouse poor. In addition to the normal relief program, aldermen occasionally assisted particular distressed groups, such as war refugees or imprisoned debtors.[15]

Private benevolence increasingly supplemented public assistance. If the efforts of the municipal government seemed sadly lacking in purpose and result, the proposals of private individuals and the activities of charitable groups and *ad hoc* organizations were more productive. The movement for home manufactures, for example, represented at the same time an attack on poverty. Reacting in 1764 to declining trade, unemployment, high prices, scarcity of specie, restrictions on paper money, and new commercial regulations such as the Sugar Act, New York merchants formed a Society for the Promotion of Arts, Agriculture, and Economy. The society encouraged domestic industries and farm products with the promise of premiums, bounties, and prizes. It established a linen factory which employed more than three hundred indigent workers for eighteen months during 1766 and 1767. In addition, the organization founded a trade school for pauper children, lent spinning wheels to poor women, and gave cash premiums to the ten female workers who produced the most linen yarn in 1765. With the passage of the Townshend Acts in 1767, the activities of this society were supplemented by a special committee of citizens, appointed "to consider of the Expediency of entering into Measures to encourage Industry and Frugality, and employ the Poor." Similarly, New York's radical Committee of One Hundred selected a subcommittee in 1775 to collect charitable donations and find work for indigent and unemployed laborers, for which purpose they established a company called the "New York Society for employing the Industrious Poor, and Promoting Manufactory." [16]

Numerous other suggestions addressed themselves to the plight of New York City's poor, and while few produced results, all are indicative of urban poverty. Schemes for employment abounded: ideas for putting idle craftsmen to work; plans to send inactive seamen and vessels to the Greenland whale fisheries; proposals for manufacturing silk, paper, wool, nails, and other products. One commentator in 1768 recommended the establishment of a bank and loan office to ease the hardships of "infectious" poverty. Others made a determined attack on the theater as an obstacle to charity, for "the money thrown away in one night at a play" would support many poor families in "tolerable comfort" during a long and severe winter. Some letter writers, such as "Benevolence" in the *Weekly Post-Boy,* questioned the efficacy of the acquisitive economic system: "How often have our Streets been covered with Thousands of Barrels of Flour for Trade, while our near Neighbors can hardly procure enough to make a Dumplin to satisfy Hunger? Whether this is as it ought to be, I leave to any indifferent Person to judge." Another observer, perhaps viewing poverty and distress in the city more pessimistically, asserted the only remedy to be "that old-fashioned but prevailing weapon, Prayer." [17]

Religious benevolence maintained a variety of programs for the poor. Early in the century the Society for the Propagation of the Gospel in Foreign Parts established charity schools in New York City for Indian, Negro, and poor white children. Anglicans used annual church collections to support a charity school of their own. Other churches, notably the Presbyterian, Dutch Reformed, and French Huguenot, raised relief funds for the poor of their congregations and sponsored charity sermons for imprisoned debtors and similarly dependent groups. As the eighteenth century progressed, Quakers turned from "in-group" charity to more general humanitarian objectives. In 1773 a group of pious New Yorkers formed an American Society for Promoting Religious Knowledge among the Poor. Undoubtedly the religious ferment of the Great Awakening stirred social consciousness and promoted benevolence. George Whitefield himself appeared in the city in 1754 to support worthy causes.[18]

Private charity supplemented the relief activities of municipal government, *ad hoc* committee, and organized religion. Mutual-benefit societies and immigrant-aid associations cared for sick or distressed members and their families as well as newly arrived countrymen. The earliest of these groups, the Scots Charitable Society founded in 1744, went beyond mere relief by employing poor female Scots to spin cotton, linen, and wool. Occupational groups also formed for mutual relief, a trend especially apparent in the 1760's when organizations such as the Society of House Carpenters (1767) and the Marine Society (1769) appeared. In imitation of neighboring Philadelphia, New Yorkers, led by Dr. Samuel Bard and assisted by an annual subsidy from the assembly, founded the New York Hospital in 1771 to relieve "Pain and Poverty, two of the greatest Evils of human Life." Benefit theater performances supplied funds for charity schools and poor prisoners. Individual donations and bequests encouraged other humanitarian causes, as did groups as varied as Free Masons and Sons of Liberty. Successful candidates for public office often became charitably inclined; on the day following his election to the assembly in 1752, for instance, John Watts distributed £70 among "the most indigent Families" in the city. And while New Yorkers toiled to combat poverty in their own community, they found energy and resources in 1774 to make donations for the poor of Boston, who suffered under limitations imposed by the Coercive Acts.[19]

The American Revolution created new hardships for the poor of New York. As the imperial crisis neared a climax in 1775 and 1776, the city's Committee of Safety assumed overall responsibility for welfare administration, distributing firewood, provisions, and, where possible, employment among the needy. When British forces began seven years of occupation in September 1776, thousands of patriots fled the metropolis—among them about four hundred almshouse poor who were assisted to havens of safety and refuge in Westchester, Dutchess, and Ulster counties, where local committees provided for them at state expense. Legislation of 1778 made a special appropriation for these and other pauper refugees, and authorized appointment of a board of commissioners to supervise their maintenance.[20]

Meanwhile, the British found themselves burdened with a growing population of indigent loyalist refugees in New York City. The military command established a new relief structure in January 1778 with the selection of nineteen overseers to supervise the almshouse and the outdoor poor. In the absence of regular tax collections, these men energetically tapped other sources of income—rents from houses and businesses abandoned by revolutionaries, tavern and liquor license fees, Brooklyn ferry rents, fines for violation of local ordinances, charitable subscriptions, and lotteries. According to one estimate, the overseers collected and disbursed more than £45,000 in public welfare between 1777 and 1783. Clearly, the social and economic dislocations produced by the Revolution aggravated poverty and relief problems in New York, both for the revolutionaries who fled the city and for the British and loyalists who occupied it.[21]

Thus, by the time of the American Revolution, New Yorkers had had long years of experience in dealing with poverty in their city. The poor laws, residency requirements, the high costs of outdoor relief, new agencies of private charity, and, finally, the construction of a poorhouse all indicated the rising incidence of poverty and economic dependency in the colonial city. British principles and practices shaped colonial thinking about poor relief. The imitative character of colonial welfare policy ensured the establishment of a negative and nonpreventive system which emphasized removal of nonresidents, work and humiliation as a deterrent for idlers and vagabonds, and a politically inspired attention to the lowest poor taxes consistent with local needs. Municipal officials did not question public responsibility for the worthy and helpless poor; indeed, they made real efforts to assist such dependents. However, this assistance, sparingly granted, did not help the poor surmount their lowly economic condition and merely maintained them in poverty. Private philanthropy, bestowed with the best intentions, similarly aided without improving. Stale ideas and rigid practices which prevented satisfactory social solutions characterized welfare policy in colonial New York. In the post-Revolutionary period, public officials and urban reformers struggled to adapt the British welfare system to American conditions.

4

State Poor Laws, 1783–1825

The end of the American Revolution had important results for public welfare in New York City. With the outcome of the conflict no longer in doubt by the close of 1782, some 40,000 loyalists and British camp followers in the occupied city began a mass exodus to England, Canada, and the British West Indies. The final contingent of British troops withdrew in orderly fashion on November 25, 1783, leaving about 10,000 people in the ravaged and partially destroyed seaport town. On evacuation day, General Washington led "ill-clad and weather-beaten" American forces down Bowery Road into the heart of the city. Returning New Yorkers cheered the triumphant soldiers and celebrated joyously, while Governor George Clinton entertained Washington and his officers at Fraunces Tavern. But if British evacuation of Manhattan symbolized for New Yorkers the achievement of victory and independence, it also brought new urban problems and imposed new responsibilities on city government.[1]

An orderly transition to municipal government quickly began under direction of the Council for the Southern District. The state legislature had created this council in 1779 as a provisional government *in absentia* for New York City and the contiguous area under British control—namely, the counties of New York, Kings, Queens, Richmond, and Suffolk. Even before British evacuation and the formal exchange of command, the council set up headquarters on Manhattan and issued a preliminary ordinance on November 21, 1783, for governing the district. As the British left, the council assumed the burdens of city government. The council's supplementary ordinance of December 1, naming three commissioners to administer public relief until municipal authority could be reconstituted, indicated that poverty and dependency demanded immediate attention. Relief was necessary for large numbers of returning New Yorkers, many now homeless refugees, who faced winter and unemployment in an economically disrupted city. Since prewar almshouse residents had begun returning from upstate shelters, the new commissioners also supervised repair and preparation of the poorhouse to accommodate them.[2]

Within three months of evacuation, the Council for the Southern District restored municipal government in New York City. In addition to reestablishing city services, the council supervised elections for aldermen and assistant aldermen on December 15, 1783. The Council of Appointment approved Governor Clinton's nomination of James Duane as mayor, and the Revolutionary lawyer and statesman took the oath of office on February 7, 1784. On the same day the mayor met with the newly elected common council to reimplement the old city charter, a document confirmed with only minor alterations in the state constitution of 1777. Having served its purpose, the Council for the Southern District disbanded as municipal government resumed.[3]

Changes in the urban welfare program followed resumption of municipal government in 1784. In conformity with the 1731 charter, the common council replaced the existing three-man relief commission with the colonial system of elected vestrymen and church wardens. However, new state legislation of April 1784 disestablished the Anglican Church in New York and, effective the following September, abolished the offices of vestrymen and church wardens in New York City. Thus, at city elections in September, voters chose two overseers of the poor in each ward to replace the church-related officials.[4]

Meanwhile, Mayor Duane had secured common council approval of a new plan for managing the almshouse and the bridewell. In previous years the aldermen, in conjunction with vestrymen, supervised these institutions directly. Duane argued that the "multiplicity and weight of Affairs" made it impossible for the council to keep up with such duties; state law had eliminated the vestrymen; at the same time, rising numbers of dependents, amounting to nearly a thousand families early in 1784, imposed new pressures on city welfare services. Thus, in the spring of 1784—indeed, shortly after abolition of the vestry system—the council selected thirteen commissioners of the almshouse and bridewell. The mayor and aldermen maintained overall supervision of the public buildings but entrusted the commissioners with immediate maintenance and operation of the welfare institutions. The Duane proposal especially enjoined the new appointees to pay "diligent Attention" to "strict Œconomy" without neglecting benevolent purposes.[5]

Implementation of the mayor's plan caused a short period of administrative confusion in welfare policies. State poor laws charged the elected overseers of the poor with responsibility for public assistance. But the common council had appointed commissioners to supervise the almshouse, the central relief agency in the city. Obviously, duties of overseers and commissioners overlapped and the line separating jurisdictions of the two bodies seemed unclear. Municipal officials quickly recognized the inefficiency of what amounted to dual relief administration and asked the legislature to permit a unified welfare system for the city. The legislature responded on March 18, 1785 by abolishing the board of overseers of the poor in New York City. The new law vested overseers' powers in the mayor and common council and authorized that body to appoint special commissioners to administer state poor laws in the city. The commissioners of the almshouse and bridewell were so appointed, adding overseers' duties to those they previously exercised in managing the city's welfare institutions.[6]

Thus, in little more than a year after resumption of municipal government in New York City, the administration of public poor relief underwent two important changes. First, the secularization of relief officials brought the welfare system under closer public supervision. Equally important, centralized and specialized management vested in thirteen appointive almshouse commissioners eliminated overlapping jurisdictions and made relief administration more efficient and responsible.

Despite improvements in city welfare administration, state government did not make similar advances. Drawn from English and colonial precedent, the state poor laws provided the archaic and inflexible framework within which municipal relief officials worked. The legislature passed the first comprehensive post-Revolutionary act "for the settlement and relief of the poor" on April 17, 1784. Except for the secularization of administration, this statute essentially reimplemented the last important provincial poor law of 1773 and in this sense only reaffirmed colonial settlement and relief practices. The law made each city, town, and "district" responsible for support of its own poor. It stipulated annual elections throughout the state for overseers of the poor, the local officials who administered poor relief and enforced state-imposed welfare requirements. Rather than dictating uniform relief methods, it permitted each locality to determine its own welfare program. Thus, rural communities and small towns utilized outdoor relief and a number of other less admirable practices: for children, apprenticeship and indentured servitude became common; under the "contract system" overseers boarded paupers in the homes of others at a fixed rate; under the "auction system" pauper labor was sold off to the highest bidder. Larger towns such as Albany and New York City found poorhouses necessary as well. The statute also granted local control over assessment of taxes, work programs for the poor, and apprenticeship practices for dependent children.

But if the 1784 poor law encouraged local initiative in relief techniques, the monolithic residency requirements had the opposite effect. As in England and colonial New York, one had to settle legally in a district to be eligible for public support. According to the law, a migrant might obtain such official residence by renting a house or tenement valued annually at five pounds or more, or by purchasing property worth at least thirty pounds. In either case, law demanded occupancy of the rented premises or owned property. Other acceptable methods of securing legal residence included: holding public office for at least one year; paying taxes for at least two years; serving for not less than two years under a written indenture of apprenticeship; and continuous residence within the district for forty days after registration with overseers of the poor.

Long years of poor-law experience in the colonial period had convinced New Yorkers that successful operation of the welfare system depended on strict enforcement of residency requirements. Overseers' expulsion powers lay at the heart of state relief administration and deeply influenced welfare procedures at the local level. In every community overseers investigated relief applicants for eligibility; those without official residence were removed to the place of their last legal settlement, whose overseers became legally obliged to provide support. Overseers also had power to expel any nonsettled person, whether chargeable or not, although they usually exercised this authority only when it appeared likely that public assistance might be needed. The requirement that newcomers in any district register with local overseers brought potential migrant paupers to official attention and made the "warning out" system more ominous. Although overseers' victims rarely knew enough about the law to complain, those dissatisfied with decisons could appeal to justices in the district which initiated the removal.

Even for those dependents who had an unquestioned residential status, the law imposed additional requirements. For example, the state made immediate relatives of paupers legally responsible for support. Thus the law bound financially able parents and grandparents to maintain indigent offspring. Similarly, children and grandchildren became responsible for elderly family members. Overseers penalized parents, particularly fathers, who pauperized families through desertion by confiscating and selling property and goods at auction.

In general, New York's 1784 poor law reemphasized the harsh provisions of earlier welfare practice. Rather than establishing minimum standards throughout the state, the statute allowed each locality to create its own relief program. Predictably, a haphazard system lacking uniformity and logic resulted, which prevailed well into the nineteenth century. Settlement and removal policies occupied most of the attention of lawmakers and law enforcers. Indeed, the contradictory nature of overseers' tasks—responsibility for supplying poor relief but also responsibility for denying many of those in need—ensured inefficient administration and encouraged an unworkable and irresponsible welfare program.[7]

A general poor-law revision in 1788 brought few positive changes in state welfare administration. On the contrary, although many features of the old law remained, most additions, clarifications, and definitions resulted in an even harsher and less humane relief system. For instance, residency requirements became stricter. An annual rental value of twelve pounds replaced the former five-pound provision. The forty-day waiting period after registration with overseers, the most common method by which newcomers secured legal residence, was extended to twelve months. In addition, the law retained other settlement alternatives intact. Through more precise definitions, it also attempted to eliminate the uncertainty surrounding categories of dependents whose status had caused overseers special problems. Thus illegitimate children acquired the legal settlement of the mother. Nonresident seamen and immigrants obtained settlement in the place in New York State where they first resided for at least one year. This last provision had an important effect on poor-relief administration in New York City, the major immigrant port in the nation and in which immigrants formed a large part of the pauper population. Basically, it induced municipal officials to emphasize removal of poor immigrants before the one-year period had elapsed—an early form of immigration restriction.

The revision of 1788 carefully detailed removal procedures. Overseers implemented removals by reporting nonresident paupers to local justices of the peace; when investigation substantiated overseers' reports, justices ordered local constables to transport paupers to the constables of the adjacent town; this process continued, town by town and county by county, until the pauper arrived at his place of residence or until state borders had been reached. Transported paupers who returned after removal, apparently a common enough problem to cause concern, received public whippings (up to thirty-nine lashes for men and up to twenty-five for women) before being ousted a second time. When nonresidents became so sick or infirm as to prevent removal, or died before transportation could be arranged, the law required the town of legal settlement to pay relief expenses or, in the event of death, funeral costs.

Effective enforcement of the settlement provisions depended on an accurate flow of information to overseers about migrants and newcomers. One portion of the 1788 law addressed itself to this need, requiring residents and innkeepers in every town to inform local overseers in writing "the name, quality, condition and circumstances" of visitors of more than fifteen days. Because the burgeoning population of New York City presented special problems, the law obliged ship captains to report the names and occupations of all passengers to municipal officials within twenty-four hours of arrival. Penalties levied amounted to £20 for each American citizen omitted from such passenger lists and £30 for each foreigner overlooked. As a second check on new immigrants in the city, householders had to report foreign visitors to the mayor within twenty-four hours. If an immigrant needed public assistance or could not "give a good account of himself," the law compelled ship captains to return such indigent foreign passengers to the places from which they came—a requirement, in other words, for trans-Atlantic removals. To ensure faithful compliance with this clause—and admittedly compliance with such an unrealistic provision was difficult to secure—the state demanded that shipmasters post bonds of £100 with the mayor of the city.[8]

When rigidly enforced, the settlement clauses of the New York State poor laws had the general effect of reducing the geographical mobility of poor immigrants and lower-class native Americans. But the 1788 poor law revision had one redeeming feature. It recognized that many poor persons could not find employment in the city or town where they were legally settled and were "not able to give security that they and their families shall not become chargeable to any other city or town where they can find employ." Designed as a measure to relieve unemployment and reduce welfare expenses in depressed localities, a passport system adopted by lawmakers permitted movement within the state for persons in search of work. Certificates of settlement, issued by local overseers of the poor, enabled job hunters to migrate without fear of removal, as long as they did not require public assistance. However, when such transient workers became relief applicants, overseers removed them immediately to the place which issued the certificate.[9]

Other portions of the 1788 poor law retained key features of the earlier statute. For instance, the new law repeated exactly the earlier requirements regarding parental desertion, apprenticeship practices, appeal procedures, and the responsibilities of relatives. The 1788 revision also retained previous provisions granting overseers blanket control of local relief programs. Within the framework mandated by state law—namely, that eligible dependents be cared for, that nonsettled paupers be removed, and that overseers keep uniform records—few other requirements hampered local initiative in welfare policy. As a result, relief programs varied widely throughout the state and represented a patchwork of public assistance. The law empowered communities to maintain poorhouses, but, except for the larger cities and towns, few districts used this authorization until later in the nineteenth century. Most towns continued to utilize one or more forms of outdoor relief.

With a unique set of welfare problems, New York City re-

quired efficient relief adimnistration. A special section of the 1788
law, applying only to the city, vested the commissioners of the
almshouse and bridewell with the same powers overseers exercised
in other towns. Since 1785 these powers had been exercised by
the mayor and common council, who had delegated them to the
commissioners. After 1788, state law recognized the commissioners
as independent and responsible relief officials in New York City.
Thus, from the immediate post-Revolutionary period population
pressures, immigrant needs, institutional facilities, and altered
administrative practices made welfare programs in New York
City markedly different from those in other parts of the state.

The rising number of immigrant arrivals in New York City alone
demanded special provisions. The transoceanic removal policy
for alien paupers quickly proved unworkable. Legislators repealed
it in 1797 and demanded instead that ship captains place bonds
with the mayor to indemnify the city in the event immigrants required relief. An element of imprecision, however, crept into the
wording of the new amendment, which did not make clear whether
shippers had to place bonds for each immigrant or for each cargo
of immigrants. Furthermore, to escape the bonding procedures,
ship captains often landed alien passengers at isolated spots in
New Jersey, Connecticut, and Westchester County and on Long
Island. From these places the new arrivals traveled overland to
the city. A new law in 1799 remedied these defects by permitting
New York's mayor to require ship captain bonds of up to $300
per immigrant, returnable if the newcomer did not need relief
within two years. The law imposed $500 fines on captains for
each nonbonded immigrant, as well as $500 fines for each alien
passenger landed within fifty miles of New York City "with the
intent to proceed to the said city otherwise." [10]

These new provisions, of course, reinforced the main thrust
of the state poor laws, namely, the emphasis on settlement and
removal. Shipmasters continued to avoid reporting and bonding
requirements by landing immigrants outside the city limits. In
response, a new policy gradually emerged in the nineteenth century. The common council permitted captains of immigrant ships

to make payments of three to five dollars per passenger in lieu of admittedly hard-to-collect bonds. Yet critics also castigated these "commutation" payments as an inducement to foreign governments "to rid themselves of their paupers at a trifling expense." Thus, lack of effective enforcement and eventual breakdown of the bonding system merely increased the numbers and worsened the plight of poor immigrants in New York City.[11]

State officials occasionally tried to help New Yorkers confront the immigration problem. In the late 1790's Governor John Jay reacted to the pleas of municipal officials and urged the state legislature to assume some financial responsibility for alien dependents, suggesting that they be treated as "the poor of the state." The legislature responded in 1798 by authorizing a 1 per cent tax on auction sales in New York City to support the "foreign poor" in the metropolis. Although the tax produced several thousand dollars each year, local welfare officials usually found that immigrant needs continued to outrun available funds.[12]

Despite such efforts, therefore, immigration continued to impose an "unequal burden" upon the port city. A poor-law amendment in 1821 merely confirmed actual practice by stipulating that nonresident paupers be returned to New York City if they had first entered the state through that port; the law did not say what was to be done with such dependents once returned to the city (although city officials aided them as if legally settled), nor did it provide the city with any additional financial assistance to maintain these immigrant paupers. Municipal leaders fought such legislation without success.[13]

The legislature made only a few minor alterations in New York's poor laws during the first quarter of the nineteenth century. A liberal amendment of 1809 provided that nonresident paupers too sick to be removed must be supported as if legal settlement had been obtained. A special law enacted during the War of 1812 exempted families of militia and army men from removal and made such families eligible for relief as if legally settled. General poor-law revisions of 1801 and 1813 brought no other substantial changes in the state welfare structure. Not until 1824 did state lawmakers overthrow the relief framework inherited from colonial times.[14]

By the 1820's municipal officials and humanitarian reformers acknowledged the need for complete overhaul of the poor laws. Rising immigration after the War of 1812 combined with economic depression and extensive unemployment to produce a welfare crisis, particularly in New York City, where pauperism had increased to "an alarming extent." Groups such as the New York Society for the Prevention of Pauperism generated public concern and molded public opinion against the state poor laws. The heated debate about pauperism and relief in contemporary England confirmed American suspicions about the efficacy of the welfare system, and demands for abolition of the British poor laws stimulated a similar reaction in the United States. In New York City these demands took the form of harsh proposals to reduce relief and taxes by enforcing settlement clauses rigorously, limiting immigration, and imposing a system of "coercive labor" as a deterrent to welfare. Most participants in the debate believed that relief encouraged dependency and stifled self-help efforts; few advocated a more liberal welfare program for New York's poor. All were ready to condemn the system, wrote the editor of the New York *Daily Advertiser* in February 1820, "but there is a task of more importance, and certainly of much more difficult performance, and that is to *devise a better system*. Some plan is indispensable—because the poor we are to have always." Some observers labeled as specious any program that would tear down the system of government responsibility without providing adequately for legitimate needs. Such a myopic approach, these analysts argued, could hardly cure poverty. In New York City, however, demands for a more punitive system drowned out advocates of increased public responsibility.[15]

Even before 1820 intense discussion of the poor laws had been carried from newspaper columns to the halls of the state legislature. Within the context of the growing debate, the lawmakers in April 1823 directed Secretary of State John Van Ness Yates to investigate and report on welfare administration throughout the state. Yates conducted his inquiry by means of questionnaires sent to every city, town, and poor-law district in the state. He queried local officials particularly about the efficacy of poorhouses and the workability of the removal system. Yates requested statistics on taxes, relief expenditures, and numbers of paupers. He also welcomed suggestions for welfare reform from mayors, county supervisors, and overseers. As the answers arrived, Yates began the arduous task of compiling the information into a concise report and formulating recommendations for a major poor-law revision.

The Yates report represented one of the most ambitious and comprehensive public welfare surveys in the early nineteenth century. (A comparable investigation of Massachusetts poor laws conducted about the same time by Josiah Quincy of Boston was similarly important.) Presented to the legislature in February 1824, the Yates report first noted defects in existing welfare practices. Yates listed the failure of outdoor relief as a serious deficiency in the current system. Both the contract and auction methods had proved cruel and inhumane, for many keepers allegedly treated their poor "with barbarity and neglect." Similarly, masters neglected the education and morals of apprenticed children, who, Yates reported, "grow up in filth, idleness, ignorance and disease, and . . . become early candidates for the prison or the grave." Cash payments to the outdoor poor were excessively expensive and encouraged pauperism. The report recognized a second major defect in outmoded and unworkable removal policies. Such practices not only seemed inconsistent with benevolent purposes, but involved costly administration and extensive litigation as well. Furthermore, existing programs of public assistance did little to stem "the growing evils of pauperism." A successful welfare system, Yates argued, must combine economy with humanity, and relief for the infirm with employment for the idle and moral instruction for the young.[16]

To achieve these desired objectives, the Yates report proposed important structural changes in the state poor laws. It advocated the establishment of county poorhouses throughout the state in place of outdoor relief. In addition, it urged abolishing removals for technically nonresident paupers, suggesting instead that coun-

ties assume responsibility for such dependents. Within a year
the legislature incorporated the Yates recommendations in a new
poor law. The 1824 statute, along with a number of supplementary
amendments in the next few years, revolutionized welfare administration in New York State. Legislators and other public officials
hoped the new system would prove less costly and more humane
than the one it replaced. They optimistically envisioned the poorhouse as a haven for those in real need but a deterrent to unworthy
paupers.[17]

Despite the optimism of Yates and reform-minded legislators
that the new provisions would end pauperism in the state, public
officials and humanitarian leaders in New York City objected
strenuously to the changes in the poor law. Indeed, in his reply
to the Yates questionnaire, New York's Mayor Stephen Allen urged
adoption of legislation which contradicted the most important revisions made by the 1824 law. For example, Allen urged that poorhouses be discouraged because they undermined the spirit of self-
reliance among the poor. Similarly, he suggested a law which
strengthened removal practices and stiffened settlement requirements. Predictably, passage of the Yates poor law brought immediate roars of disapproval from New York City, where paupers
numbered seventy per thousand of population. New Yorkers particularly protested the abolition of settlement and removal policies,
arguing strongly that such changes imposed the full burden of
the immigrant poor on the city. Attempts at amendment failed,
as did an alternative effort to secure an increase in state financial
aid to support foreign-born paupers. Given the special circumstances of New York City as an immigrant port, the poor-law reform of 1824 hardly seemed a reform to those concerned with
public welfare in the metropolis.[18]

Throughout the period from 1783 to 1825—a time of economic
transition, social transformation, and great urban growth—the
poor laws of New York State remained static and inflexible. The
statewide welfare structure emphasized legal settlement of the
poor rather than aid to dependents, removal rather than relief,
which in any case remained the responsibility of local communi-

ties. Not until the very end of the period did legislators throw off the shackling traditions of medieval England and colonial New York. But even the welfare changes emerging from the Yates investigation had little positive effect on relief in New York City. The city already had a poorhouse; weak enforcement of settlement provisions had permitted large numbers of nonresident paupers, both native-born and immigrant alike, to gather in the port long before the 1824 law legalized such migrations. Both the pre- and post-1824 systems were rooted in the conception of poverty as a moral evil; under both, municipal officials skimped on relief for fear that it stimulated "the crime of pauperism." This, then, comprised the harsh, ineffective, even irrelevant welfare structure within which New York City's public servants carried out their legal responsibilities to the poor.[19]

5

The Municipal Welfare Structure

If the residency clauses of the state poor laws imposed a harsh uniformity upon public assistance programs, other portions of the same legislation permitted local initiative in putting those programs into practice. In most sections of the state, overseers of the poor utilized one or more forms of outdoor relief. In New York City the pressures of a rising population and the reality of a more interdependent economy made institutional facilities necessary as well. In both rural and urban areas, the extent and quality of welfare programs depended on the humanity and good will of local officials. In many places, the stiff residency rules merely provided overseers with an excuse to avoid state-mandated duties, a rationale to maintain low taxes. However, in numerous other places—in villages and cities alike—expanded services accompanied increased need. With some exceptions, relief administrators in New York City seem to have acted responsibly and with paternalistic, yet often contemptuous, concern for the poor. Motivated as much by humanitarianism as by the desire to protect the reputation and nurture the urban aspirations of their growing city, officials adjusted municipal welfare programs to changing circumstances.

Changes in the administrative structure of urban relief reflected the impact of urbanization on social organization and city government. Throughout the late eighteenth and early nineteenth centuries, New York's commissioners of the almshouse supplied direction and energy to the urban welfare program. In the still relatively small town of post-Revolutionary years, the almshouse board represented voluntary community service by respected and concerned citizens often lacking requisite expertise. When added to the inefficiency of a large and unwieldly commission and the rising political controversy which often carried over into official deliberations, inadequate execution and inexperienced leadership became troublesome. In the first decade after 1800 social welfare clearly emerged as New York's most serious urban problem. City fathers responded by turning public assistance over to a small board of salaried professionals. But heightened partisan tensions in the larger and more socially diversified city soon replaced professionals with politicos. Surprisingly, the inarticulate poor caught in the middle of this often vocal contest between reformers and politicians did not seem to suffer overmuch. Throughout the struggle the almshouse commissioners—whether volunteers, professional experts, or patronage appointees—transacted the everyday business of relief with few interruptions.

The first alterations in relief administration stemmed from the unprecedented welfare needs of an unsettled population in the months immediately following British evacuation of the city. As previously indicated, Mayor James Duane set up the almshouse board in 1784 to handle daily supervision of that central institution and other public buildings. Approved by the common council, the Duane plan vested thirteen commissioners with authority to make all rules for governing the almshouse and the bridewell; to determine admission policies, while vigilantly enforcing vagrancy laws; to appoint or discharge officers of both institutions; to purchase all supplies and provisions; to manage pauper manufactures and sell any finished products; and to keep records of all policy decisions and business transactions. In short, the council entrusted the commissioners with the task of "directing all Things which shall relate to the internal Œconomy of the said Alms House and

which may in their Judgement best promote the benevolent Purposes of the Institution." To ensure orderly administration, the
common council required the commissioners to visit the almshouse twice daily on a rotating basis and inspect it once a week
as a body.[1]

State legislation of 1788, which vested the almshouse commissioners with the same powers exercised by overseers of the
poor in other communities, strengthened the New York City relief
officials, increased their duties, and gave them a measure of independence. Yet administrative autonomy, when combined with
amateurism, had its perils. With the common council no longer
looking over their shoulders, the commissioners neglected some
duties and occasionally engaged in fraudulent activities. The
board often made contracts with one of their number for supplying
the almshouse with clothing or provisions, a practice subject to
numerous abuses. For instance, municipal officials discovered in
1790 that one-time treasurer of the almshouse board Willet Seaman
had supplied the institution with shoes at excessive prices and of
"bad Quality and unfit for use." The poor quality of butter, flour,
and other supplies similarly caused embarrassment among the commissioners and raised eyebrows at common council meetings. The
commissioners also appeared lax in enforcing settlement laws and
in examining paupers for institutional aid, for numbers of dependents without official residence found their way into the almshouse.[2]

Furthermore, the very size of the almshouse board, totaling
thirteen commissioners, made its operation unwieldy and inefficient.
The whole conception of a board of voluntary commissioners had
been unsuccessful, a common council committee reported in 1800,
because "very little responsibility" attached to any commissioner
individually, and the burdens and chores of office were "shifted
from shoulder to shoulder, till at last . . . left wholly unsup-
ported." The city government could do little to correct any of
these problems, since the commissioners—although appointed by
the common council—were removable only for proven "mal-
conduct." [3]

Under such circumstances, the common council sought structural changes in the administrative apparatus to encourage efficiency and permit closer municipal supervision of welfare policies. Jacob de la Montagnie, one of the city's representatives in the state assembly, promoted such reforms in behalf of the municipal government. On March 12, 1798, Mayor Richard Varick sent Montagnie specific instructions for welfare reform: "On the subject of the Alms House, if you cannot get a new Law—Let the other be amended authorizing the Com. Council to reduce the number [of commissioners] & to make such reforms & alterations in the system as they shall deem proper." With such changes, the common council—"if properly disposed"—might eliminate the more flagrant abuses in the city welfare program. "It would be well," Varick added, "to have the Commissioners removable." [4]

These legislative efforts met success in April 1798, when an important new law empowered the city council to appoint up to five almshouse commissioners, and "to make and ordain such ordinances and regulations as they shall think necessary for the better government of the said alms house and bridewell, and the keepers, officers and servants thereof." Thus, the legislature gave greater supervisory powers to the municipal council to offset the ineffectiveness of almshouse officials. Several weeks later the alderman selected five new commissioners to replace the former board of thirteen. [5]

Reduced numbers, however, did not satisfy reform urges. The common council soon made further changes in the composition of the almshouse board. In 1800 a committee of aldermen reported, after considerable study, that ineffective welfare administration stemmed from the absence of full-time, salaried commissioners; few holders of the office appeared willing to sacrifice their private affairs "to an object of general concern." The common council accepted the committee's report and agreed that a "professional" staff of welfare workers seemed necessary. Drawing upon authority conferred by the act of 1798, the council adopted new welfare rules, and reshuffled the almshouse board once again. [6]

The new policy took effect in July 1801, when the council replaced the incumbent commissioners with three new men, two of whom served in salaried capacities. According to the new common council directive, the first commissioner acted also as superintendent of the almshouse, a new position replacing the former keeper of the institution. The second commissioner, designated purveyor of the almshouse, handled the business functions of public welfare in the city. The council hoped the third commissioner would be "a judicious and discreet Man, qualified to act in Council with the other two and occasionally to join with them in performing the duty of Commissioners of the Alms House but without any Salary." Former alderman and street commissioner Richard Furnam received appointment as first commissioner and superintendent; Elijah Cock, a storekeeper and a member of the almshouse board since 1784, became second commissioner and purveyor; Thomas Eddy, Quaker merchant and former superintendent of New York's Newgate state prison, declined appointment as first commissioner but accepted the third, unsalaried position. This restructuring of the almshouse board in 1801 marked the first effort at professionalization of welfare administration in New York City.[7]

The improvement proved short-lived, for by 1808 partisan bitterness negated social-welfare reforms. Poverty programs and political patronage became closely intertwined. In a legal opinion requested by a partisan common council early in 1808, the municipal attorney argued that less than five commissioners did not comport with the meaning of the act of 1798. Buttressed with apparent legality, the common council revoked the 1800 organizational reform in February 1808 and restored a separate superintendent and the five-man board of unsalaried, nonprofessional commissioners. These five soon resigned in a dispute with the new superintendent, William Mooney, and the common council reverted for a time to a three-man almshouse board. In March 1811 the aldermen again amended the almshouse ordinance to provide "that there should not be not more than five nor less than three commissioners." The city council then selected two additional commissioners, bringing the total number to five, at which strength the board remained until after 1825. Clearly, factionalism in city politics had caused the failure of welfare reform. Just as clearly, patronage and graft became a regular part of almshouse business.[8]

The duties of the commissioners of the almshouse and bridewell included management of the two institutions, execution of state poor laws, and supervision of public welfare in New York City. As overseers of the poor, the commissioners administered relief appropriations and approved almshouse expenditures. They examined paupers for official residence and authorized admissions to the poorhouse. In conjunction with justices and constables, they executed removals of nonsettled dependents. One of their important activities related to apprenticeship programs; thus, the commissioners bound out almshouse children with craftsmen and families within the city and, after legislative permission, throughout the state. This function also involved adjusting differences between apprentices and masters, and investigating charges of mistreatment and indenture violation. The commissioners occasionally made special provisions for orphans and almshouse infants by placing them with foster parents in the city. Finally, they maintained bond registers for ship captains and the fathers of illegitimate children.[9]

The commissioners usually met weekly at the poorhouse and spent most of their time handling administrative chores. Minutes of board meetings, which have survived intact for the years 1791–1797 and in fragmentary form for the period 1808–1829, illustrate weekly activities in detail. At meetings the commissioners discussed almshouse management, gave instructions to the keeper or superintendent, issued orders for support or removal, corresponded with overseers in other communities, drew up indentures, and received immigrant bonds. In addition, the commissioners examined paupers admitted to the almshouse during the preceding week by the superintendent and the poor people who without fail came to such meetings to request assistance.

The almshouse board conducted much of its business by committee. Before the 1800 welfare reorganization, separate standing committees purchased food, clothing, and firewood; others audited almshouse accounts and investigated treatment of indentured children. Between 1796 and 1800, visiting committees of two inspected the almshouse and bridewell daily. During winter months and other periods of distress, committees of the board visited indigent families throughout the city to distribute groceries, firewood, clothing, and cash. However, reduction of the almshouse board to three in number in 1800 made committees unfeasible, and after that date the three-man board usually visited the poorhouse and conducted other important business as a body.[10]

After 1800 the almshouse commissioners began delegating tasks to subordinates. Throughout most of the period, a salaried clerk of the almshouse kept minutes of board meetings and maintained the voluminous records required of the commissioners. Beginning in 1808 the board hired full-time investigators to examine paupers, determine official residence, and handle administrative details. Other board employees worked in the almshouse and dispensed relief in the slums. As the city welfare program expanded, the almshouse board became increasingly bureaucratic. The force of the urban environment—and the reality of dealing with poverty in that environment—gradually transformed the commissioners into policy makers who assigned routine chores to lesser officials.[11]

The men who served as commissioners of the almshouse and bridewell usually commanded prestige and position in the urban community. During the period as a whole, the overwhelming majority of commissioners came from mercantile and business backgrounds. Between 1784 and 1825, a total of 49 men served on the almshouse board; of these, 43 are identifiable. The group numbered 17 merchants, while 2 others not positively identified may have been merchants. City directories listed 18 others as manufacturers, retailers, and skilled craftsmen. Six more held other public offices, but most of these had some business connections as well. Only 2—both lawyers—came from the traditional professional class. This occupational breakdown seems to indicate that influence and importance attached more readily to men in mercantile and business pursuits than to those in the professions. The willingness of some merchants and other business-oriented citizens to serve as almshouse commissioners reveals a concern about the deleterious effects of poverty on urban prosperity. In most cases, these men also participated actively in city politics and sought power and opportunity.[12]

Although the commissioners of the almshouse directed the municipal welfare program, a number of other city agencies dispensed public relief as well. Throughout the post-Revolutionary and early national periods, city aldermen also functioned as magistrates, or justices of the peace—offices which entailed some relief-granting powers. Alleging poverty, citizens often bypassed the commissioners of the almshouse and petitioned the council directly for economic aid, patronage jobs, tax remission, and lowered occupational license fees. Similarly, most humanitarian societies petitioned for financial assistance, some annually. The council had a charity committee which received such petitions and recommended decisions to the larger body.[13]

The common council's almshouse committee, although it existed for less than a decade, also performed some welfare functions. This committee emerged from a temporary group established in 1811 to supervise construction of a new almshouse and formulate improved welfare practices. Upon completion of the new structure in 1816, the council replaced the construction committee with a permanent almshouse committee, which seemed to absorb, for a time, some of the duties of the commissioners of the almshouse. The council abolished the committee in 1819, and several attempts to revive it during the 1820's failed.[14]

Special committees handled some portions of the relief function at other times. Responding to a yellow fever epidemic in Philadelphia, a group of citizens in 1793 formed a health committee, soon joined by a seven-man delegation from the city council. The committee worked to prevent the spread of infectious disease in New York City and, when these efforts failed, distributed public relief and voluntary donations to the poor during the serious epidemics between 1795 and 1805. Other periods of extreme distress generated new public responses. A committee of supply, for example, coordinated an expanded public assistance effort during a severe winter in 1805; a committee of ways and means did the same during the embargo crisis of 1807–1808. At various times, other common council committees inspected the almshouse, studied methods for improved welfare administration, and assisted relief officials. Thus although the commissioners of the almshouse possessed primary responsibility for urban relief, other municipal agencies developed during times of special crisis to act in conjunction with the commissioners or assume some of their duties.[15]

The commissioners of the almshouse supervised municipal welfare programs, but successful implementation of policy depended on the alacrity and effectiveness of another official—the superintendent of the almshouse. Before the 1800 welfare reorganization, management of the almshouse had been entrusted to a keeper, an employee with little decision-making authority who carried out instructions of the commissioners on all matters relating to internal affairs of the institution. Samuel Dodge, the only man to hold this position in the post-Revolutionary period, had been keeper of the house prior to 1776 as well as a state-appointed relief commissioner for paupers removed from New York City during the conflict. At the end of the war the almshouse board reinstated Dodge as keeper, in which position he served until 1801. As the nineteenth century began, the common council replaced the keeper with a superintendent, an officer with more independence and wider powers.[16]

Inefficient management of municipal welfare in the 1790's had decided the common council on more wieldly, more streamlined administration. Thus, they created the office of superintendent to restore order and economy to the relief program. Moreover, by making the superintendent at the same time one of the commissioners of the almshouse, they hoped to ensure effective policy and knowledgeable decisions. To guarantee proper performance in office, the common council—and later the commissioners of the almshouse—defined the superintendent's powers and responsibilities in detail.

The municipal welfare reform of 1800 provided the first occasion for the common council to describe the superintendent's job. The new plan entrusted the superintendent with overall management of the almshouse. He appointed all employees of the institution, including clerks, cooks, matrons, and domestic servants. He approved all expenditures for food, fuel, medicine, and other supplies and presented quarterly financial accounts to the common council, along with an almshouse census. He examined relief applicants for legal residence and handled outdoor relief at the direction of the commissioners. He maintained order and discipline among inmates, supervised employment for the able-bodied, and indentured pauper boys and girls as apprentices and domestic servants. He secured medical aid for the sick and disabled, nursing care for infants, and schoolmasters for children. After administrative changes in 1808, the commissioners of the almshouse delineated the superintendent's duties in very similar fashion, although they delegated some functions to subordinate officers—clerk, steward, and recorder. In general, the municipality required the superintendent "to direct, superintend and carry into execution all the Laws, rules and regulations of the Alms House and to preserve peace and order and proper Government therein." [17]

The job demanded much, but from the common council point of view the clear designation of responsibility to a single individual corrected the deficiencies which characterized public welfare in the 1790's. Unfortunately, the common council negated its reform by retaining appointive powers, thrusting the almshouse and its officers into the cauldron of New York's partisan politics. Despite the obvious need for responsible, competent, and impartial appointees, politics usually dictated the selection of superintendents. Indeed, the job of almshouse superintendent, with its subsubstantial salary and numerous opportunities for patronage and graft, became a sought after political plum. Between 1801 and 1809 the superintendent's office changed hands five times, usually as the immediate result of a municipal election.

Under the new almshouse plan adopted in 1800, a Federalist common council selected Richard Furman as first almshouse commissioner and superintendent. However, by 1805 Republicans had gained control of the municipal government, and in May the council's Republican majority replaced Furman with Philip Arcularius, a tanner by trade and a local Republican leader. The removal created heated political controversy in the city, with editor William Coleman of the Federalist *New-York Evening Post* leading opposition to Arcularius' appointment. Coleman praised Furman's management of the almshouse, criticized the application of political partisanship to a charitable institution, and labeled Arcularius "a man respected by no one . . . hated by many, despised by most, ridiculed by all." Particularly "odious," Coleman wrote, the common council had turned out of office a patriot officer of the Revolution and replaced him with a "Hessian Sutler." Two months after the appointment, one of the *Evening Post* correspondents suggested that Arcularius' performance in office sustained the critics and revealed his total inability for the position. According to this Federalist opponent, the new superintendent spent little time at the almshouse and left most business to his assistants. "He usually comes after breakfast, walks about the rooms for half an hour, goes to market, perhaps returns for an hour, perhaps not. After dinner he comes again, takes a turn or two, goes home and takes his afternoon nap; perhaps makes a short visit at sunset and thus ends his day." [18]

The *Evening Post* continued the campaign against Arcularius long after the new superintendent took office, charging him with administrative irregularities and inhumane treatment of the paupers. Other newspapers also joined the attack, as did unknown persons who posted critical handbills on pillars at City Hall and about the city. Meanwhile, the Republican-oriented *American Citizen* defended the incumbent and levied counter-charges against Furman. Arcularius and his Republican supporters pointed mainly to financial misdealings during Furman's tenure as superintendent. With no checks on spending, Furman and the Federalists allegedly siphoned almshouse money for huge salaries and electioneering. "Here then," wrote "Samuel Adams" in the *American Citizen,* "was Mr. Furman in clover, with no fence and without any other animal to interrupt his feeding." The controversy ended in a libel case between Arcularius and Coleman, a suit eventually won by Coleman and hailed as a successful battle for a free press. With the

Federalist victory in the 1806 aldermanic elections, "the perse-
cuting spirit of party" swiftly emerged once again. The new
council removed Arcularius ("his only crime was *republicanism*,"
said the editor of the *American Citizen*) and reappointed Furman
to the almshouse post.[19]

Furman's second incumbency as superintendent did not last
very long. The Republicans swept back into power at municipal
elections in 1807. Needless to say, they removed Furman once
again in February 1808, this time replacing him with William
Mooney, an important Tammany leader. The council also selected
former superintendent Arcularius as a commissioner of the almshouse. These purely partisan appointments roused the ire of editor Coleman, who resumed his diatribes against the Republicans
and singled out Mooney for special treatment.[20]

The opposition to Mooney found unexpected support among the
commissioners of the almshouse. Early in 1808 five new commissioners had been appointed in a politically motivated welfare
shakeup. After a preliminary survey, the new commissioners found
almshouse management "susceptible of many alterations and
amendments"; to make proper reforms the commissioners demanded "full powers to do and perform every act and thing necessary for the better regulation, improvement and Government of
those establishments." The common council passed a new ordinance on March 14, 1808, granting such wide powers to the commissioners it had just selected, reserving to itself power over appropriations and appointments only. With this buttressed authority, the commissioners rewrote the almshouse rule book and
redefined the superintendent's duties and those of other welfare
employees.[21]

However, the new superintendent considered the commissioners
meddlers "plotting against him," refused to cooperate, and ignored instructions for internal reforms. He further labeled the
almshouse board a "Five-headed monster," likened the commissioners to the French Directory, and on at least one occasion
threatened to "blow their brains out." The commissioners, in turn,
complained to the common council about Mooney, alleging: "he

remains contumaceous, and disobeys the orders and entreaties of the Commissioners." They further argued that he had "not the qualifications and capacity, necessary to perform the duties of that office, with the prudence economy and sagacity" which the public interest required. Finally, they requested the council to clarify whether the powers of the commissioners included that of removal. Obviously, partisan appointments had led to a power struggle between an authoritative superintendent determined on iron-fisted rule and equally authoritative commissioners bent on undiluted control of the entire welfare program.[22]

Mooney and the commissioners traded charges and countercharges through May, June, and July of 1808. In July the city council conducted a special investigation of the case, interrogating particularly the almshouse employees. Mooney himself appeared before the alderman in his own defense. The investigation did not clearly prove Mooney a lax or incompetent administrator, nor did it positively reveal a conscious neglect of the public interest. Apparently Mooney drank heavily, although one subordinate claimed with perhaps more than a little sarcasm that he had "observed him a whole morning without taking a drink." More revealing, perhaps, almshouse clerk Josiah Shippey, Jr., observed of Mooney "that when anything on the part of the Commissioners irritating came to his knowledge, he would go to the side board & take a drink." The investigation did clarify the bad feelings between Mooney and the commissioners. Unquestionably, the superintendent had ignored legitimate instructions. Equally apparent, the ensuing power struggle had disrupted the city's normal welfare procedures. But despite evidence of Mooney's improper conduct, the common council resolved in a nine-to-four partisan vote on July 25, 1808, to close the inquiry. Two days later the almshouse commissioners resigned to protest the whitewash.[23]

Within a year new commissioners equally disapproved of superintendent Mooney. An "alarming increase" in almshouse expenses caused special concern. A committee of aldermen investigated Mooney a second time and found that almshouse costs had almost doubled between 1804 and 1809, rising from $45,000 to more than

$86,000; the average number of paupers supported in the insti-
tution had only increased from 763 to 865 during the same period.
The committee further asserted that the greatest portion of the
increase went for "those articles which are used as the gratifica-
tion of luxury or intemperance" by the superintendent, his wife
and five sons, and his numerous political friends. As evidence, the
investigating aldermen compared the 322 gallons of liquor bought
for the almshouse during Furman's superintendency in 1804 with
the 1,200 gallons purchased and consumed between August 1808
and July 1809. During one year of Mooney's superintendency consumption of rum doubled over Furman's tenure in 1804, while
brandy and gin purchases increased five and six times, respectively.
Similarly, the committee discovered heavy and unprecedented food
expenditures for the "Middle House," where Mooney lived with
his family. Almshouse record books also revealed large and un-
accounted for distributions of cash to the outdoor poor, suggesting
peculation and fraud.[24]

The revelations of Mooney's excessive expenditures, which apparently had financed numerous political banquets, drinking bouts,
and "midnight orgies," led to the superintendent's discharge in
September 1809 by a thirteen-to-one vote of the council. William
Coleman, who recognized a good political issue when he saw one,
kept the Mooney case in the columns of the *Evening Post* long after
the event, castigated the ousted superintendent—a Tory during
the Revolution—as "a zealous red coated subject of King George,"
and criticized Democratic-Republican incompetence and waste
in general. Even the Republican editor of the *American Citizen*
criticized Mooney's almshouse administration. Mooney, in turn,
defended himself against all charges in the *Public Advertiser*,
a new Republican organ. The commissioners of the almshouse
temporarily assumed direction of welfare institutions until the
reappointment of Richard Furman for a third term in December
1809—"an act," wrote the editor of the *Commercial Advertiser*,
"of public as of individual justice." [25]

Furman's third term lasted twelve years, considerably longer
than his first two appointments. He owed his long tenure partly to

Federalist control of the common council before 1814 and partly
to state legislation in that year which stipulated a seven-year term
for the superintendent's job. Anticipating the need for stable and
continuous management of the new almshouse at Bellevue on the
East River, the common council had requested the legislature to
remove the office from political machinations. The minority of
Democratic aldermen had originally favored the council's petition,
but within a year they reversed field. Needing an election issue
in 1814, Democratic councilmen protested Furman's long-term
appointment as an "aristocratic" experiment and a "dangerous
prerogative" which violated democratic principles and subverted
the rights of the people. They protested vainly in 1814, but the
legislature did repeal the allegedly "Anti-Republican" law in 1821
when petitioned again by a Democratic council. At the expiration
of Furman's seven-year term in 1821, the same council appointed
Arthur Burtis to the position, which he held until after 1825.[26]

The superintendent of New York City's almshouse functioned
as the chief welfare administrator throughout the early nineteenth
century. The commissioners of the almshouse made policy and
possessed ultimate authority under the city council, while the
superintendent implemented relief. The effectiveness of the urban
welfare program depended, of course, upon the capabilities and
the energy of the superintendent. Poverty programs and politics
went hand in hand, and aldermen usually picked almshouse commissioners and superintendents for partisan reasons. Yet, except for
the two-year incumbency of William Mooney, and to the extent
permitted by municipal appropriations, these officials seemed to
exercise their charge responsibly, even with care and humanity.
State law established the legal fabric for poor relief, but under
this larger framework specialized institutions and local administrators emerged in response to urban needs. Within this formalized
structure, then, welfare officials conducted the daily business of
public assistance.

6

The Urban Welfare Program:
The Almshouse

When Sweden's Baron Klinkowstrom visited New York City in 1819, he observed approvingly that despite large numbers of poor persons, "no one has ever been found lying starved in the streets." Although this may have been an overly optimistic appraisal, the Baron's impressions did not vary significantly from those of other foreign and native travelers in New York during the same period. Anne Royall, the professional travel writer from Alabama, wrote in 1824 that it appeared "the pride of New-York, to have no poor seen in the streets." Such comments struck close to the truth, for the municipal government made a conscious effort to keep the poor from public view. By the 1820's city marshals canvassed the streets daily, vigorously enforcing vagrancy ordinances. In addition, the extensive urban welfare program kept eligible citizens from publicly displaying their poverty. Thus temporary paupers with official residence secured home relief, while the more permanently dependent found immediate refuge in the almshouse.[1]

The almshouse lay at the heart of public welfare in New York City. Constructed in 1736, the city's first poorhouse served multiple purposes during the rest of the colonial period. Along with paupers and their children, the building housed prostitutes, vagrants, and assorted disorderly characters; not until 1775 did city fathers provide a separate place—the bridewell—for such persons. Both institutions, along with the city jail finished in 1759, clustered in the triangular park at the northern edge of town where City Hall would later be built. (This architectural arrangement provided a symbolic representation of the social attitudes which lumped together poverty and crime, charities and corrections, until well into the twentieth century.)

In immediate post-Revolutionary years, both the almshouse and the bridewell quickly proved inadequate. The British had left both buildings in a dilapidated condition. The social and economic dislocations stemming from the Revolution multiplied candidates for the two institutions, and both soon maintained greater numbers than could be comfortably accommodated. Vagrants, wandering beggars, and nonresident paupers—most left behind by the British, the common council claimed in 1784—posed special problems. Vigilant municipal officers rounded up such "idle wicked and dissolute Persons" for a term at hard labor in the bridewell or transportation from the city. But many escaped official notice and gained admission to the almshouse. In 1789 the almshouse commissioners noted with concern that their bailiwick had become "too much of a common Receptacle for idle intemperate Vagrants," many without legal settlement, who "by pretended Sickness or otherwise" imposed upon the benevolence of the community and siphoned assistance designed for "real Objects of Charity." The swarms of poor immigrants who began to arrive in New York after 1790 helped swell the institution as well, and by 1795 foreigners comprised about half of the almshouse paupers. In January 1796 some 770 dependents crowded a sixty-year-old building capable of handling less than half that number.[2]

Welfare officials adopted a number of temporary measures to relieve pressures on the almshouse. The common council, for example, provided extra funds for outdoor relief as a means of shortening the admission list; bank loans negotiated by the city supplied this additional money. Careful examination of almshouse residents periodically resulted in expulsion of those without official residence or who had parents or children able to support them. For those who remained, other expedients offered partial solution and eased overcrowding. Thus the commissioners of the almshouse removed sick paupers to the empty barracks built by the British at the northern edge of the park. They appropriated several rooms of the bridewell, sending occupants to the city jail; later they renovated the ground floor of the jail for the poor. When this added space proved insufficient, the commissioners used the almshouse school room and several additional sections of the barracks for similar purposes. Strangely, these same barracks served as an early form of public housing, for the almshouse keeper rented a number of apartments to "persons able to pay a moderate rent." [3]

By January 1794 the common council publicly acknowledged the "Ruinous Condition" of the almshouse and agreed that further repairs would be useless. Given the deteriorated state of the building and the simultaneous rise in demands placed on the institution, the council followed the only acceptable course of action—construction of a new poorhouse. In April 1795 the state legislature authorized a municipal lottery (a much-used method of supporting public projects in early America) to raise funds, and work began on the new building early in 1796. Workmen completed the new three-story almshouse one year later at a total cost of $130,000. In May 1797 the paupers moved to their new home, located immediately behind the old structure, and watched as contractors razed their former refuge.[4]

The first decade of the nineteenth century witnessed rapid expansion of the physical city and a 50 per cent population increase. Several summers of epidemic fever and several years of severe economic depression combined with haphazard urban growth to intensify municipal welfare problems. Especially damaging to prosperity, the federal shipping embargo caused widespread unemployment among seamen, artisans, and day laborers and brought heavy demands for public relief. In response to obvious need, city officials enlarged the public assistance program. In the two years after 1807, when the embargo affected urban economic life, the

common council expanded aid to the outdoor poor and systematically provided work relief for the first time. However, institutional
relief broke down under the new pressures. Indeed, the new almshouse had quickly proved obsolete; even before the turn of the
century more than 870 paupers crowded the new institution. During twelve months after 1812, more than 2,800 dependents found
refuge within its sheltering walls. Motivated by such institutional
inadequacies, by the belief that outdoor relief was more costly
than almshouse care, and by a humanitarian concern for the poor,
the common council decided once again on new facilities.[5]

New York's aldermen did not consider enlarging the almshouse,
which had been built in 1796–1797. Nor did they think of erecting a new building in City Hall Park, which urban growth had
transposed from suburb to center. In all its deliberations on the
subject, the council indicated instead a firm desire to move the
institution from the heart of the city to a more "recluse" situation.
Councilmen clearly reacted to earlier complaints that visitors to
City Hall had "their feelings constantly shocked" by haggard
paupers and undisciplined children peering from almshouse windows, hanging on the fences, and wandering in the park. After
considering several possible locations outside the city limits, the
common council finally selected a six-acre site at Bellevue, just
north of the settled city on the East River. The property, purchased from merchant Samuel Kipp for $22,494, seemed especially
desirable, because the city already owned considerable land at
Bellevue. The East River estate of Quaker merchant Lindley Murray had been leased by the city in 1794 and purchased outright
in 1798; meanwhile the buildings on the property had been used
as fever hospitals during the serious yellow fever epidemics in the
years after 1795. The Kipp property adjoined the Murray estate
and provided the isolated location the city sought.[6]

Extensive plans reflected the city's intentions for the new establishment. The common council conducted an elaborate corner-
stone-laying ceremony on August 1, 1811, and then appointed a
special Bellevue committee to supervise construction. To save
money the committee used convicts from the jail and vagrants

from the bridewell as forced labor for unskilled tasks such as digging foundations and carrying building materials. The work of construction progressed rapidly until interrupted by the War of 1812, during which many laborers joined the militia. Many others lost jobs when the common council cut city expenditures to concentrate on strengthening harbor defenses. Not until April 1816 did the Bellevue almshouse stand ready for occupancy. Meanwhile, the old bridewell and the jail, "two black, dismal looking edifices," continued in use and remained, as a visitor from Massachusetts sarcastically remarked, "elegant appendages" to City Hall. The common council donated the old almshouse, renamed the New York Institution, to a number of the city's literary and scientific societies.[7]

The newly finished poorhouse, and the spirit of public benevolence which it seemed to reflect, caused wonderment and amazement. Spread over several acres, an eleven-foot wall enclosed the establishment on three sides, while the fourth side opened onto the East River. In addition to the large stone almshouse—the largest structure in the city—the complex of buildings consisted of a workhouse, a penitentiary, two hospitals, and a number of smaller structures, including bakery, icehouse, greenhouse, soap factory, stables, fire station, chapel, and superintendent's residence. Total cost of the new relief institutions amounted to $421,-109—a fabulous sum for the time. When he visited New York shortly after its completion, Yale's President Dwight remarked that "there is no eleemosynary establishment in the American Union equally splendid." In 1821 another visitor, Zerah Hawley, reported that the almshouse made "a very grand and beautiful appearance" from the river.[8]

To contemporaries the facilities appeared admirable indeed, but the cycle of obsolescence continued unabated. What at first seemed lavish and expansive soon proved cramped and outmoded, seemingly confirming the opinion of those who claimed that public facilities for the poor simply created a class of paupers. By the 1830's the city had grown out around Bellevue and the number of dependents had outgrown Bellevue. As early as 1830, the com-

mon council discussed but never completed removal of the almshouse to Barn Island, later Ward's Island, in the upper East River.
In 1848, however, the city finally completed new buildings for the
poor on Blackwell's Island, now Welfare Island, and transformed
Bellevue into a public hospital.[9]

The city's rapid growth had made larger institutional facilities
necessary, for as population increased so did demands on the
welfare system. The proportion of institutionalized dependents to
total population, for example, remained relatively stable through-

Table 1

NUMBER AND ORIGINS OF ALMSHOUSE PAUPERS, 1798–1816

Year	New York City	New York State	Other States	Foreigners	Totals
1798	262	54	74	246	636
1799	323	49	72	236	678
1800	451	56	84	283	874
1801	460	65	90	290	903
1802	450	60	90	295	895
1803	461	70	93	297	931
1804	462	54	87	306	904
1805	474	69	90	308	941
1806	476	70	97	302	955
1807	480	75	101	320	976
1808	487	105	98	327	1,017
1809	504	107	104	336	1,051
1810	509	90	110	357	1,066
1811	604	103	104	406	1,217
1812	730	103	120	456	1,409
1813	624	78	129	434	1,265
1814	642	88	125	346	1,201
1815	701	101	115	405	1,322
1816	772	105	150	498	1,525

Source: *Commercial Advertiser* (New York), January 25, 1817. Almshouse superintendent Richard Furman prepared these statistics for the common council to
buttress a municipal petition seeking additional legislative assistance for the "foreign
poor." The census was taken on January 1 of each year except 1816, when it was
made on December 31. Some small computational errors exist in the totals for 1799,
1801, 1803, 1804, and 1806, attributable either to newspaper misprints or Furman's
faulty addition.

Table 2

JOHN STANFORD'S ALMSHOUSE CENSUS, 1816–1826

	May 1, 1816	May 1, 1817	May 1, 1818	May 1, 1819	Jan. 1, 1820	Jan. 1, 1821	Jan. 1, 1822	Jan. 1, 1823	Jan. 1, 1824	Jan. 1, 1825	Jan. 1, 1826
white men	249	368	264	361	457	478	463	480	499	511	521
white women	287	394	393	413	489	493	420	489	515	480	533
black men	21	29	33	35	36	38	35	28	16	21	25
black women	46	47	62	55	62	77	40	33	31	41	30
white boys	227	396	371	356	457	369	339	379	382	370	368
white girls	192	242	227	242	334	253	249	259	235	207	234
black boys	15	13	19	18	21	14	19	16	17	10	21
black girls	6	11	15	13	13	26	9	8	4	8	10
children "at nurse"	199	—	—	—	—	—	—	—	—	—	—
maniacs	—	—	—	—	27	30	30	25	33	42	—
Totals	1,242	1,500	1,384	1,493	1,896	1,778	1,604	1,717	1,732	1,684	1,742

Sources: *New-York Evening Post*, June 12, 1816, May 14, 1817, May 20, 1818, May 20, 1819, January 11, 1821, January 9, 1822, January 15, 1825; *Commercial Advertiser* (New York), January 5, 1820, January 19, 1826; *New-York Daily Advertiser*, January 15, 1823, January 8, 1824. Errors in the totals for 1818, 1821, and 1825, owing either to a printer's mistake or Stanford's arithmetic, remain unchanged.

out the period. The rate generally held close to 1.5 per cent, although it rose significantly to above 2 per cent during the depression year of 1820. The continual rise in the actual number of almshouse residents similarly shows how population pressures made expansion of the public assistance program necessary. In March 1786 the original structure housed 381 dependents. By January 1800 almost 900 paupers crowded the new building in City Hall Park. The number increased markedly in following years, amounting to 941 in 1805, 1,066 in 1810, 1,322 in 1815, and 1,896 in 1820. Officials noted a decrease for 1825, when the almshouse poor totaled 1,684.[10]

But although these statistics are accurate, they are somewhat misleading. In the first place, the common council derived the annual published figures from official almshouse censuses, which gave only the number of pauper inmates at the time of census taking. The manuscript census records, and occasionally annual reports of almshouse commissioners, presented a more informed view of the extent of institutionalized social welfare in New York City. These records and reports included the total number of dependents supported in the house during the year, noting the number discharged and deceased as well as those actually resident at the time of census taking. Thus 3,449 paupers needed institutional care for various lengths of time between April 1, 1818, and April 1, 1819, but because 1,577 had been discharged during the year and another 379 had died, only 1,493 remained on the latter date when the superintendent took a census. Similar figures for other years suggest that the almshouse sheltered a great many more dependents than indicated in the published statistics.[11]

Secondly, figures for the later part of the period, especially the decade after 1815, are misleading because they fail to consider the degree of social-welfare specialization achieved by the common council and almshouse commissioners. In the eighteenth century and early in the nineteenth, city officials housed dependents and vagrants of all descriptions in the same institution—the almshouse. But in the years after the War of 1812, and particularly after construction of the welfare institutions at Bellevue, public assistance in New York City became diversified, more sophisticated perhaps. Indeed, as Anne Royall wrote in 1824, "it would require the constitution of Sampson to visit all the public institutions of New-York." [12]

A look beyond the poorhouse statistics clearly reveals the trend toward specialization. For instance, magistrates sent all beggars and vagrants without exception to the bridewell or the new penitentiary at Bellevue. The commissioners maintained some sick and injured paupers in the New York Hospital or the City Dispensary, while others remained in the almshouse hospitals. Mentally disturbed patients were treated in the "maniac asylum" of the New York Hospital, in the Bloomingdale Asylum, and after 1825 in the new Bellevue Hospital. Nurses and foster parents cared for many almshouse infants and some older children went out as apprentices. Other children who might formerly have required almshouse aid received care in the Orphan Asylum and the House of Refuge, two private institutions founded in 1806 and 1824, respectively. Two other charitable societies, the Institution for the Instruction of the Deaf and Dumb (1817) and the New York Eye Infirmary (1824), provided facilities for other dependents previously aided in the poorhouse. Numbers of other benevolent organizations aided the needy and eased pressures on public institutions. The residue of public paupers remained in the almshouse; the superintendent recorded only these in his annual census reports.

A simple count of almshouse paupers, therefore, provides only a partial measure of the extent of municipal relief. Fortunately, beginning in 1817 almshouse chaplain John Stanford made an annual independent census which included most of the specialized institutions. These reports presented a more realistic picture of public assistance. But neither Stanford's set of statistics nor those of the superintendent included the outdoor poor—always much more numerous than those supported in the almshouse or other institutions.

Poorhouse expenses rose alongside climbing pauper statistics. Until the 1820's officials prepared and audited the city budget on

Table 3

JOHN STANFORD'S CENSUS OF NEW YORK CITY INSTITUTIONS, 1816–1826

	May 1, 1816	May 1, 1817	May 1, 1818	May 1, 1819	Jan. 1, 1820	Jan. 1, 1821	Jan. 1, 1822	Jan. 1, 1823	Jan. 1, 1824	Jan. 1, 1825	Jan. 1, 1826
almshouse	1,242	1,500	1,384	1,493	1,896	1,778	1,604	1,717	1,732	1,684	1,742
Orphan Asylum	93	113	124	133	133	128	136	166	160	150	159
city hospital	301	268	247	241	259	224	215	239	265	256	250
debtor's prison (including liberties)	95	300	273	382	423	517	216	120	205	300	178
bridewell	215	127	75	102	99	106	141	125	106	116	162
state prison	654	752	650	617	599	580	553	580	608	642	496
penitentiary	—	189	268	334	358	377	344	342	331	338	294
Bellevue Hospital	—	—	—	—	—	—	—	—	—	—	84
House of Refuge	—	—	—	—	—	—	—	—	—	—	63
Totals	2,600	3,249	3,021	3,302	3,767	3,710	3,209	3,289	3,407	3,486	3,428

Sources: *New-York Evening Post*, June 12, 1816, May 14, 1817, May 20, 1818, May 20, 1819, January 11, 1821, January 9, 1822, January 15, 1825; *Commercial Advertiser* (New York), January 5, 1820, January 19, 1826; *New-York Daily Advertiser*, January 15, 1823, January 8, 1824.

a fiscal rather than calendar-year basis. Almshouse costs for fiscal year 1785–1786 totaled £5,017 (at this time the New York pound was equivalent to $2.50). By 1796–1797 expenses had more than

Table 4
ALMSHOUSE EXPENSES, 1798–1816

Year	Expenditures
1798	$32,970
1799	33,414
1800	42,372
1801	35,500
1802	34,989
1803	37,000
1804	34,000
1805	66,408
1806	42,786
1807	46,136
1808	57,007
1809	78,781
1810	60,128
1811	68,600
1812	74,488
1813	70,000
1814	92,700
1815	77,000
1816	79,973

Source: *Commercial Advertiser* (New York), January 25, 1817.

doubled to £11,694. During the depression year 1818–1819 annual financial needs soared to $105,509. Indeed, from the close of the Revolution to after 1825, social-welfare costs constituted the greatest single municipal expenditure year after year, amounting usually to about one-fourth or one-fifth of the city's total budget.[13]

Just as the superintendent's census-taking techniques disguised reality, the annually published almshouse financial accounts tended toward understatement. For one thing, the commissioners always separated almshouse costs from outdoor relief, a standard item which occasionally amounted to as much as $25,000. Building repairs and construction costs of new poorhouses in 1796–1797 and 1811–1816 went on separate budget lines. The city treasurer similarly treated common council donations to private charitable societies, grants which amounted to $3,820 in 1816–1817 and $5,280 in 1818–1819. Clearly dictated by the welfare needs of the urban community, these expenses did not appear in the annual almshouse accounts. Then, as now, public assistance seemed costly. The amount city officials spent for public welfare reflected their seriousness of purpose, but also revealed the extensiveness of economic dependency.[14]

Liberal expenditures and extensive institutional provisions for the poor early gave New York City a reputation for municipal benevolence. The almshouse became a regular point of interest for foreign and native travelers. Most such observers found the paupers to be treated with kindness and care, but some asserted the house to be excessively neat and well managed. Anne Royall, for example, reported on Bellevue in 1824: "The alms-house is well regulated, and no gentlemen's parlour looks neater, the floor being scrubbed with sand daily. The paupers looked plump and hearty, and were comfortably clothed; most of their beds were of feathers." She questioned several of them about their treatment and "they eagerly replied that they never lived better, nor had a wish ungratified." In the same year Samuel Griscom, a visitor from Philadelphia, found the almshouse wards "kept with a good deal of neatness; particularly those occupied by the aged; some of whom seem to enjoy themselves very well and one old lady said she would not give sixpence to call the king her uncle." De Witt Clinton's strongest impression upon examining the house in 1823 was one of docile and extremely obese women cultivating potted plants and flowers "with great solicitude." Other visitors and even inspection committees from the common council usually found the institution clean, orderly, and properly managed.[15]

Yet such observations often contained unintended revelations about almshouse care. Obesity and "plumpness" among the paupers might very well have indicated poor diet. The New York almshouse may have appeared superior only in comparison to conditions elsewhere. The admitted extra efforts of commissioners and superintendent to make the house presentable during visiting hours help explain the favorable reports. More important, contradictory statements about living conditions in the institution have survived in the writings of those who attended the poor regularly. Indeed, the favorable impressions of occasional visitors rarely matched the less optimistic but more informed views of men who visited the almshouse on a systematic basis.

In describing the building and its pauper inmates, regular observers catalogued the entire range of filth, misery, and misfortune. Great numbers of paupers entered the house enfeebled, diseased, and dying; crowded living conditions hardly promoted good health. Even Anne Royall, an apologist for the institution, criticized inadequate health measures and inhumane child care. The almshouse chaplain, the Reverend Ezra Stiles Ely, constantly complained in his diary about the horrible odors of sickness and death which penetrated every part of the building. On more than one occasion the offensive air of the place made his stomach sick, his breathing labored, and his sermons short. Even the common council admitted that the place had "that offensive smell common to Prisons." Ely described the almshouse congregation in 1813: "The air was full of smoke, and of that flavour which is far worse: I was unwell, and surrounded by age, widowhood, decrepitude, the consumption perpetually altering his voice, blindness, poverty, and disease of almost every name." On several occasions the city council had to instruct the superintendent to furnish paupers "with the necessary apparel to cover their nakedness." For poor blacks, whether diseased or healthy, city officials reserved the worst section of the house—a filthy, damp cellar. Constantly overflowing privies contaminated drinking water and made the almshouse grounds "a sink of pollution." [16]

The combination of misery and poverty with overcrowded and insanitary conditions produced a disordered and ill-disciplined welfare institution. Ely recorded a number of vivid descriptions of the house. In 1812 he found that "the greater part of the wards abound with the vile; and here and there a solitary believer is vexed with the filthy conversation of this second Sodom." Although the paupers possessed none of the "sins of high life," they more than made up these deficiencies "by the lusts of the flesh." "Drunkenness and Lewdness," he wrote in 1813, "are the common vices of the place." Since "even unmarried persons sleep together," most native paupers were "the offspring of the house." Similarly, John Stanford, who succeeded Ely as almshouse chaplain, modestly confirmed in his 1823 report to the Society for Supporting the Gospel among the Poor that the "greatest part" of the institution's residents "cannot be commended for their good conduct." [17]

Given these conditions, the commissioners of the almshouse imposed strict regulations to maintain their version of decency and order, to restrain immorality, intemperance, and other "vicious habits." Thus under the rules the superintendent segregated paupers according to sex, age, health, race, and character. He prohibited marriage and promiscuity among the inmates on penalty of immediate expulsion, although he allowed those already married to live together as far as was practical. (Considering the tenor of Ely's complaints, one wonders about the effectiveness of such regulations.) Those who behaved in an orderly fashion and performed required tasks faithfully received small rewards, but drunkenness, profanity, criminality, quarreling, and begging met appropriate punishments. For example, disobedient or ill-tempered paupers lost meal privileges or won solitary confinement in the "Dark Room" on bread and water. More serious offenders might be forced "to wear an Iron Ring around their Leg, with a Chain and wooden Block fixed thereto." Rule breakers also faced corporal punishment, extra work loads, confinement in bridewell, or expulsion from the house. Several times a year the commissioners assembled the almshouse people to read aloud the rules and regulations accompanied by "pressing injunctions" for "decency, sobriety, and cleanliness." [18]

New York City's welfare officials heartily subscribed to the moral interpretation of poverty and implemented policies which presupposed individual shortcomings as the major cause of de-

THE URBAN WELFARE PROGRAM: THE ALMSHOUSE

pendency. They echoed Ely, who argued in 1812 that "if man will not work, when able, he should not eat." Almshouse rules demanded some kind of work of all able paupers "to inure them to Labour." One of the superintendent's assistants rang a bell each morning as a signal for work to begin and took attendance daily to ensure compliance with the work requirement. In 1795 the almshouse commissioners reported that "the Business of sewing, spinning and picking Oakum is daily attended to by all who are able to work and are not employed in the Wash House the Cookery the Bakery or the Nurseries." Of 1,563 paupers in Bellevue in December 1821, a total of 145 men worked at twenty-one different occupations. They were bakers, barbers, tailors, cooks, shoemakers, carpenters, sawyers, weavers, masons, wheelwrights, coopers, blacksmiths, gardeners, cartmen, laborers, and grave diggers. Some 231 women performed such tasks as knitting, sewing, spinning, cooking, nursing, sweeping, washing, and scrubbing. In 1811 a writer in the *New-York Evening Post* enthusiastically urged municipal purchase of some newly invented textile machines which would permit almshouse children and "infirm" paupers to "earn a living"—a suggestion later adopted by city officials. Obviously requested by the common council as a deterrent to welfare, a state law of 1822 authorized the superintendent to demand work as an eligibility requirement for relief.[19]

By careful utilization of involuntary pauper labor, the commissioners supplied many needs of the almshouse. Pauper carpenters kept busy making coffins, an extremely useful occupation considering the high almshouse mortality rate, which averaged 10 per cent or more during the decade after 1815. Eventually, paupers manufactured most of their own clothing and all of their shoes. Inmate labor also provided food for the institution. Large garden plots tended by paupers produced vegetables in quantity, while cows pastured nearby supplied fresh milk. Under supervision of bridewell keeper William Sloo, vagrants netted shad and other fish in the Hudson River for almshouse meals.[20]

Where pauper food-producing efforts proved impractical, the commissioners made other arrangements. For example, local butchers annually submitted bids to furnish the almshouse with beef and meat products. The commissioners purchased other supplies, such as grain and molasses, in large quantities at wholesale prices. Rich New Yorkers, such as merchant Alexander Robertson, often donated food for the almshouse poor; Robertson celebrated the marriage of his daughter in 1791 by the "uncommon method" of sending to the house 150 loaves of bread, 300 pounds of beef, 130 pounds of cheese, three barrels of strong ale, and three barrels of apples. Many local market ordinances stipulated that bread, butter, flour, vegetables, and other food products, if found on inspection to be of improper weight or quality, be confiscated for the poor. In an effort to eliminate the nuisance created by hogs roaming the streets, the common council in 1786 ordered such animals seized and delivered to the almshouse. Extraordinary circumstances occasionally provided a special source of supplies. A large, decorated ox paraded through the streets by Republicans at Jefferson's election in 1801 ended up on almshouse supper tables. In April 1806, when American seaman John Pierce was killed in New York harbor by the guns of a British frigate, an angry crowd immediately seized ten cartloads of provisions purchased for the British blockade squadron and brought them to the almshouse "amidst the loud huzzas of the multitude." [21]

Almshouse residents had needs beyond the immediate requirements of food and shelter. Since the welfare institution constantly bulged with afflicted persons—diseased, blind, insane, crippled, or aged and dying paupers—the understaffed almshouse medical department worked overtime. In the colonial period the common council had paid a local physician to act as "Doctor of the Poor." City aldermen expanded this practice after the Revolution. Thus in 1784 they appointed Dr. Peter Van Bueren as almshouse physician at an annual salary of £80 to handle cases which transcended the skills of the institution's resident apothecary. Between 1788 and 1796 the poorhouse served as a kind of medical school, for the resident physician "received no emolument but what arose from the privileges granted to a number of Students of Physic and Surgery in the City, to attend the practice of the houses." By 1796, however, the newly opened New York Hospital had drawn the "attention of the students," forcing the common council to restore the physician's job as a salaried post. For the position, the aldermen selected William McIntosh, himself a former pauper and later the almshouse apothecary whose medical studies the city council had financed.[22]

In the early nineteenth century, growth of the pauper population necessitated further expansion of the almshouse medical department. For example, after 1800 established medical men of good reputation—doctors such as David Hosack, William McNevin, and Felix Pascalis—served as unpaid "visiting" physicians. New medical arrangements took effect in 1817 soon after completion of two hospital buildings at Bellevue. The new plan stipulated four medical appointments: a resident physician and a resident surgeon, each to live at Bellevue and each salaried at $250 annually; and a visiting physician and a visiting surgeon—"honorary," unpaid consultants. While respected physicians normally held the advisory positions, the full-time jobs usually went to young doctors or medical students who accepted a small salary "on account of the information to be obtained in the line of their professions."[23]

In addition, the almshouse provided some specialized medical services. The superintendent kept a midwife on call, and pregnant women "in their hour of nature's peril" might choose between the almshouse physician and the Widow Spencer. The commissioners regularly permitted doctors from the City Dispensary and the Kine-Pock Institution, two private medical charities, to inoculate paupers against smallpox. Epidemics of yellow fever often forced the common council to expand almshouse facilities for sick dependents. Although mentally disturbed patients received no special treatment, the city council did provide separate accommodations for such "crazy paupers"—usually primitive basement quarters.[24]

Educational facilities in the poorhouse reflected municipal concern about pauperism. The rationale for pauper education also revealed contemporary opinions about the causes of dependency. The standard argument generally held that pauperism stemmed from ignorance, immorality, and crime. The absence of schools for the poor, a common council committee asserted in 1803, "has no doubt been the source of many crimes and tends to debase the mind, and cherishes every evil propensity." City officials conceived of education as an all-purpose reform which would shape and firm the character of poor children and stimulate virtuous and industrious habits. Thus the almshouse schoolmaster, beginning soon after British evacuation, imparted daily lessons in spelling, reading, writing, arithmetic, and the "principles of religion and morality." [25]

In an era before public education became common, schooling for most children depended on private support. During the first quarter of the nineteenth century, almshouse education became closely connected with the fortunes of the Free School Society. In the absence of real municipal or state aid for education, this society had been organized in 1805 by a number of prominent citizens to build schools for the poor throughout the city. The common council seconded the Free School Society's efforts and appropriated several city lots and unoccupied buildings to the new group. In return the society agreed to educate poorhouse children. This arrangement became impractical with completion of the Bellevue almshouse and the consequent move from the center, where the society's schools were located, to the outskirts of the city. The almshouse commissioners, however, kept the school program going independently; by 1823 they supervised instruction of 350 children in four classrooms at Bellevue. But this plan faltered as well because the teachers, recruited from among almshouse residents, lacked training and seemed to "have no excitement to the performance of their duties." In 1823 the Free School Society again assumed responsibility for pauper education and sent trained teachers to handle the poorhouse schools.[26]

The municipal government also displayed considerable interest in the spiritual welfare of public dependents and sought to inculcate among them "a due sense of religion." Thus the commissioners furnished the institution with "pious books" and encouraged literate paupers to read them to the others. As early as 1785 the city fathers permitted Protestant clergymen to preach in the house; they hoped particularly to reclaim the impious and intemperate Irish Catholic immigrants, who formed, by the 1790's, the largest single group of public dependents. Such services were held irregularly until formation in 1812 of the first city mission organization —the Society for Supporting the Gospel among the Poor of the City of New-York. This association, established primarily to conduct religious services for the poor in public institutions such as the almshouse, bridewell, city hospital, and state prison, received generous financial support from the common council after 1814 in the form of annual salary grants to the Reverend John Stanford, the official preacher. Such aldermanic zeal stemmed largely from the conviction that religious exhortation kept order and discipline in the poorhouse and fostered morality and good habits among the paupers—in effect, a belief that religion might cure poverty.[27]

The almshouse served not only the varied needs of the poor, but many other practical functions as well. The common council occasionally held official meetings at the house; more regular were the dinners, political gatherings, and boisterous assemblies of hard-drinking, incumbent councilmen. Such politicking at public expense seemed especially apparent when Tammany leaders Arcularius and Mooney served as superintendents, but it appears to have been common throughout the period. Until 1796 the municipality used the old almshouse in City Hall Park as a polling place for the sixth ward. Stables at Bellevue housed the "public horses," fire engines, and other municipal equipment. Following the suggestion of city inspector John Pintard in 1804, the resident physician made daily meteorological reports at the "City Observatory" in the almshouse garden. City officals experimented at the house with new fireplace improvements, especially those of Count Rumford, and with new kinds of fuel, such as coal. The house served as an asylum for lost children, and public notices advised that parents could apply there for them. During the early part of the period, slaves and unruly servants might be committed to the house by masters upon payment of proper fees, although the almshouse commissioners often objected to use of the institution for this purpose. Finally, the almshouse contained a morgue, or "dead house," where coroners held inquests and physicians performed autopsies. Thus the institution not only housed the poor but became an all-purpose municipal building serving the varied needs of city government.[28]

Although few villages and towns built poorhouses before the state welfare reform of 1824, population pressures in New York City early made institutional facilities both logical and necessary. Despite its shortcomings, New York's almshouse represented official determination to comply with state-imposed poor laws. It also reflected the dual motivations which often sustained humanitarianism and philanthropy: the benevolent concern, on the one hand, to aid the poor and rescue the downtrodden; and the not so benevolent effort, on the other hand, to protect society and prevent undesirable or socially disturbing behavior. The almshouse, by assisting helpless dependents and by minimizing begging and other forms of "visible" poverty, performed both functions. The municipal program for outdoor relief stemmed from similar motives and served similar purposes.

7

The Urban Welfare Program:
Outdoor Relief

In describing New York's public institutions in 1797, the visiting duc de la Rochefoucauld reported a revealing conversation with one of the almshouse commissioners. "The poor-house of New York," the commissioner observed, "produces paupers." This comment suggests that as early as the 1790's municipal welfare officials questioned the efficacy of institutionalizing the urban poor. In the early nineteenth century such ideas found more frequent expression, became more convincing to contemporaries.

The emerging argument consisted of a number of closely related propositions: that almshouses brought no permanent solutions but merely perpetuated pauperism; that certainty of public aid in time of crisis destroyed initiative, thriftiness, and self-reliance; that relief stimulated, indeed strengthened and deepened, the very dependency it aimed to overcome; that real benevolence demanded close scrutiny of all relief applicants to determine those "worthy" and "deserving" of aid; that such assistance be as sparing as possible; that immorality and "lewdness" in the poorhouse generated a new crop of infant paupers each year; that almshouse admissions be authorized only after all other alternatives had been exhausted. Such fundamental assumptions underlay all public assistance in

New York City. Thus the almshouse commissioners spent considerable time examining welfare applicants for official residence, apprenticing pauper children in local trades, and searching for parents, relatives, ship captains, or others who might be legally responsible for support. Some dependents they directed to private charities; generous subsidies helped others migrate from the city. In addition, the municipality financed an extensive program of outdoor or home relief, a program conceived as less troublesome, less expensive, and less enduring than institutional care.

Outdoor relief rivaled the almshouse in importance. That institution, of course, served real needs and drained substantial sums from the municipal treasury annually. But the number benefiting from almshouse care could not compare with those aided, at less cost, by outdoor relief. Each year, particularly during the winters, municipal funds brought provisional assistance to thousands of indigent immigrants, slum dwellers, and jobless, unskilled laborers. Outdoor relief also seemed the most effective method of supporting temporary dependents produced by war, economic depression, or such local disasters as epidemic and fire. Although officials occasionally provided cash or, more rarely, jobs on public projects, such assistance usually took the form of food, clothing, and firewood.

Along with their many other duties, the commissioners of the almshouse administered the outdoor relief program. In immediate post-Revolutionary years, the commissioners examined applicants who appeared at weekly meetings in the almshouse. The city council set up a special "donation fund" upon which commissioners drew to supply those deserving aid. During winter months the commissioners formed visiting committees to canvass the slums, distinguish between "real or pretended" distress, and grant aid where "absolutely necessary." In February 1796, for example, one such committee visited and subsidized forty families, "either by giving them money, where they supposed they might be trusted with it, or by leaving orders on neighboring grocers." On other occasions the almshouse keeper distributed food parcels from municipal larders according to pauper lists made up by the commissioners. Keeper and commissioners also gave out potato "tickets" and wood "tokens," permitting the outdoor poor to draw potatoes from the almshouse and firewood from public wood yards in the city.[1]

After the welfare reorganization of 1800, the commissioners delegated responsibility for outdoor relief to the almshouse superintendent. Thereafter he supervised investigation of pauper applicants and made relief decisions. To assist in these duties the superintendent hired several aides. Some handled food distribution from the almshouse; others—early case workers perhaps—visited poor families and dispensed advice and assistance. In normal times such relief appeared parsimonious at best. For example, superintendent William Mooney permitted the assistant charged with visiting to dole out only two dollars per day in cash relief. Those with greater needs were instructed to apply at the almshouse. Heavy relief demands during hard times, of course, forced expansion of this usually closefisted program.[2]

In addition to commissioners and superintendent, city councilmen shared in the distribution of outdoor relief. As early as 1786 aldermen distributed public funds to the poor of their respective wards. The council considered such aid necessary to prevent further admissions to the already overcrowded almshouse. In an effort to make the common council share responsibility for rising welfare costs, superintendent Philip Arcularius in 1805 suggested the propriety of limiting outdoor assistance to those specifically recommended by aldermen. However, councilmen preferred to reap the political benefits of cash distributions in their wards to the more exacting and less popular task of detecting "impositions." (Indeed, some evidence suggests that aggressive city leaders, men like Edward Livingston and De Witt Clinton, consciously built political support among the lower classes through social programs.) That political considerations motivated some was confirmed by a council action of 1812 which prohibited cash relief by aldermen because "the public treasures may be employed by unprincipled members of the Board, under the guise & semblence of public charity, to ensure their own re-election." Yet newspaper

accounts in January 1814 indicated that the practice had been
resumed, in this instance amounting to two hundred dollars per
ward.[3]

Thus various groups of municipal officials normally shared control of the outdoor relief program. But times of urgent need required coordinated action. Four such major crises in urban relief,
some extending over several years, stand out in the early history
of New York City: a decade of yellow fever epidemics after 1795;
a serious shortage of food and firewood during the early months
of 1805; the suspension of commerce caused by the federal shipping embargo, 1807–1809; and several years of severe depression
after the War of 1812. Each crisis revealed the ineffectiveness of
shared assignments and the irresponsibility of municipal miserli-
ness. Each demanded additional humanitarian exertions by both
public and private agencies. And each produced new efforts to
confront poverty and dependency in the city.

The summer and autumn epidemics of yellow fever which hit
New York City almost annually for a decade around the turn of
the nineteenth century brought unprecedented pressures for municipal relief. During these periods of disease, affluent and middle-class citizens sought havens of health and safety in the sub-
urbs and surrounding rural counties. Typically, city inspector John
Pintard estimated that almost 27,000 residents, about one-third of
New York's population, fled the city during the epidemic of 1805.
Stringent quarantine regulations suspended the vital commerce of
the port. Merchants and employers left town with their families.
With shops closed and business offices empty, virtually all economic activity ceased. These conditions quickly brought unemployment and subsequent dependency to the working class remaining in the disease-infested town. Equally predictable, the
"laboring poor," particularly wretched immigrant residents along
the waterfront and blacks in the Bancker Street slum, became the
most frequent victims of the "implacable foe." Under such circumstances, demands for public assistance mounted rapidly with
each new appearance of the dreaded fever.[4]

A special committee of health coordinated medical and relief measures during each of these epidemics. This committee had been formed by a number of concerned civic leaders in September 1793 (when yellow fever was ravaging Philadelphia) to draft effective precautionary procedures. Recognizing the threat to public safety, the New York city council shortly added seven aldermen to the voluntary citizens group. For the next eleven years, until formation of an official board of health in December 1804, the semi-autonomous health committee functioned as a major relief agency. Ignorant of the origins of yellow fever, the committee implemented quarantines and vigorously enforced new sanitation ordinances. But the disease came almost yearly, despite precautionary measures which appeared to some both primitive and tardy. Increasingly, therefore, the health committee provided the sick and poor with medicine and relief after an outbreak occurred. These tasks they performed responsibly and with as much efficiency as might be expected.[5]

During the epidemic of 1795, the health committee temporarily replaced the almshouse commissioners as dispensers of public charity. Although in mid-July some medical men believed reports of a suspicious fever, by the end of August few doubted arrival of the contagion. With sanitary and quarantine measures in effect, the health committee proceeded to prepare as a hospital the newly leased municipal buildings at Bellevue. The disease spread rapidly and, as Mayor Richard Varick wrote, seemed "most fatal among the poor emigrants who lived and died in filth and dirt." Some 750 persons died during the three-month epidemic; 438 had been so poor that the city buried them at public expense. The health committee made other provisions for survivors. The Bellevue buildings eventually accommodated 238 fever victims. Committee members, each assisted by "two confidential citizens," sought out the sick and indigent. These little groups made daily rounds of the city, securing medical treatment for the afflicted and distributing relief where needed. Donations poured into health committee coffers, including $7,000 from the people of Philadelphia (New Yorkers had sent a $5,000 donation to Philadelphia during the 1793 epidemic). With these resources, plus about $10,000 of municipal appropriations, the committee met the relief crisis head-on. When the fever appeared at an end in November 1795, the health committee handed over its pauper lists to the almshouse commissioners, who resumed their normal duties.[6]

In each of the following two summers, slight outbreaks of the disease occurred in the waterfront area near the Battery. But in each case the health committee quickly removed the sick to a new "pesthouse" on Bedlow's Island in the harbor, and yellow fever deaths remained low each year—sixty-nine in 1796 and about twenty-five in 1797. A more severe test of municipal energy and initiative occurred in the late summer and early autumn of 1798, when New York experienced perhaps its most severe yellow fever epidemic.[7]

The 1798 contagion first appeared in July and August in the dock areas, this time on the East River shore of Manhattan. The first signs of disease touched off the now usual flight from the city, disrupting normal business activity and leaving working people unemployed and increasingly dependent on public assistance. Once again the health committee superseded the commissioners of the almshouse as a relief agency. Beyond working diligently to cleanse the city of summer filth, the health commissioners met daily at the almshouse to receive and act on relief applications. The common council purchased the Bellevue estate previously leased from Lindley Murray and the health committee supervised rapid construction of additional buildings on the property for indigent fever victims. The committee hired three physicians and a large number of nurses to care for the sick poor at Bellevue and in slum homes. For healthy dependents the committee set up three "cook houses" where soup, bread, and other food supplies were distributed. In addition to 800 paupers supported in the almshouse, between 1,600 and 2,000 New Yorkers sought daily meals at these soup houses during September and October. Some 500 families also drew daily rations from almshouse stores. Common council appropriations supported most of the relief effort, but as in previous years donations from wealthy New Yorkers and collections in other towns also financed some of the health committee operations. This private benevolence consisted not only of money, foodstuffs, and firewood, but such special items as catnip, castor oil, even six bottles of "Syrup Rasbury [sic] Vinegar." That such nostrums tempered the severity of the sickness is unlikely, however, for the death toll mounted to almost 2,000 for the two-month outbreak.[8]

The impact of the epidemic lasted well into the winter, as indicated in Mayor Varick's acknowledgment of a substantial contribution from an Albany relief committee: "We are extremely anxious and unprepared for the wintry blasts." Although the almshouse commissioners resumed their duties at the end of the epidemic, the health committee continued to receive and distribute donations until February 1799. The 1798 fever emergency also forced city authorities to think more realistically about effective precautions and preventives. Thus a special common council committee on epidemics and disease, borrowing a technique which had been used successfully in Philadelphia, recommended purchase of a number of large tents "adequate for 5000" which might be pitched outside the city as a refuge for "the poor class of citizens." [9]

The next few years brought only mild outbreaks of yellow fever, but much more serious epidemics occurred in the summers of 1803 and 1805. Earlier patterns were repeated. "Our city," wrote a New York physician on September 20, 1803, "has received greater damage this year than in any former season of yellow fever; the wealthy early abandoned the city, and the poor are daily falling victims to its ravages." A reactivated health committee quickly reopened the Bellevue buildings for the sick, set up sheds and tents four miles from the city for working-class families still in health, and distributed weekly rations from the almshouse to those remaining in the city. During the 1805 epidemic the newly formed board of health, headed by Mayor De Witt Clinton, replaced the earlier semi-official health committee but performed essentially similar duties—supporting fever victims in Bellevue and dispensing food and other relief from the almshouse. The common council also utilized public work relief for the first time in an emergency situation, employing at least thirty jobless men at cleaning and repairing city streets. In addition, the Secretary of the Navy permitted the use of federal buildings in the navy yard for fever patients. The relief and medical expenditures of health commissioners and aldermen during the 1805 epidemic amounted to $25,000, a considerable sum for the time. At the peak of the outbreak in October 1805 almshouse superintendent Philip Arcularius claimed that "improper Objects of Public Charity" needlessly siphoned city funds. "Improper Objects," according to Arcularius, consisted of nonresidents (especially free blacks), seamen and their families, parents who refused to apprentice their children, and those unable to "give satisfaction of their being in want." Despite the nonbenevolent attitude of the city's chief welfare official, the municipal government generally expanded public responsibilities for social welfare during these recurrent periods of urban crisis.[10]

The early winter months of the same year—1805—brought another welfare emergency to New York City. This time severely cold weather during January and February and a simultaneous scarcity of firewood stimulated relief needs. Municipal officials always knew that welfare demands, particularly outdoor relief, increased markedly with the slowdown, even occasional suspension, of business and commerce each winter. The special problem of fuel for the poor had prompted numerous benevolent proposals in post-Revolutionary years. In a letter to the *Daily Advertiser* in January 1791, "A Poor Man's Friend" had proposed a public fuel dispensary to meet winter relief demands. The anonymous correspondent envisioned, perhaps realistically, that such a plan would bring more effectual relief than "all the charity sermons preached thro' the winter." In an open letter to Mayor Clinton appearing in the *New-York Evening Post* on October 12, 1804, "Civis" castigated wood sellers as "monopolists" and forestallers who reaped unconscionable profits from shivering slum dwellers; at the same time, he revived the plan for a coordinated municipal fuel program as "the cheapest way of relieving the poor." Three days later, on October 15, city inspector John Pintard presented the common council with a special report containing identical proposals on the subject of fuel for the poor.[11]

In his report, Pintard pointed out that the insular situation of New York City brought annual fuel shortages. Winter ice floes and freezing weather slowed wood shipments at the very time fuel demands rose. Consequently the price of firewood soared to exorbitant levels which laboring men could not meet. It therefore became the "duty" of municipal government, he wrote, "to devise some practicable mode of relieving the wants of the miserable, and if possible without increasing the public burthens." Pintard urged the city council to buy 500 cords of firewood at wholesale prices before winter arrived. The cut logs might then be "judiciously resold" at prices determined by the circumstances of the buyer, repaying municipal outlays and leaving a sufficient portion for free distribution to absolute indigents. "Robust paupers" from the almshouse might be made to saw, pile, and deliver the wood, also saving considerable expense.[12]

Although the common council appointed a special committee to consider the scarcity of fuel, the aldermen did not adopt John Pintard's plan. Nor did the committee devise any other productive measures. Doubly unfortunate, the severe cold of winter clogged the harbor with ice and caused suspension of wood deliveries from Westchester and New Jersey. These conditions intensified an already serious fuel crisis and forced the city government to seek legislative assistance. A common council petition of January 23, 1805, claimed "the most severe privation at present experienced by the poor is the scarcity of wood" and sought permission to cut up state-owned wooden fortifications at the Battery for fuel. Mayor Clinton buttressed the petition with a simultaneous letter to the city's assemblymen seeking active support of the measure. Without such help and without a break in the weather, Clinton argued, "ten thousand souls" would be forced onto relief rolls within a few days. Such arguments seemed persuasive, for the legislature unanimously endorsed the municipal request a week later.[13]

The needs of the poor, however, went beyond firewood during the winter emergency of 1805. As happened each winter, business

curtailment threw many laborers, particularly the unskilled, out
of work. Once again the commissioners of the almshouse yielded
relief functions, this time to a special common council "committee
of supply." Entrusted with vast powers to deal with the relief
crisis, the new committee met daily at the almshouse. It immediately sponsored a widened welfare program lasting two
months. During the week ending January 29, for example, the
committee of supply gave food allowances to 5,400 persons and
distributed wood to 1,200 families. Private donations of cash,
food, clothing, and firewood increased the committee's coffers
and supplemented municipal appropriations. For the first time, a
general citizens meeting produced relief committees in each ward
(a technique of voluntarism much used in following years).
These ward committees collected funds and sought out the
needy in their neighborhoods. In addition, a new organization
named the Samaritan Society spontaneously appeared to supplement public assistance; at the end of the crisis, the society just as
spontaneously dissolved. The committee of supply and the common
council, also for the first time, attempted to coordinate public
relief efforts with those of numerous private charitable groups.
And finally, editor William Coleman of the *Evening Post* drew
public attention to the plight of the poor and urged on the benevolent workers with his pen in an early newspaper crusade against
poverty. City dwellers again responded positively, although somewhat belatedly, to urban problems. Above all, the emergency of
1805 revealed the effectiveness of cooperative welfare efforts by
both public and private agencies.[14]

Worsening American diplomatic relations with England marked
the early years of the nineteenth century. The Jeffersonian Congress
reacted to international violations of neutral rights by clamping
an embargo on American commerce in December 1807. Passage
of the Embargo Act posed severe relief problems for New York
City during the winters of 1807–1808 and 1808–1809. In these
preindustrial years commerce stimulated and sustained New
York's prosperity. Profits of merchants and the jobs of most urban
workers depended on maritime commerce and supplementary

trades. Thus extended disruption of normal economic activity brought large-scale unemployment among seamen and long-shoremen, laborers and artisans. The city felt these effects almost immediately. One observer estimated in January 1808 that the number of destitute, dependent New Yorkers had increased tenfold during a few weeks of embargo enforcement.[15]

Political protests and relief demands emerged almost immediately among those thrown out of work by the embargo. For example, after widely circulated public notices a large group of seamen, perhaps two hundred in number, met in City Hall Park on January 9, 1808, to demonstrate opposition to the shipping suspension and determine a course of action. The meeting provoked controversy and middle-class concern for public order, but the assembly proved mild enough. The jobless sailors asserted a desire to "choose some kind of employment rather than the poor house for a livelyhood" and called on Mayor Marinus Willett to provide them with work for the duration of the winter. The mayor disapproved of the sailors' "mode of application," which seemed to threaten orderly processes of government, an especially disturbing consideration in the wake of working-class nativist riots which had disrupted the city about a year earlier. However, Mayor Willett addressed the meeting, declared support of the embargo a patriotic duty, and announced, although somewhat ambiguously, that the city would "provide for the wants of every person, without distinction, who may be considered proper objects of relief." [16]

Yet the park protest produced quick municipal action. On January 11, two days after the seamen's meeting, the common council promulgated a three-point relief program to counter the disastrous effects of the embargo; first, federal officers at the United States naval yard in New York agreed to hire unemployed seamen at city expense (a measure of social control as much as of benevolence, for aldermen envisioned that with sailors at work and "subject to the orders and discipline of the Navy, no ill consequences can result to the peace of the city, from their tumultuous associations"); second, the municipality provided jobs for the unemployed on such public projects as filling in the Collect Pond, building the new City Hall, and cleaning and repairing city streets; and third, from a soup kitchen in the almshouse welfare officials began issuing food rations several times a week to those in need. To supervise and coordinate this emergency relief program, the city council once again sidestepped the commissioners of the almshouse—this time appointing a special aldermanic committee of ways and means to deal with the crisis. The committee met daily for three months and spent $14,228 on food, firewood, cash donations, and salaries for indigent workmen. Simultaneously, the state legislature provided work for jobless men on defense projects in the city's harbor. Some New Yorkers even demanded a federal welfare program, for as editor James Cheetham of the Republican *American Citizen* observed in 1809, "the NATION should provide for the distress which the nation inflicts." Little sympathy for such views could be found in Congress, however, and relief during the embargo remained essentially a local affair. As spring replaced winter the acuteness of the 1808 crisis passed. On April 1 the common council dissolved the ways and means committee and suspended the emergency relief program.[17]

During the following winter, with few signs of improvement in Anglo-American relations, economic crisis deepened and posed even more burdensome problems for city government. As early as December 1808 the commissioners of the almshouse urged the council to reopen the municipal soup kitchens. In January 1809 almshouse superintendent William Mooney reported the institution crowded with more than a thousand paupers. "The outdoor poor," he further told the council, "are already incalculable and rapidly increasing. There wants consists [sic] of every necessary of life." Reacting to these reports, the city council speedily reimplemented the welfare plan of the previous winter and borrowed funds to finance it.[18]

Once again massive outdoor relief formed the basis of the program. Between January 6 and March 31, city officials spent $7,601 in distributing 76,019 individual food allotments (each ration consisted of one pound of bread, one-half pound of pork, and one quart of bean porridge) and $4,581 in supplying nearly 1,800 cartloads of firewood; in addition, cash donations amounted to $602, bringing total expenditures to almost $13,000. Institutional costs mounted quickly as well during the same winter, for between November 1808 and January 1809 almshouse censuses showed a 25 per cent increase in paupers, the count rising from 841 to 1,050.[19]

Despite the apparent magnitude of the public-relief program during the embargo crisis, the almshouse commissioners noted in 1809 that the streets still swarmed with beggars. Yet the commissioners often seemed less concerned with the welfare of such visible paupers than with the image of the metropolis; they feared that large numbers of beggars would lead visitors to believe "that the poor are but illy provided for" in New York City. However, a number of city natives, including editor James Cheetham, held just such views. Public relief, Cheetham asserted, had been "sparingly administered" throughout the emergency; "in times of public calamity," he wrote, "there is a cruelty in parsimony for which no apology can be found." Others echoed the Republican scribe, including municipal voters who turned out the Republican city administration in the 1809 elections. One newspaper correspondent urged, in terms suggestive of twentieth-century welfare-rights organizations, that the "suffering" poor demand relief "as a right." Obviously, assistance needs exceeded both municipal willingness and existing tax revenues. Thus the embargo crisis stimulated, as did earlier relief emergencies, private benevolence; existing charitable societies expanded aid programs, new voluntary groups such as the important Assistance Society emerged, and ward committees sprouted once more to help those who did not normally depend on public relief or private charity. Clearly the embargo brought unexampled economic misery to New York City and other seaport towns, conditions which required but did not always receive energetic relief.[20]

The fourth major crisis in urban relief occurred during the War of 1812 and in the years immediately following. The war itself produced destitution because it disrupted regular economic activ-

ity and, for those in military service, normal family patterns. Almshouse superintendent Richard Furman told the common council
in November 1814 that "owing to the distresses occasioned by the
War . . . the applications for public charity will be far more
numerous than at any former period." Furman's forecast did not
miss the mark. Between April 1, 1812, and April 1, 1813, the
city supplied some outdoor relief to 1,973 families totaling 8,253
persons at a cost of $12,613. Within two years each of these
figures had doubled. Between April 1, 1814, and April 1, 1815,
almshouse commissioners granted assistance to 3,516 families (or
16,417 individuals); total outlay for home relief came to $25,485.
To handle increased numbers of welfare applicants, as well as to
ensure against "improper" donations, the city council in January
1816 permitted almshouse superintendent Furman to appoint
knowledgeable citizens in each ward to aid in examining neighborhood paupers and distributing relief in the slums. Completion of
the new Bellevue almshouse in 1816 temporarily reduced institutional pressures, but postwar depression forestalled any reduction in numbers of outdoor poor.[21]

Contrary to traditional views, the Panic of 1819 did not destroy
New York City's prosperity and touch off years of economic misery.
Severe depression, stemming largely from altered trade patterns
and changes in European economic and monetary policies, de-
scended on New York and other coastal cities as early as 1816 and
1817; only gradually did economic distress make its way to
interior sections of the country where it affected land and cotton.
Thus for New Yorkers the urban-relief problems of the War of
1812 continued almost uninterrupted into postwar years.[22]

The year 1817 seems to have been a crucial one in the social
welfare history of New York City. Not only did assistance demands
and relief expenditures top those of most other years of the same
decade, but the state legislature simultaneously reduced the
financial resources available to the municipality for welfare purposes. As previously noted, a law of 1798 had imposed a 1 per cent
tax on auction sales in the port, a measure specifically designed
to raise funds for support of indigent immigrants who had not

become official city residents. The tax provided the common council with substantial sums annually for public assistance. The auction duty produced $32,455 in 1815, but the peacetime resumption of trade, particularly the dumping of British goods in New York, quickly pushed up municipal income from this source; in 1816 auction-duty funds soared to $72,705. Between 1798 and 1816 the tax brought in a total revenue of $526,252. Claiming "good reason" to believe that the city did not need such large sums for the "foreign poor," the state comptroller urged repeal of the auction tax and suspended payments to the city treasurer on November 11, 1816. Obviously the loss of revenue adversely affected the city's welfare program at the beginning of another winter season.[23]

The common council took immediate action for restoration of this important source of municipal revenue. Learning of legislative intentions before the comptroller's action, the aldermen met on November 9, 1816, and appointed a committee to draft a protest against the suspension which took effect two days later. The municipal petition argued the absolute necessity for some state support for the urban welfare program. The poor laws required removal of the state's nonresident, immigrant paupers to New York City only "because they can be sent no farther." Statistics provided by almshouse superintendent Furman substantiated the assertion that such foreign-born paupers imposed a constant and heavy drain upon municipal resources. Countering the idea that the rapid rise in auction sales after the war produced more funds than could be used effectively, the aldermen argued that the transition from "a state of universal war to one of universal peace" encouraged heavier immigration. Thus the number of immigrant paupers, whose support was envisioned by the auction law, would increase at the same time the relief fund grew. A second council committee, which included Richard Furman, traveled to Albany to lobby and protest in person.[24]

The protests of councilmen and city assemblymen brought results which hardly satisfied municipal officials. In February 1817 a joint senate-assembly committee recommended that the auction-tax suspension be rescinded, a measure the legislature later approved. However, the legislature thwarted municipal expectations with a simultaneous decision to appropriate only $10,000 annually to New York City from the tax. Not only had the city's welfare program been deprived of accustomed state funds during the severity of winter, but the restored tax provided only a fraction of earlier revenue. In both of these ways, the auction-duty controversy and its outcome had important negative consequences for social welfare in New York City in 1817 and after.[25]

With the auction duty suspended, and then only partially restored, difficulties began almost immediately. Unemployment and postwar depression had already set in. Unprecedentedly heavy immigration swelled New York's lower classes. According to one official estimate, more than seven thousand European immigrants arrived in the city during 1816; few had skills, even fewer had jobs, and most sought public assistance during the early winter months of 1817. Winter relief demands, usually very high anyway, much exceeded those of earlier years. An *ad hoc* citizens committee, formed in February 1817 to gather contributions for the poor, estimated that 15,000 persons (about one-seventh of the city's population) depended on public and private charity. Public relief costs in the 1816–1817 fiscal year soared to $125,045, a sum not duplicated until after 1825. Private charities responded to the emergency and similarly increased their efforts and their costs. The citizens committee, working through the now time-tested technique of small ward groups, raised more than $8,000 for the poor and supplemented the municipal assistance program.[26]

The relief crisis of 1817 stimulated strong forces for charity reform in New York City. Burgeoning assistance needs increasingly accompanied by the city's rapid population growth. Simultaneously, city officials and humanitarian leaders questioned the purposes and challenged the results of welfare and aid programs for the poor. Some New Yorkers remarked that pauperism increased at a greater rate than total population, that the sufferings of the poor seemingly grew "by the very means taken to subdue them." Despite the obvious relationship between lengthened welfare rolls and depressed economic conditions, such attitudes flourished. Given the commonly accepted moralistic assumptions about the causes of dependency, the new "solutions" offered appeared entirely predictable—less welfare and more moral reform.[27]

By 1817 a harsh moralism on social questions characterized both public and private welfare efforts. For instance, the common council appointed a special committee in May 1817 to study poverty and poor relief. At the end of its investigation, the committee recommended a number of welfare "reforms." These included: strict enforcement of the settlement laws and rapid removal of vagrants and nonresident paupers; centralized distribution of all charity and relief funds, preferably by the almshouse commissioners, to prevent duplications and "impositions"; and appointment of special investigators to screen carefully the needs of welfare applicants. The common council accepted these suggestions and added one of its own—reduction of city expenditures which, they said, had been rising steadily, "particularly from the great addition of foreign Poor." Opting for immediate retrenchment, the Democratic council slashed by 25 per cent the salary of almshouse superintendent Furman, an old Federalist, reducing his income from $2,000 to $1,500. The council contemplated similar cuts in public relief.[28]

Humanitarian leaders of private charities, almost without exception, had arrived at an equally rigid, moralistic position on poverty by 1817. The *ad hoc* citizens committee, previously mentioned, investigated the causes of poverty during the 1817 crisis "to devise some plan to prevent in future a recurrence of so great an evil." This group of distinguished civic leaders, unwilling to admit economic inequities, fastened on alcoholism as "the most prominent cause" of pauperism and rising relief expenses. Their solution, therefore, primarily consisted of unsuccessful efforts of secure limitations on the number of liquor licenses and closer supervision of the more than 2,000 "grog shops" and "tippling houses" in New York City. Religious and missionary groups, education societies, and the city's numerous other charities had reached similar moralistic conclusions. Perhaps an even more typical response to the relief crisis of 1817 can be found in the formation of the Society for the Prevention of Pauperism, a group dedicated not to distributing charity but to eliminating poverty causes. Yet the society proposed only to improve the morals of the poor rather than eliminate the social and economic evils of the environment, only to promote pious, virtuous, and diligent habits rather than counter economic inequality and social injustice in the industrializing, urban community. Unquestionably, heavy relief expenditures in 1817 and heated controversy about social welfare practices catalyzed New Yorkers' attitudes about poverty and pauperism.[29]

Throughout the period before 1825, New York City officials pursued a dual welfare program. For the helpless poor the almshouse supplied a refuge, a secure haven from the harsh realities of existence in the rising city. For those whose need was more temporary, and thus less severe, outdoor relief provided an alternative to institutionalization. Even after the state poor-law reform of 1824, which urged the abolition of outdoor relief, welfare officials in New York City found it impossible to abandon home assistance. At the beginning of the period municipal officials promoted welfare aid of this kind as a less expensive mode of complying with state poor laws than sending all dependents to the almshouse. Yet as each succeeding relief crisis affected a larger population, expenditures for outdoor assistance mounted to what seemed alarming proportions. Gradually the sincere and benevolent attitudes which had motivated public and private humanitarians turned sour and gave way to a doctrine of moral improvement as the best method of helping the poor. The crisis in outdoor relief in the early nineteenth century, perhaps more than any other development, stimulated proliferation of private charity and helped shape the humanitarian rationale.

III

PRIVATE HUMANITARIANISM

8

The Humane Society and Urban Reform

Public assistance programs represented but one kind of response to urban poverty and deepening dependency. Private humanitarianism complemented municipal action in important ways in the early decades of the nineteenth century. During these years immigration, industrialization, and urbanization destroyed the orderly society of the eighteenth-century town and brought social change, confusion, and chaos to New York City. Urban humanitarians and civic leaders reacted to the disturbed and disordered state of the city by supporting a variety of charitable, reform organizations. These voluntary associations supplemented municipal relief activities, assisted groups whose dependency had not yet been recognized as a governmental responsibility, and attacked worsening social conditions in the urban environment. The Humane Society of New York City was the most consistently important of these groups, and, because of the diversity and inclusiveness of its interests, the most representative. From its origins in 1787 until the 1830's this society responded in positive ways to poverty and other social problems which characterized American urban growth.

The plight of imprisoned debtors stimulated formation of

the new society in 1787. The outmoded penal system of New York State, and especially the imprisonment of debtors, constituted one of the more obvious injustices of the post-Revolutionary period. During the 1780's, despite some commercial advances, the United States experienced severe economic depression and dislocation. Debtor interests aligned against creditors in almost every state, and the contest occasionally ended in violence, as in Shays' Rebellion in Massachusetts. The paper money that financed the Revolution had been repudiated; merchants and creditors demanded specie in payment of debts; and as a result debtor prisons filled rapidly. This situation prevailed in New York.[1]

Municipal authorities confined convicted debtors in a section of the city jail, a dark and dismal structure located near the present site of City Hall. Not only was the imprisonment of debtors irrational but state law obliged debtors to provide their own keep (a practice that contrasted with the treatment of criminals and public paupers, whose needs were supplied by city and state governments). Furthermore, many prisoners left families destitute, without support, and in such cases the almshouse or some other form of public relief remained the only recourse. In some instances, the families of debtors even lived in the jail with the prisoners, a similarly unhappy practice. In 1798, for example, at least thirty families resided in the New York City debtor's prison—all supported by charity. The Enlightenment had yet to extend its rational and reforming influence to the prison systems of the United States. Imprisonment for debt remained, one editor wrote, a "remnant of feudal and aristocratic tyranny." [2]

Observers continually emphasized the filth and horror of the city's prison. In March 1790 Marinus Willett, sheriff of New York County, wrote of conditions in the debtor's cells in a letter to De Witt Clinton, who represented the city in the assembly: "The wretchedness there is past my power to attempt a description— if distress ever claimed Legislative assistance, the melancholy situation of the confined debtors in this place demand[s] attention." Willett urged Clinton to support a bill to relieve and improve "the deplorable state of those unhappy people." When one re-former inspected the jail in 1811, his "olfactory nerves were assailed with a noisome effluvia," and another visitor depicted "squalid Misery seated on her filthy throne, with Poverty and Vice, Oppression and Sickness, officiating as her ministers." A third wrote that sight of the prison would convert men to the reform cause more readily than logic and rational argument. Some prisoners themselves wrote letters to the newspapers com-plaining about poor treatment, inadequate facilities, and, more specifically, the use of large, open tubs for toilets. As late as 1820, a grand jury of the court of general sessions reported the debtor's jail to be in a state of physical decay and ruin.[3]

The debtors themselves formed a varied group. Most were imprisoned for small sums. A petition to the legislature in 1788 noted that of 1,162 persons sent to jail for debt in New York City during 1787 and 1788, a total of 716, or 62 per cent, were committed for "sums recoverable before a justice of the peace," many under twenty shillings. Another report revealed that during 1809 some 1,152 debtors had been confined to prison for sums under twenty-five dollars. According to one observer, other prison-ers by fraud, dishonesty, and speculation "lost their fortune and what is worse that of others." A third group consisted of sailors confined as a result of false suits brought by their captains "with a view of securing their persons until they depart from the port." And finally, reformers alleged that young and "abandoned" girls were committed for very small debts by brothel keepers for the purpose of extorting the "wages of wickedness" with the threat of a jail term. Law-enforcement officers (sheriff and jailers) threw these debtors, male and female, indiscriminately together—a practice, wrote "Humanitas" in 1810, which made the prison a "school of lewdness and vice." [4]

Some historians, notably Edward T. Randall, have attempted to show that the number of persons imprisoned for debt in the United States has been overestimated. Bonds posted with the sheriff enabled convicted debtors to live within legally established bounds, "gaol limits," or "liberties." Many debtors, therefore,

although officially in custody, enjoyed real freedom while their
financial affairs were straightened out. The annual reports of the
Humane Society, however, reveal substantial numbers of imprisoned debtors in New York City who did not live on the jail

Table 5

CONFINED DEBTORS SUPPORTED BY THE HUMANE SOCIETY, 1787–1818

Year	Debtors Supported	Year	Debtors Supported
1787	123	1804	184
1788	104	1805	227
1789–90	131	1806	183
1791	71	1807	298
1792	90	1808	1,025
1793	78	1809	607
1794	108	1810	524
1795	—	1811	536
1796	126	1812	399
1797	170	1813	—
1798	154	1814	199
1799	139	1815	501
1800	136	1816	1,120
1801	200	1817	328
1802	145	1818	267
1803	131		

Sources: *Daily Advertiser* (New York), February 21, 1789, May 13, 1791, April 5,
1792, February 11, 1793, February 11, 1794, March 11, 1795, February 17, 1798,
January 28, 1799, January 9, 1800, March 8, 1804; *Commercial Advertiser* (New
York), January 7, 1801, February 20, 1807; *New-York Evening Post*, January 9, 1802,
January 8, 1803, January 23, 1805, March 15, 1806, January 13, 1808, February 13,
1809, March 8, 1810, February 8, 1811, February 12, 1812, January 16, 1813,
January 9, 1815, February 19, 1816, February 18, 1817, February 14, 1818, Janu-
ary 21, 1819.

limits and who depended on charity for various periods of time.
In at least two years, 1808 and 1816, the society assisted more
than a thousand prisoners. To be sure, many debtors lived on
the jail limits in New York City, but the volume of aid dispensed
annually by the Humane Society to imprisoned debtors casts

doubt on Randall's basic argument—that all but a few debtors escaped jail.[5]

The unfortunate condition of these imprisoned debtors attracted the attention and sympathy of benevolent New Yorkers. The formation in 1787 of the Humane Society (originally named the Society for the Relief of Distressed Debtors) manifested this concern. Among the founders of the society were Judge John Sloss Hobart, political leaders Melancton Smith and Robert Troup, merchants Moses Rogers, Matthew Clarkson, and Lawrence Embree, and clergymen Abraham Beach, William Linn, and John Rodgers—the latter the first president of the organization. Mayor James Duane became a member in November 1788; Quaker humanitarians Thomas Eddy and John Murray, Jr., joined soon after, followed in 1798 by another civic leader, Dr. David Hosack.[6]

Composed of twenty-four members or managers, the society established a dual objective: providing debtors with the necessities of life (food, firewood, clothing, and bedding); and, second, securing release of "deserving" prisoners confined for small sums by assuming their debts, supplying attorneys and legal advice, and appealing to the humanity of creditors. The society also formed a visiting committee to examine the jail regularly, assure proper treatment of prisoners by the jailers, determine the needs of the debtors, and distribute relief among them.[7]

During the early period of its existence, the society depended upon the sporadic financial support of the urban community. Yet the calls for charity did not go completely unanswered. On Thanksgiving Day of 1789, President Washington made a donation of fifty guineas to the society. Collections made by a musical society, a debating society, the Mechanics Society, the Tammany Society, and various groups of Free Masons, and donations from charity sermons in numerous churches, provided a partial income. A charity box in the city's courthouse encouraged donation of jury fees from sessions of municipal, state, and federal courts. In 1794 the society placed a second charity box in the Tontine Coffee House on Wall Street, the original merchants' exchange in New York City. With these meager resources, the society assisted 123 destitute debtors during its first year by providing 2,042 pounds of beef and pork, 2,826 pounds of bread, 42 pounds of cheese, 24 bushels of potatoes, 32 cabbages, 8 bushels and 17 quarts of cornmeal, 8 loads of wood, and 6 shirts.[8]

The volume of aid dispensed by the society progressively mounted during the 1790's, as the published annual reports of the organization reveal. During 1789 some 131 prisoners received assistance; 170 debtors were aided in 1797; and in 1801 the society gave relief to 200 poor prisoners. Similarly, the financial resources of the society increased substantially in that same decade. In 1788 expenditures totaled £62; in 1794 donations totaled £327 (expenses amounted to about half of that sum); during 1798 relief costs came to $1,013. Most of this assistance took the form of food and firewood, although the society supplied some clothing and blankets and obtained the discharge of several prisoners each year. In 1803 the Reverend John Rodgers, Presbyterian minister and president of the society from its origin until 1809, reported "the pleasing reflection that the imprisoned debtor is comfortably fed and warmed." [9]

But the society did not limit itself solely to relief activities. During the 1790's, as a result of petitions and memorials to the state legislature, these New York humanitarians secured some moderate reforms in the penal code. The society showed particular concern with the lack of distinction between those confined for small and large debts and the willful debtors and victims of misfortune. Legislation of February 13, 1789, introduced at the instigation of the society, limited imprisonment to thirty days for those owing less than ten pounds—later changed to twenty-five dollars—the so-called Ten-Pound Act. Additional efforts to make creditors legally responsible for the support of confined debtors met consistent defeat in the legislature. The society also expressed alarm at the prevalence of vice, immorality, and drunkenness in the jail. The availability of liquor to prisoners constituted one of the many "irregularities" that prevailed in the institution. With the presumed assistance of the jailers, debtors allegedly exchanged or sold food received from the society for alcohol. A law of March 21, 1791, also passed at the request of the society, prohibited the sale or use of spirituous liquors in the prison and imposed $250 fines upon the sheriff for each violation.[10]

In other reforming efforts, the society persuaded the common council to supply the prison with fresh water and sick prisoners with medicine. But only the argument that diseases contracted in prison made alms seekers of liberated debtors prompted council action. During the yellow fever epidemics of the 1790's, the society financed some sanitary measures in the jail (repeated whitewashing of cell walls). These efforts, however, did not prevent several prisoners from being "delivered up to the malignancy of the common enemy" in the summer of 1798 before the municipal government removed the debtors to a more healthy abode. Even during this early period, the society did not confine assistance to destitute prisoners alone. Widening their horizons somewhat in 1790, the managers of the society, in conjunction with the Medical Society of New York, led in founding a public dispensary to serve the medical needs of lower-class citizens. The idea was first suggested by John Rodgers, who became the first president of the new facility in addition to his other duties. The medical men devised a plan of operation, the Humane Society conducted a successful fund-raising campaign, and the New York Dispensary opened early in 1791.[11]

As the urban community expanded after 1800 and as the plight of the poor in New York City became more extensively apparent, the society began to enlarge upon its original design. The society's annual report for 1802 acknowledged that the problems of the debtor had not been solved and that "their desolate condition will continue to call for the protecting and the supporting hand of benevolence." But the society further announced a plan to extend assistance to poverty-striken inhabitants throughout the city.[12]

The establishment of a soup house in September 1802 reflected the expanding functions of the society. Located near the jail on Frankfort Street and patterned after similar institutions in Europe, the soup house provided prepared meals for prisoners—a method "more economical and less liable to abuse" than the former practice of supplying debtors with uncooked food. In addition, the urban poor could purchase soup at the rate of four cents per quart. In winter months and during periods of epidemic and depression, soup was distributed free of charge. The society also printed soup tickets to be given to street beggars in place of money and provisions, which were "too frequently employed to purchase *liquor* instead of supplying the *real* wants of *life*." In recognition of its enlarged program of charitable assistance, at a meeting on March 7, 1803, the society formally changed its name to the Humane Society—a name the organization had been popularly called as early as 1789.[13]

The soup house became the central point of the Humane Society's widened orbit of charity. During the yellow fever epidemic of 1803, and a double catastrophe for the poor in 1805 (a severe winter with inadequate fuel supplies and a yellow fever epidemic during September and October), the institution delivered thousands of quarts of soup to the indigent and un-employed. In February 1805 the society opened a second soup house on Division Street between the seventh and tenth wards, two sections heavily populated by the poor. During 1805 the society distributed 33,642 quarts of soup from its two kitchens in addition to the normal aid to imprisoned debtors. In April of the next year, the society erected a new, brick structure on Tryon Row, replacing the old Frankfort Street soup house. The common council, displaying a high regard for the essential public services performed by the Humane Society, appropriated $600 for construction and donated city property adjacent to the jail as a building site.[14]

The monthly reports of the visiting committee, which now had the additional duty of supervising the soup house, provide a rough index to the extent of the society's relief activities. During 1806, for example, the soup kitchen supplied 183 debtors with 9,095 quarts of soup and the poor of the city with 4,823 quarts; in 1811 some 536 debtors received 21,601 quarts of soup, with 2,698 additional quarts issued for tickets or sold to the indigent. Thus, except for periods of extreme crisis among the poor (such as in 1805), the society continued to emphasize the relief of imprisoned debtors.[15]

New state legislation of 1817 abolished imprisonment for debt in cases involving sums under twenty-five dollars and caused a distinct change in the Humane Society's pattern of relief. Poor persons confined for debts smaller than twenty-five dollars had composed the bulk of prisoners aided by society. In most cases food from the soup house sustained these prisoners during the whole of their thirty-day term. The new law eliminated these debtors from prison. The number of confined debtors declined sharply, and reports in December 1824 declared the debtor's jail temporarily vacant.[16]

As a result of the new law, the focus of the society's relief efforts shifted permanently from imprisoned debtors to the poor of the city. During 1818 the society distributed 41,407 quarts of soup, but only about one-sixth of these went to prisoners. Needy New Yorkers received the largest portion—a total of 33,168 quarts. In the depression year of 1820 soup distribution to the indigent amounted to 69,279 quarts. In 1822 the society claimed that it never refused any applicant for relief and that "no human being is therefore in danger of perishing from want in this city." The soup house statistics, of course, provide only a partial measure of poverty in the metropolis. But it is evident that the Humane Society and other private charities, through timely assistance, prevented many poverty-striken New Yorkers from becoming public charges.[17]

In 1806 the Humane Society took on another function—the supervision of efforts to resuscitate victims of drowning. At a time when mercantile activity constituted the heart of New York's commercial life, with harbor, docks, and wharved ships crowded with busy workmen, and at a time when few people knew how to swim, many drowned. During the last half of the eighteenth century groups were organized in European and American sea-ports to rescue and revive drowning people. New York thus followed the example of Amsterdam (1767), London (1774),

Philadelphia (1780), Boston (1785), and Baltimore (1790).[18]

Contemporary medical theory supported the idea of resuscitation. Dr. David Hosack, one of the leading spirits of the humanitarian movement in New York City and a member of the Humane Society, published in 1792 a treatise on the causes of "suspended animation" from drowning. According to Hosack's analysis, drowning caused a suspension of all vital bodily functions. Recovery could not be accomplished by rolling the body over a barrel or hanging it by the heels, two methods most commonly applied. But revival could be achieved, Hosack wrote, by restoring the suspended functions to activity. Therefore, body heat must be revived by wrapping the victim in blankets, respiration by inflating the lungs with air, blood circulation by bloodletting, and action of the brain and nervous system by injecting warm solutions into the stomach and tobacco smoke into the bowels.[19]

The Humane Society adopted Hosack's four principles. To attain the desired results it sent to Europe for several sets of revival apparatus (consisting of bellows, pipes, and syringes) and stationed them at locations along the waterfront. Posters tacked up about the city and notices published in newspapers, city directories, and guidebooks listed instructions for using the equipment and the names of physicians for emergency calls. There is little reliable evidence, however, that Hosack's method was used with any success in New York City, although European societies using similar techniques claimed that three-fourths of all victims recovered.[20]

As the nineteenth century progressed and the social conditions of the urban community worsened, the Humane Society moved from charity to reform. The city's judicial system received special attention. In 1815 the clerk of the fifth-ward court, Ebenezer Burling, presented an extensive report to the society on the injustice, malpractice, and fraud prevalent in the city's courts. Burling complained chiefly about the "avarice" of the marshals, "who too often appear to forget that the Law was made for the benefit of Society." In the first place, the city government appointed too many marshals; furthermore, they exercised excessive influence

over the courts and judges; they received no salaries but instead
depended on court fees for income; they insisted on serving unnecessary subpoenas in order to charge witness fees, and even
named themselves as witnesses; they persuaded many defendants
to demand jury trials, thereby earning additional fees for serving
subpoenas; and rather than paying sums collected in executions
for debt immediately into the court, the marshals became "Brokers
among the Common Prostitutes . . . Lending other people's
money at an exorbitant interest." Although he recognized "how
dangerous it is to touch the interest of Men that Love Money
more than the good of Society," Burling made two suggestions for
judicial reform. First, the improper activities of the marshals had
to be terminated, by law if necessary. Second, the number of
marshals appointed to each court had to be limited, "that they
may *not* for want of employment be compelled to commit
Depredations on Society to obtain a Support." These ideas were
communicated to the common council, which on several occasions
requested (unsuccessfully) legislative changes to reduce the
number of courts, eliminate unnecessary litigation, and suppress
the "sinister purposes" of marshals and justices.[21]

In another reforming effort, the Humane Society promoted a
mechanical invention for cleaning chimneys as a substitute for
"climbing boys." A committee of the society composed of Dr.
David Hosack and Dr. John W. Francis investigated the subject
and reported to the society in June 1819: chimney sweeping
constituted an unnatural, hazardous, and "pernicious" occupation;
physical deformities, diseases of the lungs and chest, and a
shortened lifespan full of "moral depravity" appeared to be the
normal expectations for young boys so employed. Following the
example of a London society founded in 1808 for similar purposes,
the Humane Society recommended a chimney-sweeping machine
invented and sold by one F. A. Evrard of New York City in place
of child labor.[22]

Not content with rescuing chimney sweeps from baneful
occupations, reforming the courts, and supplying the needs of
debtors, drowning victims, and the poor, the Humane Society

attempted to eliminate some of the supposed causes of poverty and misery in the city. In 1809 a special committee of the society, headed by Thomas Eddy, reported the most prominent of those causes to be "the excessive multiplication of petty taverns, and the injudicious system of confining in the same apartments of our prison, persons suspected or convicted of various degrees of guilt." The liquor problem seemed an endemic characteristic of New York City's working classes and drinking the reason for "the misery and poverty, of most of the laboring poor." The committee recommended reformed licensing procedures and higher excise taxes to suppress these evils. The group also uncovered shocking and degrading conditions in the city prison, conditions greatly aggravated by mass confinement of prisoners in large compartments. To reform the penitentiary system, the committee demanded more humane treatment for convicts and construction of a new prison with small, individual cells. Finally, the committee appealed to the community to unite behind plans for immediate, effective, and drastic reform.[23]

The Humane Society report stimulated action. Soon after the investigation, officers of several humanitarian organizations met to discuss implementation of the suggested reforms. Delegates from twenty-one societies gathered at the New York Free School on the evening of January 10, 1810. This meeting of humanitarians and reformers resulted in petitions to the common council and state legislature demanding legal measures to suppress gambling and masquerade balls (thought to contribute to immorality) and to reform debtor legislation, liquor-licensing techniques, and prison methods. Typically, however, unified action of city reformers proved insufficient to overcome the inertia of aldermen and legislators.[24]

The Humane Society of New York City functioned effectively in supplementing municipal poor relief and stirring reform sentiment. The organization, therefore, enlisted broad support within the urban community. The common council assisted the managers of the society in a variety of ways. Donation of cash and property for construction of the new soup house in 1806 manifested early municipal approval. City government permitted the society to purchase soup provisions at reduced prices from almshouse supplies, and the managers occasionally met in rooms at City Hall. In return, managers gave soup tickets to aldermen and assistants for distribution to the poor in their respective wards. During the winter of 1818, a petition from the society convinced the municipal government to install six stoves in the debtor's prison to replace the large, drafty, and wasteful fireplaces that had filled the jail more with smoke than heat. Although the common council rejected the Humane Society's first formal application for monetary assistance in 1808, spokesmen for the society continued to argue that food distributed at the soup kitchen to "crowds of necessitous persons" lessened considerably demands upon the almshouse. In later years municipal purse strings loosened, and the society's petitions for financial aid were granted with regularity after 1817—usually $200 to $400 annually. Despite some opposition to appropriations of this nature among councilmen, most aldermen considered the Humane Society "only a branch to the Alms House." [25]

The Humane Society received support from other segments of the community as well. De Witt Clinton—as mayor, as state legislator, and as governor—aided the organization by backing its objectives, by introducing some of its reform proposals into council and legislature, and by becoming a manager of the society. Other public officials supported charity and reform, among them the keepers of the debtor's prison, William Parker and later James Bell, men who had daily opportunity to observe the hardships imprisonment imposed upon indigent debtors. Bell, for example, made an affidavit early in 1817 at the solicitation of the Humane Society, asserting that during 1816 a total of 759 persons had been imprisoned in New York City for debts under twenty-five dollars. All, Bell wrote, would have starved but for the charity of the Humane Society. This evidence helped to speed reformed debtor legislation in 1817. Similarly, almshouse physician Dr. Felix Pascalis attended the debtor's jail, sympathized with the prisoners, and actively supported the society, as did a group of ninety-nine lawyers who organized in 1822 an informal legal-aid society to secure release of unjustly or illegally imprisoned debtors.[26]

The newspapers of the city, in two distinct ways, added support to the society and the goals it pursued. First, by editorializing on the merits and utility of the society and by soliciting public assistance in its behalf, the press contributed the weight of its influence and opinion to the advantage of the organization. Second, and perhaps more important, the editors printed numerous lengthy communications advocating reformed debtor laws. The topic was one of considerable contemporary interest, and scarcely a week went by without at least one anonymous contribution on the subject. "Humanitas," "Benevolus," "Veritas," "Civis," "Ambrose," "Howard," and many others all wrote long series of articles condemning imprisonment for debt. The widespread exposure the debtor's situation received helped create an atmosphere fostering legislative reform. The catalog of horrors to which imprisoned debtors were allegedly subjected also generated support and public patronage for the Humane Society.[27]

Additional support for the society came from *Forlorn Hope,* a unique newspaper established in 1800 and published in the prison by William Keteltas, a convicted and confined debtor. Founded to promote prison reform, this journal demanded a federal bankruptcy law and state legislation for relief of debtors. During its short period of existence (March 24 to September 13, 1800), *Forlorn Hope* rapidly broadened its objectives and advocated a great variety of social reforms—temperance, education for women and Negroes, abolition of slavery and the slave trade, suppression of gambling, abolition of capital punishment, aid to orphans, propagation of the gospel among debtors and criminals, and legal aid for prisoners. Editor Keteltas recognized the importance of the Humane Society and continually editorialized in its behalf. The masthead of the paper depicted two chained, disheveled figures with a caption reading: "We should starve were it not for the Humane Society." [28]

Although the society found support throughout the community, membership of the organization came almost exclusively from the business and professional classes. Of the 109 men who served as managers of the society between 1787 and 1831, all but seven are identifiable. More than half of the managers, or a total of fifty-eight, were merchants and businessmen; sixteen were attorneys, eleven ministers, nine physicians, and six politicians; only two— a tanner and a painter—came from the artisan or mechanic class. The managers numbered among themselves many men of standing and prestige in the urban community, men who participated actively in other humanitarian and reform organizations. These included, in addition to members already mentioned, merchants Divie Bethune, Leonard Bleecker, Thomas Franklin, John R. Murray, and John Pintard; attorney Peter A. Jay; clergymen John H. Hobart and John B. Romeyn; Cadwallader D. Colden, mayor of the city from 1818 to 1821; Jacob Sherred, also a president of the Mechanics Society; and Samuel Osgood, politician and first Postmaster General of the United States. Yet the Humane Society, although organized and managed by men from the business and professional classes, derived broad support and patronage from the community at large; in this the society reflected a general response to recent urban dislocations and demands for improvement and reform.[29]

In the period after 1825, a scarcity of funds forced the Humane Society to reduce its general relief program, although imprisoned debtors, at the rate of twelve a day, continued to receive food from the soup house. In 1831 the society's major reform goal of almost fifty years was finally achieved. After great public and legislative controversy, a law passed on April 26, 1831 (effective the following March), abolished the last vestiges of imprisonment for debt in New York. However, the Humane Society continued to operate its soup house for the poor, a technique adopted by municipal government and other New York City charities during depression years of the late 1830's and early 1840's.[30]

Students of urbanization, sociologists and historians alike, have suggested that social groupings and voluntary associations such as the Humane Society filled an important social need in nineteenth-century American cities. Under the impact of heavy immigration, rapid urbanization, and early industrialization—social changes New York City began to experience in post-Revolutionary years—established institutions no longer served to integrate and regulate the growing community. Native and immigrant new-comers upset traditional order. Social control broke down under the new pressures. The humanitarian, benevolent, and reform organizations founded in New York City, characterized by an overlapping leadership and membership, bulwarked by a strong sense of morality and stewardship, thus assumed important functions.[31]

The Humane Society typified associative humanitarianism in New York City in the early decades of the nineteenth century. During its long existence, from about 1787 until after 1831, the society engaged in a wide range of philanthropic activities and aided various categories of dependents in the absence of munici-pal responsibility. Simultaneously, the society's petitions and re-ports stimulated legal and social reforms. Composed of men of influence and position in the community, the society became a model reform group, widely imitated in organization and tech-nique. The Humane Society, like many similar voluntary associa-tions in New York and other cities, reflected a deepening aware-ness of the disordered conditions and the new requirements of American urban life.

9

The Proliferation
of Urban Philanthropy

If the Humane Society typified urban philanthropy and reform, a myriad of other charitable societies and social-welfare institutions in New York City reflected the same tendencies. The associative pattern of private humanitarianism which began in colonial years became more pronounced in the early nineteenth century. Some groups, imitating the Humane Society, assisted the poor in general. Others focused on specific categories of dependents such as widows and orphans, or offered specialized relief and services such as medical care, education, fuel, work, and religion. Extreme crises always spawned short-lived relief committees supplying immediate needs. Religious and fraternal societies aided parishioners and members. Mutual-benefit societies and occupational organizations provided effectually for many urban workers and served as an early form of prepaid medical and unemployment insurance. By 1825 New York City boasted more than one hundred such voluntary associations—a traditional American technique of confronting common problems.

The network of private benevolence penetrated every corner of the rising seaport community. Most groups toiled, some with more energy than others, to ameliorate the condition of the poor with timely relief. But many also labored to bring moral reform to the slums, to eliminate the "vicious, intemperate, and idle habits" which presumably caused poverty, by imposing middle-class values upon alms seekers. To a remarkable degree, a small coterie of civic leaders directed the affairs of all the important voluntary associations. Middle-class and business-oriented, concerned about moral conformity, social order, and the reputation of their city, humanitarian leaders sought simultaneously to aid and indoctrinate the poor. Viewing charity as a Christian duty, they used benevolence, often unconsciously, to promote moral stewardship and social control. More often, they consciously combined charity with moral instruction and religious exhortation. Each philanthropy worked in its own special way to improve the human condition, restore urban order, and ensure security for established society. Like the Humane Society, these voluntary associations taken together represented a positive, yet cautious and conservative, response to urbanization and social change.

Relief emergencies prompted appearance of a number of charitable societies. In every case, benevolent men and women acted on the conviction that public assistance lagged behind human needs, that even existing private charities neglected some poor city dwellers. For example, the Samaritan Society emerged during the 1805 relief crisis to supplement public aid and "succour the extremity of want among the poor of all descriptions." Leonard Bleecker, a religious activist and one of the city's leading stock and insurance brokers, sponsored an organizational meeting on January 16, 1805, at the Tontine Coffee House. The gathered humanitarians determined upon an immediate relief plan to parallel public efforts during the winter emergency. Leading citizens agreed to serve on nine ward committees; their function—to investigate needs of the poor, solicit contributions from the rich, and distribute relief in conjunction with the common council's special "committee of supply." On February 19, Bleecker reported the achievements of a month of humanitarian exertion: each evening a board of directors appropriated funds to the ward committees, which in turn dispensed relief daily; more than five hundred families received $1,900 worth of food, firewood, blankets, and clothing; members of ward committees, guarding against "impositions" and aid duplications, visited each poor family before granting any relief. In all cases, the society noted with special pride, visitors "sought to disseminate the light of religious instruction among the gloomy recesses of ignorance and wretchedness." With the exception of the Humane Society's soup houses, most private charity during the winter of 1805 passed through the hands of these early visitors to the poor. The Samaritan Society became, for the moment, as one editor put it, "the great fountain of benevolence." Yet when winter ended, the fountain evaporated; the Samaritan Society disappeared without a trace of further activity.[1]

The embargo crisis of 1807–1809 brought a similar organizational response to poverty and unemployment. While public assistance carried the burden during the first winter of the shipping suspension, two new private groups emerged during the second on an invigorated wave of urban benevolence. In January 1809 Quaker merchant and reformer John Murray, Jr.—a moving spirit in humanitarian work throughout the early decades of the nineteenth century—sponsored a series of public meetings which resulted in formation of a "General Committee of the Benevolent Associates for the Relief of the Poor." Murray's new group, concerned about "those whose distress does not usually obtrude itself upon the public," reimplemented the committee system which the Samaritan Society had used successfully. Forty civic leaders composed the "general committee"; these forty then nominated five additional men to each of ten ward committees, which in turn split into smaller district committees. They envisioned a division of humanitarian labor, with the general committee collecting donations and small neighborhood groups visiting the poor and distributing relief. Ideally, visitors served also as employment agents, arranging jobs for those the embargo put out of work. Simultaneously, they made the usual pleas for industriousness and sobriety in the slums. Revealing ambitious plans, the general committee demanded new poor relief taxes and asked the common council to place "the whole public charity" under its direction.

After deliberating for a week, the aldermen politely declined both suggestions: new taxes were unnecessary, since private charity had lessened pressures on the almshouse; and almshouse commissioners had had more experience in centralized relief giving than the new citizens group. Municipal rejection of the petition seemingly dealt a deathblow to the whole scheme. By the first of March the *ad hoc* general committee had disappeared, leaving the field clear to a second new group—the Assistance Society.[2]

The formation of the Assistance Society in December 1808 provides further evidence of increased economic dependency in New York City during the embargo years. The society's first public statement on December 10 acknowledged the magnitude of public relief and the utility of private charities; but it also asserted that the crisis created by national policy had pushed poverty beyond the relief capacities of established agencies. Thus the society stated its objective as supplying "the deficiencies of other charitable societies" by "embracing impartially all persons in want and distress." A board of twelve directors managed the society's affairs and invited citizens to participate in the humanitarian experiment as "annual subscribers." Members soon began soliciting funds with charity sermons and door-to-door campaigns, and annual supporters were enticed with the privilege of "recommending beggars to the notice of the committee." Throughout the remaining months of the shipping prohibition (the embargo was lifted in March 1809), the Assistance Society from its storefront headquarters on John Street served as a central relief agency.[3]

The society's reports indicated the extent of its activities. Throughout the early winter months of 1809 the society assisted several hundred families each week, usually with cash, food, and firewood. During the week of February 22, 1809, for example, 789 families totaling 3,137 persons received help; the charity list the following week showed 827 families. During the whole of 1809 the society made 17,763 separate grants to poverty-stricken New Yorkers at a total cost of $3,544. In each case a committee of visitors personally investigated recipients to prevent misapplication of charity. Visitors also distributed Humane Society soup tickets, acquired by the Assistance Society at reduced prices. In addition, the society purchased a number of spinning wheels and lent them to able-bodied but unemployed workers. By the summer of 1809 the economic emergency had passed and the Assistance Society modified its relief program, confining attention thereafter to the "sick poor." [4]

The Assistance Society remained active until after 1825, occasionally reinstituting general relief during periods of extreme distress. By 1815 society directors had mapped out the city into six districts, or "walks." Two "pious and discerning" visitors implemented the relief policy in each walk. During its first four years, according to the annual report of 1813, the society assisted more than 28,000 persons. However, this figure is misleading. Visitors aided numerous families more than once, yet recorded each grant separately in the society's books. Nor was relief distributed in any indiscriminate fashion, especially after the first surge of humanitarianism in 1809. Relief recipients, the directors asserted in 1811, "must be actually in a state of suffering, laboring under affliction, and though willing, yet altogether incapable of subsisting by their own exertions." [5]

Indeed, the common attitude among nineteenth-century humanitarians that poverty stemmed from moral defects marked Assistance Society statements and reports. "Vice and improvidence are the general sources of want and distress," the first annual report claimed in 1810. Thus visitors combined relief with preachments on "habits of sobriety and industry." They prayed with the poor in their homes, urged regular church attendance, and distributed Bibles and religious tracts (despite the admission that most of the poor could not read). In general, the Assistance Society sought "to combine moral improvement by the recommendation of religion, with temporal relief distributed in the most economic and cautious manner." [6]

Unlike the Humane Society, Assistance Society leadership came largely from the working class. Of the thirty-nine managers of the society between 1809 and 1825, all but two are identifiable. Twenty-four managers—artisans and mechanics—worked as masons, printers, carpenters, sailmakers, butchers, tailors, bakers, tallow chandlers, and cartmen; nine merchants, two municipal employees, a teacher, and a physician made up the rest of the list of directors. This characteristic of the Assistance Society clearly reflects the organizational reaction to urbanization and urban social problems. People at every social and economic level felt the pinch of hard times and responded to new urban pressures. Thus the organizational thrust—adoption of voluntary associative behavior patterns—cut across the structure of urban society.[7]

Post-embargo relief emergencies stimulated new philanthropic efforts. In December 1813, for instance, amidst general hardship of war with Britain, New Yorkers founded a short-lived Fuel Association. It followed the pattern of previous groups organized spontaneously to meet some pressing demand. Leonard Bleecker put relief forces into motion in mid-December by sponsoring two public meetings, a now standard technique of humanitarian action. Composed of one delegate from each of ten city wards, a general committee solicited donations, purchased fuel, and supervised distribution to subcommittees in each ward. In turn, ward committees received relief applications and dispensed firewood to the "meritorious" poor. Within two months the Fuel Association sent 1,315 loads of wood to nearly 1,000 needy families. After serving immediate purposes, the society disbanded in March 1814 and, despite attempts to revive it in 1816, never reappeared.[8] In similar fashion, the crisis year of 1817 produced temporary charities for general relief. Several prosperous butchers financed a new soup house, where for three weeks in February and March ten cooks boiled meat and vegetable soup day and night. The benevolent butchers dispensed more than a hundred thousand quarts of soup to the poor, who stood in long lines for daily handouts. Simultaneously, a citizens committee of one hundred mobilized community resources for relief through the usual ward committees. During a two-week period of extreme distress in late February, these committees collected and spent more than $8,000 for relief.[9]

Organizations for general relief of the poor followed a recognizable pattern. Each crisis, each severe winter, each depression, generated special humanitarian exertions. Excepting the Humane Society and the Assistance Society (whose purposes were more than temporary), each charitable effort adopted the citizens-committee format. This organizational pattern, accompanied each time by smaller working ward committees, appeared in 1805, 1809, 1813, and 1817. On other occasions of widespread distress—during the War of 1812, during yellow fever epidemics, and after serious fires leveled portions of the city—humanitarians used similar techniques. Each time charity leaders drew upon experience and expertise acquired in previous experiments. Usually spontaneous in nature and concerned with immediate needs of the poor in general, each of these groups spent money and dissipated energies rapidly. Necessarily, they ignored more specialized and more permanent requirements of poverty-stricken New Yorkers. To supply such permanent and specialized relief the urban environment produced private charities of a different kind.

Humanitarianism energized associative philanthropy for specific purposes on many fronts. Some New Yorkers, but not many, early recognized the relation between economic dependency and poor health. Despite general complaints that the almshouse catered to large numbers of able-bodied paupers, most residents of the institution suffered debilitating diseases and injuries. Health problems contributed to the dependency of many families in need of home relief as well. Thus, medical charities added an important thrust in attacking poverty and destitution.

New Yorkers listed the City Dispensary among the most useful medical philanthropies. Founded during the winter of 1790–1791 by joint efforts of the Society for the Relief of Distressed Debtors (later the Humane Society) and the Medical Society of New York, the new institution provided medical treatment for the "industrious poor" in their homes and in an outpatient clinic located a block from the almshouse at the corner of Beekman and Nassau streets. Modeled upon a similar institution established in 1786 in Philadelphia, the dispensary depended upon voluntary services of physicians. Twelve dispensary directors divided the city into six districts, while the Medical Society appointed two physicians to make house calls in each. Three other physicians, each serving one day a week, handled outpatients at the dispensary. In addition, an "apothecary" lived at the clinic and furnished medicine and emergency aid around the clock. New Yorkers approached the dispensary idea with great optimism, for they expected the new institution to provide necessary care at "trifling expense" while protecting the poor from "merciless and unfeeling quacks." The Humane Society sponsored a public subscription to raise initial funds and the dispensary opened on February 1, 1791.[10]

As the city expanded in later years, dispensary directors added new medical districts and established additional clinics. Dispensary services multiplied as well. By the end of 1791 dispensary physicians had established a resuscitation program for drowning victims based on Dr. David Hosack's principles of "suspended animation." In later years, of course, the Humane Society assumed direction of the rescue apparatus. More significant for urban public health, in 1805 the City Dispensary absorbed the Kine-Pock Institution, a three-year-old smallpox inoculation center. The medical philanthropists conducted annual inoculation campaigns. They printed handbills and posters describing the advantages of vaccination, distributing them liberally throughout the city, especially in the outer wards, where the poor resided in greater numbers than in other sections of town. During yellow fever epidemics dispensary physicians worked energetically against the new urban scourge. Reflecting these widened services, the annual count of dispensary patients increased rapidly in the early nineteenth century. During 1791, the first year of operation, 310 patients sought medical aid. But in 1824 dispensary physicians treated 7,635 persons for a multitude of health problems, and vaccinated another 6,080 against smallpox—a record of considerable accomplishment for a private charity with a public purpose.[11]

Because of the City Dispensary's clear commitment to public health, the common council supported it more generously than any other private charity. At first the council made small annual cash grants of $25 to $125 to assist dispensary activities, especially the inoculation program. After 1816 the council paid an annual subsidy of $500 to $1,000 to support widespread vaccination of the poor as a public health measure. In addition, the common council supplied accommodations for the institution. A $200 grant in 1805 enabled the medical men to enlarge their clinic for the newly acquired "kine-pock" department. In 1810 the dispensary moved into the municipal building on Chambers Street and Broadway, which also housed the city's board of health. Such municipal approbation in reality made the City Dispensary a semi-public agency.[12]

A second medical institution—the New York Hospital—served similar public purposes and drew substantial financial support from public sources. Finding inspiration in Philadelphia's new city hospital, New Yorkers in the late colonial period advocated a similar establishment for the "labouring poor." "It is truly a reproach," wrote Dr. Samuel Bard of King's College (now Columbia) in 1769, "that a City like this, should want a public Hospital, one of the most useful and necessary charitable Institutions that can possibly be imagined." The arguments of Bard and others bore fruit in the 1770's when New Yorkers built a hospital with provincial and municipal assistance. Before plans could be fully implemented, however, the American Revolution intervened and British occupation forces used the new building as a barracks. Not until 1791 did the New York Hospital reopen, and only then because of state financial aid.[13]

That the New York Hospital depended on state support reflects one important characteristic of American philanthropy in the early national period. State laws imposed responsibility for poor relief on public agencies, but local officials often administered relief in minimal fashion. More often, they neglected such specialized services as health care. Thus private charities like the New York Hospital reduced demands for public facilities, earning support of aldermen and legislators. Legislative appropriations helped give birth to the New York Hospital in the 1790's and kept it alive well beyond 1825. In 1788, for instance, the legislature granted the hospital an annuity of £800 from liquor taxes. Laws of 1792 and 1795 increased the yearly grant, first to £2,000 and then to £4,000, now drawn from auction taxes. A law of 1796 added another £1,000 to the annual appropriation. Legislation of 1801 and 1805 brought total state support to $12,000 per year, while an act of 1806 extended the life of the annuity for fifty years. In 1810 the legislature granted an additional ten-year annuity of $3,500. Between 1810 and 1820, therefore, the New York Hospital had an annual income of almost $16,000 from the state legislature alone. The common council provided additional, but less substantial, support. From the beginning the New York Hospital became a semi-public institution, with most of its income derived from public sources, but with direction held firmly by twenty-six "governors" elected annually by members of a private voluntary association—the Society of the New York Hospital.[14]

Located on Broadway one block north of the old almshouse, the New York Hospital provided free treatment for the "sick poor." In contrast to the City Dispensary, which handled only outpatients, the hospital institutionalized those with serious illness and injury. Some patients paid for care at the rate of $2.50 per week, but most came from immigrant ships and city slums and had no funds for medicine, doctors, or nurses. By arrangement with federal officials, the hospital also treated sick and disabled seamen at government expense. Physicians donated time and services in return for the privilege of using the hospital as a teaching institution—an early medical school.[15]

Gradually, the New York Hospital added a number of specialized facilities. In 1802 the hospital absorbed the newly founded Lying-in Hospital (1799) and established a separate ward for poor, pregnant women. (The Lying-in Hospital retained its identity and a separate board of directors, but transferred its income to the larger institution.) When a group of women formed the New York Asylum for Lying-in-Women in 1823, it too came under the protective care of the New York Hospital. In 1807 hospital governors built a "lunatic asylum" adjacent to the main building.

Serving both rich and poor, the new institution accepted mentally disturbed paupers from the almshouse and charged the common council two dollars per week for their care. Influenced by New York Quaker humanitarian Thomas Eddy, who consistently advocated more humane treatment of the insane, and aided by a special forty-year legislative annuity of $10,000, the New York Hospital established a new mental hospital in 1821 at Bloomingdale, several miles north of the settled city. Lengthened patient lists reflected these widened services. In 1824 the hospital served 1,575 regular patients, 32 "lying-in" women, and 230 "maniacs" in the Bloomingdale Asylum.[16]

Other medical charities also served the poor. The New York Institution for the Instruction of the Deaf and Dumb, established in 1817 by the Reverend John Stanford, banker Matthew Clarkson, and De Witt Clinton, and supported by both state legislature and common council, became a refuge for specially afflicted almshouse children and, eventually, for all deaf and dumb children who lived in New York State. Within one year of its founding in 1820, the New York Eye Infirmary treated more than 1,100 poor patients. In 1824 the Eye Infirmary set up a special clinic to treat ear diseases as well. The New York Infirmary for the Treatment of Diseases of the Lungs (1823), also designed for indigent patients, attempted to combat the major cause of death in New York City. Thus medical needs of the city's poor were furnished not only by municipal government in almshouse hospitals and special fever and quarantine hospitals, but by a group of private medical charities which by 1825 had made available a wide range of gratuitous services.[17]

A number of middle-class, religious-oriented women led and sustained another major philanthropic thrust in New York City, particularly after 1800. Although men dominated most urban charities, they left certain specialized fields for female philanthropy. The benevolent ladies devoted special attention to widows, orphans, and various categories of female distress. The organizational response prevailed once again in the form of such agencies as the Orphan Asylum Society, the Female Assistance Society, and the Society for the Relief of Poor Widows with Small Children (SRPW).

The SRPW typified female charity organizations in New York City. Isabella Graham, a pious and widowed Scotswoman with a deep social consciousness, inspired formation of the society in 1797. Composed of twenty-four "managers," the society had 152 widows with 420 children on the relief books by December 1798, one year after establishment. Relief usually took the form of firewood, food, shoes, clothing, and Humane Society soup tickets. Only in cases of sickness or to assist voluntary removals from the city did the SRPW distribute cash. In addition, a few managers and some widows conducted several small schools for fatherless children, classes which enrolled fifty-eight students by 1805. To "unite permanent advantage with present assistance," the society also provided widows with work—washing, ironing, tailoring— and set up an employment office in a building in the city's business district.[18]

Financial support for the SRPW came from all the usual sources. Charity sermons, musical concerts, legacies, annual subscriptions, door-to-door solicitations, and periodic public appeals in the newspapers all supplied a partial income. Arguing that "the assistance afforded by the Society relieves the Corporation from a considerable expense," the SRPW also secured substantial municipal patronage. On a number of occasions, the common council remitted property taxes, donated firewood from almshouse supplies, and made cash appropriations. State support helped as well, particularly 1803 legislation authorizing a £15,000 lottery which permitted the society to establish a permanent fund for widows. With such wide backing the SRPW conducted a major private relief program. By November 1821 the society regularly assisted 921 persons (254 widows and 667 children under the age of ten). In 1822 relief expenses totaled almost $3,500, a sum considerably greater than that spent by either the Humane Society or the Assistance Society.[19]

The women of the SRPW acted from the same attitudes toward

THE PROLIFERATION OF URBAN PHILANTHROPY

poverty which motivated the men—many of them their husbands —who directed other urban charities. They made the same distinctions between the "worthy" and "unworthy" poor, and they took the usual precautions against "impositions." Before granting any assistance, society managers visited each applicant to determine eligibility and virtue. In addition to showing twelve months' residence in New York City, widows had to furnish two character references. Managers further demanded evidence of the husband's death, or proof of at least twelve months' absence from home. Several restrictions limited conduct of the widows, who could be removed from the pension list for intemperance, promiscuity, begging, dancing, selling liquor, and even living in a disreputable neighborhood. In all of these ways—in its purposes and programs, its sources of support, and its social attitudes—the SRPW mirrored contemporary currents of urban philanthropy.[20]

A number of other women's charitable organizations reflected similar patterns. The Orphan Asylum Society, formed in 1806 by Isabella Graham, her daughter Joanna Bethune, and other SRPW ladies, drew substantial support from city and state governments and from the alms-giving public generally. Instructed in "religious, moral, and industrial habits" and bound as apprentices and domestic servants at the age of eight, the "infant tribe" numbered 159 by the end of 1825. The Female Association (1798) aided the "sick poor" and founded a school to teach "principles of piety and virtue" to poor girls. The Female Assistance Society (1813) duplicated the earlier Assistance Society and annually aided between 500 and 1,500 dependent but "upright" women. The "prying pitying eye of charity" sustained the Association for the Relief of Respectable, Aged, Indigent Females (1814), which supplied 150 or more women over sixty years of age with food, clothing, firewood, and Bibles "printed in large letters." The War of 1812 stimulated formation of the Association for Relief of Indigent Wives of Soldiers and Sailors (1813) and the Stocking, Hood, and Mockason Society (1814), the latter designed to furnish clothing to ill-supplied American troops on the New York frontier. The Magdalen Society (1811) established a reformatory for young prostitutes. The Society for the Promotion of Industry (1814) established workshops each winter to employ indigent but industrious women. Female philanthropy, therefore, sought out dependency often overlooked by welfare officials and sponsored numerous programs to assist women and children. Clearly the organizational response to urbanization and accompanying problems affected not only working class and middle class, but women as well as men.[21]

Other city associations supplied the poor with education and religion. The Free School Society, the Sunday School Union Society, Bible, tract, and missionary associations all sought to improve society by reforming and evangelizing slum dwellers and alms seekers. These groups (treated separately in later chapters) conformed to the organizational and attitudinal patterns of New York City's other general charities.

Philanthropic patterns and techniques had become standardized by the early decades of the nineteenth century. Some of these patterns have already been suggested. The public meeting became a recognized method of stimulating humanitarian energies. The temporary groups which sprouted during every relief emergency always established action-oriented ward committees. The excessive concern for improving the morals of the poor marked every charity: all provided admonitions and exhortations along with relief; all sought to prevent "impositions."

Many other important similarities existed among urban humanitarian associations. For example, each society was composed of annual subscribers, who elected officers and a board of managers, trustees, or governors at yearly meetings. The number of subscribers varied for each society, although some causes clearly engendered greater support than others. The Orphan Asylum Society had more than 800 subscribers in 1810, while the Humane Society could only muster 114 by 1814; in the 1820's the Assistance Society listed about 150 regular contributors, but more than 600 annually supported the Free School Society. The number of directors also differed for each association. Twenty-four trustees managed the Humane Society; a committee of fourteen directed the Assistance Society; twenty-six governors ran the New York Hospital; the Sunday School Union Society began with twenty managers in 1816 but soon added eight more. In each instance, managers served as voluntary and unpaid decision makers, while annual subscribers provided funds in the form of dues and donations.

When dues and subscriptions proved inadequate sources of income for most groups, the search for additional funds followed a general pattern. Each society turned first to the clergy and the charity sermon, an ever-popular and successful fund-raising technique. Requests for charity sermons often became so frequent that concern for parishioners' pocketbooks occasionally brought an uncharitable reply. In rejecting the SRPW's petition for a charity sermon in March 1816, the Reverend James Matthews of the Garden Street Presbyterian Church noted that his congregation had raised $5,300 for various charities during the past year and could not be expected to do more. Besides charity sermons, philanthropic societies depended for funds upon musical concerts, theatrical benefits, door-to-door campaigns, legacies, and general public appeals in the newspapers.[22]

Important financial support for humanitarian activity came from government. At one time or another, almost all private charities in New York City received some state or municipal patronage. The New York Hospital, the Orphan Asylum Society, the Free School Society, and the Institution for the Instruction of the Deaf and Dumb each secured grants and annuities from the state legislature. For many years the common council made annual appropriations to the Humane Society, the City Dispensary, the Female Assistance Society, the Society for the Promotion of Industry, and the French Benevolent Society, while other associations were supported less regularly. Societies sought such government grants with the argument that private charity lessened demands for public assistance. Alderman generally accepted this argument until the relief crisis of 1817, when both civic leaders and public officials agreed that charity stimulated pauperism by destroying self-reliance. After 1817 only the Humane Society and the City Dispensary received regular, but smaller, common council payments.

If New York's urban charities followed a general pattern of organization and operation, they also worked together closely. For instance, when the Humane Society published its 1809 report on taverns and prisons, delegates from twenty-one associations met to plan reforms. The SRPW sponsored the Orphan Asylum Society, subscribed to the City Dispensary, enrolled children of widows in free schools and Sunday schools, directed eligible dependents to the proper charity, and cooperated with the almshouse superintendent in weeding "unworthy" widows from both public and private welfare rolls. The Humane Society worked closely with its offspring, the City Dispensary. The religious-oriented groups—Bible, tract, and missionary societies—joined in a common effort to evangelize the slums.

Cooperative efforts stemmed partly from common humanitarian concerns. Perhaps even more important, organizational direction came from the same sources. A small but closely interrelated group of politicians, professionals, and merchants exercised community leadership in early nineteenth-century New York City. A coterie of men and women energized and dominated not only welfare and reform organizations, but cultural, literary, and scientific societies as well. New York's organizational network was characterized by an amazing degree of integration and overlapping at the leadership level. In his varied activities and institutional affiliations, De Witt Clinton exemplified civic and humanitarian leadership. New York's mayor for ten of the twelve years between 1803 and 1815, Clinton served at different times as president of the Free School Society, the American Academy of Fine Arts, the New-York Historical Society, the Literary and Philosophical Society, the Economical School, and the Institution for the Instruction of the Deaf and Dumb; as a manager or patron of the Society for the Promotion of Useful Arts, the Humane Society, the Orphan Asylum Society, the New York Hospital, the Lying-in Hospital, the American Bible Society, and the New-York Marine Bible Society;

and as the unofficial representative and lobbyist of all the city's humanitarian and civic organizations at Albany.

Many other humanitarian leaders had wide interests and influence. Presbyterian minister John Rodgers, one of the patriot preachers of the American Revolution, served simultaneously in later years as president of the Humane Society, the City Dispensary, the Society for Promoting Christian Knowledge and Piety, and the New-York Missionary Society. Few societies escaped the influence of Matthew Clarkson, a Revolutionary War general and postwar businessman and banker; at the same time he presided over the Humane Society, the New York Hospital, the City Dispensary, the New-York Bible Society, and the Society for the Prevention of Pauperism, Clarkson served as an officer or manager of the Manumission Society, the Free School Society, the Fuel Association, the Lying-in Hospital, the Institution for the Instruction of the Deaf and Dumb, the Marine Bible Society, and the American Bible Society. According to an obituary, prosperous import-export merchant Divie Bethune, a Scottish immigrant and an evangelical Presbyterian, worked for virtually "every society for the promotion of religion and the melioration of human misery" in the city; these included the Humane Society, the Samaritan Society, the Magdalen Society, the Fuel Association, the Free School Society, the Sunday School Union Society, the Society for the Prevention of Pauperism, and at least ten different religious-reform associations. Other New York civic leaders whose connections and influences similarly spanned the whole of the benevolent network included Thomas Eddy, John Murray, Jr., Leonard Bleecker, David Hosack, Thomas Franklin, Matthew Franklin, John R. Murray, Isaac Collins, John Pintard, Frederick Depeyster, Zachariah Lewis, John Griscom, Cadwallader D. Colden, John D. Keese, John Nitchie, and Stephen Allen. Among the women's organizations, Isabella Graham, Sarah Hoffman, Joanna Bethune, and a few others (many of them wives and daughters of the male humanitarian leaders) supplied direction and energy for the SRPW, the Orphan Asylum, the Female Association, the Female Assistance Society, the Society for the Promotion of Industry, the Female Sunday School Union Society, the Magdalen Society, and a number of female Bible and missionary groups. These men and women aggressively promoted the many-pronged associative attack on poverty, pauperism, and other evils of urban society.[23]

If leadership cemented the parallel strands of philanthropy, common interest brought men together in other urban associations. Cultural, economic, religious and ethnic diversity marked the growing population of New York City. By the early nineteenth century the drive toward organization had produced nationality groups, trade and occupational associations, mutual-benefit societies, and religious and fraternal organizations. All provide further evidence of associative urban patterns, of the network of voluntary societies. In one way or another, all served some charitable functions.

The nationality and immigrant-aid societies had a long history. The earliest such groups, the Scots Charitable Society (1744) and St. Andrew's Society (1756), like most similar organizations, had dual purposes. They served the social and fraternal needs of immigrants, and they aided indigent members and recent arrivals, in this case immigrants from Scotland. In post-Revolutionary years, numerous other "friendly" societies emerged. New Yorkers of English descent reestablished St. George's Society in 1786, an organization originally formed in 1770 but suspended during the war years. Irish immigrants founded the Friendly Sons of St. Patrick in 1784 and the New York Irish Emigrant Association (or Shamrock Society) in 1817. Citizens of Welsh background established St. David's Society before 1803. Other ethnic groups organized the German Society (1784) and the French Benevolent Society (1808). To aid immigrants of all nationalities, humanitarian New Yorkers formed in 1794 a "Society for the Information and Assistance of Persons Emigrating from Foreign Countries." [24]

These immigrant-aid societies afforded timely, if not substantial, assistance to indigent newcomers. For example, St. Andrew's Society spent more than $1,000 in charity during 1800 and $900 in 1801 and again in 1802. According to an 1811 petition to the common council, the French Benevolent Society annually supported 250 to 300 French refugee families. At a time of rising opposition to immigration, when both state laws and private agencies such as the SRPW determined relief eligibility partially by length of residence, immigrant-aid groups served useful functions.[25]

Occupational societies and trade organizations similarly aided needy members or their widows and children. One of the first such groups, the Marine Society (1769), had seventy-seven widows on its pension list in 1812; in addition, the society financed the education of seventy-six children of deceased members. In 1825 the Marine Society spent more than $2,300 for such charitable purposes. Seamen in New York established several other organizations of this kind: the Mariner's Friendly Society (1792); the Sailor's Snug Harbor (1801); the Marine Benevolent Committee, a temporary relief agency formed during the embargo crisis; the African Marine Society, which in 1811 founded a refuge for disabled black seamen and orphans; the Pilot's Charitable Society, chartered in 1817; and the New York Nautical Institution and Ship Master's Society, incorporated in 1821. The General Society of Mechanics and Tradesmen, founded in 1785, had its own "overseers of the poor" and a loan committee to assist needy members and families. By 1821 the Mechanics Society had thirty widows and seventeen children on its pension list and annually spent $2,000 for charity. After 1820 additional funds supported an apprentices' library and a school for the children of artisans. Carpenters, cartmen, butchers, tailors, teachers, shipwrights, shoemakers, printers, accountants, firemen, clergymen, and even tavern keepers all succumbed to the organizational impulse and formed benevolent societies. Each of these groups provided both relief and social outlets, while creating the nucleus for nascent labor organizations in New York City.[26]

The mutual-benefit society—a kind of cooperative insurance scheme—became popular in the United States early in the nineteenth century. When the duc de la Rochefoucauld visited New

York in 1797, he expressed surprise at the absence of the "benefit-clubs" so numerous in England and Europe. But within fifteen years, working-class New Yorkers had formed at least a dozen such organizations, including the Albion Benevolent Society, the Mutual Aid Society, the Provident Society, the African Society for Mutual Relief, the Wilberforce Philanthropic Association, the Hibernian Provident Society, the Ancient Briton's Benefit Society, the Manhattan Provident Society, and the New York Benevolent Society. The charter of the Ancient Briton's Benefit Society typically set forth the purpose of such groups: the members associated to raise a fund for "mutual relief, when rendered incapable of attending to their usual trade or calling, by reason of sickness or infirmity, and also for the purpose of preventing themselves and families from being chargeable to the public when under affliction." Usually open to any applicant these societies charged small sums as initiation fees and members made weekly or monthly insurance-premium payments of as little as twenty-five cents. During illness, unemployment, or hard times members drew upon their investment. New York's moral philanthropists promoted such self-help schemes with great energy, and several charities granted assistance only on condition that poor families join a mutual-benefit society.[27]

Church charity supplemented public assistance and private relief agencies. Most Protestant congregations assumed some responsibility for the parish poor and made annual charity collections for them. More conscientious than most denominations, Quakers handled poor relief at the Monthly Meeting. Records of the New York Meeting for Sufferings reveal a well-endowed Quaker relief fund applied not only in New York City but in other areas of the state as well. The significance of Quaker benevolence had even wider implications, since numerous Friends, both men and women, assumed leadership positions in urban philanthropies. New York's Roman Catholics annually raised $3,000 or more for poor relief among parishioners. In 1816 Catholic laymen founded the Roman Catholic Benevolent Society, a mutual-benefit association. Two additional Catholic agencies appeared in 1817: a Catholic Female Association, for the education of young girls, and the Catholic Orphan Asylum, connected with the recently built St. Patrick's Cathedral. New York's Jewish community also assisted its own poor, first through the synagogue and later through organizations such as the Hebrew Benevolent Society (1822). Each of these denominations provided charity schools and most, after 1816, Sunday schools for poor parish children.[28]

Several other New York organizations engaged in some charitable activities, although primary interest of members usually lay in other directions. One visitor suspected its "principal business" to be "influencing elections," but the Tammany Society was ostensibly founded for philanthropic purposes. Other patriotic, political organizations—the Order of Cincinnati, the Washington Benevolent Society, and the Hamilton Society—all with Federalist leanings, claimed similar benevolent objectives. Indeed, each of these groups assisted members in time of need and had pension lists of widows and children. Social and fraternal associations such as the New England Society and the Free Masons also distributed charity to ill or jobless members. But for these groups, charitable activity took a secondary place to the more central function of political or fraternal association.[29]

New York City's urbanization engendered many new problems, many new responses. The development of voluntary associations —for relief and for many other purposes—typified urban America in the nineteenth century. Societies sprouted, said the Reverend Philip M. Whelpley, "for objects as various as the forms of human want or woe." Indeed, many humanitarian New Yorkers claimed that proliferation of urban philanthropy strained their pocketbooks. "The multiplication of charitable institutions," a committee of the American Bible Society reported in 1819, "gives rise to such frequent calls upon the public bounty, that the most liberal are scarcely able to answer every demand." Yet most organizations survived, sustained by humanitarian and reformist energies. The network of benevolent associations spread its influences wider each year, as charity leaders boasted of more philanthropy in New York than in any city its size "in the known world." Charity and relief "poured upon a suffering community" through a variety of channels; but whatever their methods, associations and leaders all subscribed to the same humanitarian rationale.[30]

10

The Humanitarian Rationale:
From Benevolence to Moralism

The social and religious attitudes which sustained humanitarian activity shifted markedly in the early nineteenth century. In immediate post-Revolutionary years, the idea of benevolence as heavenly ordained motivated New Yorkers. They believed poverty a result of divine intention and looked upon charity as a Christian duty. But by the 1820's, humanitarian spokesmen had adopted harsh, moralistic positions on the causes of poverty and the efficacy of private charity and public relief. Charity reformers blamed poverty on the poor. Solutions for economic dependency increasingly became schemes for moral improvement. Philanthropic societies accompanied relief with moral indoctrination; many abandoned relief altogether for religious exhortation. Urbanization, immigration, and economic advancement combined to upset traditional eighteenth-century society and threatened to destroy urban order. As social and economic change affected the growing city, the urban leadership group turned humanitarianism into an efficient technique of social control and moral stewardship. Gradually, but unmistakably, moralism superseded benevolence as an activating humanitarian force.

The early humanitarian rationale postulated the duty and necessity of "divine benevolence." Charity sermons, annual reports, and newspaper appeals for funds all stressed the same point—that Christians had an obligation to assist the poor. "Charity and humanity are among the most necessary virtues in our society," the Humane Society asserted in its first public statement in 1788; without them one could not be a good Christian or a good citizen. The Assistance Society's report for 1809 stated it "the duty of the rich and those who are in comfortable circumstances, to provide for the relief of the suffering poor"—a duty "enforced by the precepts of our holy religion." "It will be readily granted," wrote "A Citizen" in 1814, "that the principles of the christian religion and the dictates of humanity enjoin on us a due attention to the needs of the poor and necessitous." In a charity sermon for the City Dispensary, the Reverend James Milnor emphasized the same idea: "none who are above the necessity of asking alms of others should consider themselves free from the obligation of relieving the wants of their fellow men." Similar assertions of charity as a Christian duty accompanied the public pronouncements of virtually every philanthropic society, particularly in the years before 1815.[1]

Christian humanitarians also developed a corollary "stewardship" doctrine. God "appointed" the rich as "Almoners" to distribute their abundance among the poor, the Reverend John Rodgers suggested in a 1791 charity sermon. In 1800 the short-lived newspaper *Forlorn Hope* printed an article entitled "The right improvement of Riches" which elaborated the same theme: "it is but an obligation due to our Maker, by whose infinite goodness we receive all the benefits we enjoy—and, by whose omnipotent power we exist, to render all the good we can to our fellow creatures, since we are but stewards of his bounty." New York City preachers emphasized the stewardship concept in their sermons. The Reverend John B. Romeyn, for example, used the idea in an 1810 charity sermon on "The Good Samaritan." "Riches or poverty happen at the wise disposal of God," he asserted; "the former are given in trust to alleviate the distresses of the latter." In another sermon, James Milnor listed among Christian teachings the precept that "he who is most abundantly favoured in regard to temporal things is but a steward." Similarly, charitable societies inserted the idea in reports, addresses, and, most often, fund appeals. The Assistance Society report of 1815 typically argued that God and the poor required much from the wealthy. The reminder that "they who give unto the poor, lend unto the Lord" presumably buttressed philanthropic solicitations.[2]

The stewardship principle implied that benevolence would reap future rewards. The charitable, one society report claimed, had "divine assurance of the most ample remuneration: whatsoever is bestowed in lessening the pain of the needy sufferer, is regarded with an approving eye by a watchful providence, who will most assuredly recompense the same." In the same vein, John Romeyn affirmed that on "judgement day" God would "reward charity to his poor, and punish the want of it." The prospect of eternal compensation enticed Christians to "active benevolence" and good works.[3]

Humanitarian spokesmen also developed a rhetoric with a more immediate appeal. Vivid descriptions of destitution and need stirred the sympathy of readers and listeners and helped pry open fat purses. An editorial in the *New-York Evening Post* in the midst of the 1805 relief crisis depicted "the immediate and wringing distress" that filled "the tenements of poverty." Editor William Coleman asked, "How many are there this day and this evening to be found sitting disconsolate—shivering—naked—hungry—steeped in tears—or nearly frantic at their situation?" At about the same time—January 1805—the *Commercial Advertiser* adopted similar phraseology: "Every heart should be alive to the cries of the distressed, and every hand open to administer relief to the shelterless, the naked and the hungry." Many such appeals offered graphic accounts of indigent families living in filthy cellars and hovels, suffering from "the wintry blast" and "the voracious jaws of famine." Preachers, editors, and charity leaders liberally laced sermons, editorials, and reports with descriptive material of this kind—case studies in philanthropic rhetoric.[4]

But the rhetoric of charity went beyond simple description. It postulated benevolence as the "noblest property of the human mind," the "first of all the graces," the "privilege of great and pious minds," the "connecting *link* between divinity and humanity." Charity sparked "the cheering glow of conscious usefulness." To the practitioner, benevolence brought "peculiar pleasure" and "the sublimest joy." An essayist in the *Weekly Visitor* in 1804 wrote of "the pleasing sensations that arise in the bosom of the philanthropist after rescuing an unfortunate family from ruin." In a 1793 oration, De Witt Clinton clearly expressed the early humanitarian rhetoric: "How glorious, how God-like, to step forth to the relief of . . . distress; to arrest the tear of sorrow; to disarm affliction of its darts; to smooth the pillow of declining age; to rescue from the fangs of vice the helpless infant, and to diffuse the most lively joys over a whole family of rational, immortal creatures." [5]

Drawing from the same tradition of Enlightenment rationalism, others wrote of benevolence not as a Christian, but as a human duty. The "voice of common humanity" or the "obligations of the social compact" dictated assistance to the needy. Even in the 1820's, the Reverend John Stanford argued that since the poor had helped "multiply the treasures of the rich" through labor, the rich were "morally obligated to relieve the necessitous poor." Still others found in philanthropy a kind of "patriotism," an idea emphasized during national crises such as the embargo and the War of 1812. With a variety of motivations, therefore, early humanitarians consciously promoted benevolence as necessary and beneficial, and they actively sought out the poor. "Even those whose vices have occasioned their distress, should not be suffered to die in despair," wrote "Humanity" in 1791. Such attitudes typified the humanitarian rationale in the post-Revolutionary period and in the early years of the nineteenth century. [6]

Gradually, almost imperceptibly, humanitarians moved toward moralism. Clearly, unadulturated benevolence motivated most humanitarians at the turn of the century. But just as clearly, moralism prevailed by 1820. A general acceptance, even among early humanitarians, that poverty was a natural human condition tempered sympathies and helped pave the way to moralism. New Yorkers often explained poverty as "an arrangement of divine Providence." Many sermons and reports quoted Biblical passages on the inevitability of poverty. God had ordained "various distinctions in the conditions and circumstances of his creatures"; men had to endure in "patience and submission." American Protestantism is this period, influenced by Calvinist theology and the Puritan ethic, tended to thrive on adversity. Thus, religious-oriented humanitarians found solace in the existence of poverty. "There is something rich, even in the blankness of poverty," suggested the Reverend Philip M. Whelpley in 1816, "when we reflect that the existence of suffering proves the existence of the attribute of mercy." In the same year the Female Assistance Society asked, "were there no subjects of *suffering* around us, where, or how would *sympathy, kindness* and *charity* display their sacred excellencies?" These ideas—that poverty was inevitable and that charity helped the giver more than the receiver—at once denied the perfectibility of man and revealed a kind of insensitivity to the human needs of the poor.[7]

Such insensitivity, which seemed to intensify year by year, partially explains the shift away from benevolence. In addition, increasing ethnic diversity and the rapid growth of New York after 1800 destroyed the sense of community which characterized the eighteenth-century city. Old New Yorkers found it difficult to apply Christian benevolence to ragged, uncouth, "different," and seemingly immoral newcomers. More important, rising numbers of dependents and a succession of relief emergencies imposed excessive pressures on the public welfare program. Higher poor taxes tempered middle-class benevolence and fostered close-fisted moralism. The writings of European *laissez-faire* political economists helped shape the thinking of New Yorkers as well. Particularly influential, the works of Thomas Malthus, David Ricardo, and Patrick Colquhoun criticized British poor laws and traced dependency to individual moral failings. The presumed vices which humanitarians observed in slums and immigrant neighborhoods seemed naturally and positively linked to the poverty which characterized those sections of the city. The religious ethic which demanded benevolence of the rich also demanded morality of the poor. By easy stages, charity leaders began to make distinctions between the "honest" poor and "undeserving," "vicious," "intemperate" idlers and beggars. Public officials and private charities alike began to take special precautions to prevent "misapplications" and detect "impositions."

The new humanitarian rationale which emerged in the early decades of the nineteenth century traced poverty to the poor themselves. Intemperance, idleness, immorality, impiety, and numerous other "vicious habits" became widely accepted as causes of dependency. New Yorkers with rising unanimity treated poverty as a moral problem. Government committees, society reports, the correspondence of humanitarians, even charity sermons all subscribed to such ideas by the 1820's.

Many charity reformers focused especially on lower-class drinking habits. For example, the 1817 *ad hoc* relief committee concluded its activities with a report on the causes and prevention of poverty. The committee found the "most prominent and alarming cause" in widespread addiction to alcohol, the source of seven-eighths of New York's pauperism. The other eighth stemmed in equal parts from unemployment and "possibly" unavoidable, but "difficult to enumerate," causes. According to the SRPW, urban poverty had two principal stimulants: "Intemperance among the Men, and the love of dress among the Women." In an 1824 letter to Secretary of State John Yates, Mayor Stephen Allen described alcoholism as "the foundation upon which the pauperism of this country is based." Repeated investigation, even casual observation, revealed workers and immigrants as hard drinkers. Overlooking equally persistent patterns of alcohol addiction among the upper classes, moralistic humanitarians discovered a direct link between the "grog-shop" and the almshouse. Rather than a cultural characteristic or a symptom of poverty, for New Yorkers lower-class alcoholism became "the *Cause of Causes.*" [8]

Benevolent moralists found other causes of poverty. As early as 1800 the SRPW criticized working-class extravagance. "Almost every class of mechanics live not only plentifully but luxuriously; an evil too general to be cured." The SRPW solution seemed logical; the poor had to "learn economy from adversity." In addition to alcoholism, Mayor Allen listed idleness and improvidence "among the principal sources of pauperism." Men were naturally lazy, Allen explained, yet most had to work for a subsistence. When the tendency to "inaction" surpassed the compulsion to work, dependency resulted. Similarly, a common council committee in 1821 labeled "a reluctance to labor" the reason for "a great portion" of pauperism. "Vice, ignorance, and improvidence, are the general and constantly operating causes of poverty," visiting Presbyterian preacher John H. Rice of Virginia observed in 1824. In an 1820 charity sermon for the Orphan Asylum, New York's Episcopal Bishop John H. Hobart clearly expressed the moralistic rationale: "Poverty and distress are the result and punishment of indolence, of censurable improvidence, if not of vice and crimes." But the bishop went further. "How painful indeed," he concluded, "but often how necessary, to restrain the impulses of benevolence; lest by our ill-judged bounty, we injure the best interests of society." For Hobart, and for many others, well-intended charity had only the opposite effect, strengthening extravagance, vice, and idleness.[9]

No idea emerged more strongly in the humanitarian literature of the post-1815 decade than that certainty of assistance in time of need rewarded impious, improper behavior and perpetuated poverty. Opponents of municipal relief propagated these ideas widely. Even before the nineteenth century began, some doubted the effectiveness of public assistance. Writing in the *Daily Advertiser* in December 1789, "Humanitas" considered the "public poor" usually "very far from being the greatest objects of charity." Another critic claimed in 1798 that "to find out one needful and worthy object, we must oblige a great many that are not so." In November 1817 the common council noted that excessive poor-relief expenditures, running well over $125,000 during the previous year, had elevated pauperism to a mature "System of idleness and profligacy." "Provide an asylum of any sort, and you create a class of candidates for it," wrote "Rumford" in a series of letters to the *New-York Evening Post* in 1817. Experience proved, he said, that reliance on public relief produced pauperism; "as long as food is gratuitously dealt out, there will be no lack of applicants for it." [10]

Public officials subscribed to similar principles. In his first annual address to the legislature in 1818, Governor De Witt Clinton attacked the relief system which appropriated the "fruits of industry" to idlers and beggars. In demanding "radical reform," Clinton argued that both the British and American experience showed that dependency increased in proportion to the rise in relief funds. At the very time that poor-law debates racked England (the two decades following the Napoleonic Wars), New Yorkers grappled with the same issues, and came to the same conclusions. Thus, when Secretary of State John Yates requested recommendations of New York City officials preparatory to a major poor-law revision, the reply reflected the new moralism. Mayor Allen advised severe cutbacks in public relief, severing all but the "helpless" poor from the welfare rolls.[11]

Critics attacked private charity with even greater energy and gusto. As early as 1807 moralistic preachments found a place in the newspapers. At the beginning of the embargo crisis 'Selkirk" paraphrased Malthus in arguing that "the greatest injury society sustains is the result of improper donations to the poor." The anonymous correspondent then offered suggestions to charitable societies: "make the supplies of an inferior quality, and let them be handed out sparingly. Do not give to persons able to work for a living. Do not support widows who refuse to put out their children. Do not let the means of support be made easier to one who does not work than to those who do." The implication was clear: careless charity strengthened pauperism.[12]

The belief that charity "made" paupers intensified after the War of 1812. Many charity leaders held that "the prospect of certain relief" tended to "dispel the horrors of poverty." A Free School Society report typically described the fear of suffering as "a wholesome moral discipline" which forced the poor to work and save. According to the Reverend Ward Stafford, an early city missionary, "if people believe, that they shall be relieved when in distress, they will not generally make exertions, will not labour when they are able and have the opportunity." Samuel Ackerly, a physician formerly connected with the Magdalen Society, lamented that charitable institutions made "better provisions for the vicious, than for the moral part of the community." In 1817 "a Friend to the Poor" suggested that except for clear cases of sickness, "no relief ought ever to be given but to stimulate industry by paying liberally for labour." In the same year the common council voted to suspend grants to private charities, adding that the poor had to be taught to rely upon themselves. The idea that honest, industrious workers could always find employment at substantial wages nourished middle-class moralism. By the time the 1817 relief crisis had ended, the new rationale had filtered into every part of the philanthropic network.[13]

Changing attitudes posed real problems for most charitable societies, whose programs depended on voluntary donations from citizens and common council. The emerging rationale contended that charity ruined character and promoted pauperism. Obviously, such a doctrine could destroy the financial support of many groups. (Indeed, both the Magdalen Society and the Society for the Promotion of Industry dissolved for this very reason, while many other charities barely survived.) Thus, although individual societies subscribed to benevolent moralism, most also maintained that the strictures against charity did not apply to them.

After 1815 virtually every humanitarian group claimed that it carefully dispensed relief only to the deserving poor. For example, the SRPW confined assistance to widows in "decent Poverty"; its visitors discriminated between "the real and the pretended objects of charity." The Lying-in Hospital reserved its facilities for "honest women." The Asylum for Lying-in Women accepted only women who produced marriage certificates. The Magdalen Society provided asylum only for "repenting victims of seduction." By arrangement with federal officials, the New York Hospital admitted seamen with any ailment but syphilis, on the conviction that immoral men deserved their fate. (Syphilis patients were sent to the almshouse, where they were "made to work.") The charity of the City Dispensary, James Milnor contended, could not be abused. Assistance Society reports argued that visitors carefully guarded against "deception," assuring potential contributors that "not the smallest part of their charity" would be misapplied. The Fuel Association aided only "the more respectable class of the poor." The Society for the Promotion of Industry provided not relief but work. The Humane Society offered soup tickets rather than alms to the poor as a means of disappointing "imposters." Furthermore, the society reported in 1828, "the humble meal dealt out to the lowly prisoner, can be no inducement for him to remain within his prison walls." Many other organizations used similar kinds or arguments in their annual reports and fund appeals.[14]

Intensified moralistic attitudes also gave a new emphasis to humanitarian activism. The conviction that the poor brought poverty upon themselves through improper or sinful behavior implied that moral reform would cure dependency more effectively than charity and relief. By the second decade of the nineteenth century, most philanthropies had developed dual objectives. Beyond propping up "honest poverty" with timely assistance, benevolent societies sought to purge the poor of their vices, bring moral uplift to the slums, and end poverty with virtue and religion.

To implement these new purposes, some societies adopted the technique of "district visitation." Reports that such efforts had produced positive results in Scotland, England, and Germany inspired New York's philanthropists to begin moral campaigning in the slums. Charity leaders divided the city into sections and assigned members to visit the poor in each. By the 1820's hundreds of visitors from numerous societies spread daily doses of advice and religion among actual and potential alms seekers. Assistance Society visitors worked to "reclaim the vicious" and urged the necessity of economy and cleanliness, sobriety and industriousness upon their listeners. Visitors from the SRPW and other ladies' organizations counseled, consoled, and exhorted widows, working women, and aged females. Canvassers from the Society for the Prevention of Pauperism sought information about poverty. Bible and tract societies used the visitation plan to distribute their wares. Schools and churches sent representatives into the slums to reinforce the moral lessons imparted by teachers and preachers.[15]

Societies without visitors had the same objectives. The Female Association hoped "to eradicate habits uncongenial with purity." The Magdalen Society aimed to convert young prostitutes to "principles of religion and virtue" and "habits of order and industry." The Society for the Promotion of Industry often stated its purpose as relief through self-help, the promotion of "virtue" and "self respect," and the prevention of idleness and "deviations from rectitude." Using a somewhat different tack, the Shamrock Society in 1817 urged new immigrants to "go into the country without delay" to avoid temptations to drunkenness and vice. In condemning "the man who in the bestowment of his alms, is governed by any other motive than the moral improvement of the recipient of those alms," a speaker at the American Bible Society convention in 1822 emphasized the key principle of the new benevolence. Some extremists even urged forced labor on a "tread-mill" and more frequent public executions of criminals as methods calculated to eliminate pauperism and correct lower-class morals. New York's middle-class humanitarians, then, revealed an excessive concern for regulating behavior by moral indoctrination.[16]

A few reformers and charity leaders recognized economic dependency as the result of unemployment, low wages, or poor health. The SRPW once stated that the earnings of a widow constantly at work could not possibly support a family of children. The editor of the *Morning Chronicle* suggested that for many families "the pressure of extreme want" became "the parent of vice." Almshouse physician Felix Pascalis noted in 1808 that sickness and disease in the slums "unavoidably" increased public burdens. The Society for the Promotion of Industry occasionally asserted that unemployment stimulated vice. One report of the Magdalen Society suggested that "the pressure of poverty" drove girls to prostitution. However, these few statements of economic reality were buried under a growing pile of reports, pamphlets, editorials, addresses, and sermons which blamed poverty on the poor.[17]

By the 1820's charity and benevolence had become important agents of social control and moral stewardship. Urbanization, immigration, and other social and economic forces had destroyed traditional urban institutions and traditional eighteenth-century values. In the early nineteenth century, New York City's growing population of native and foreign newcomers paid little attention to the platitudes of established leaders of church, government, political faction, business, or neighborhood. In the hard struggle for existence, virtue seemed to have little relevance. The United States had outgrown the deferential society of colonial times. Social controls broke down in the transitional city. Thus, middle-class men and women consciously promoted moral reformation and religious indoctrination as a method of restoring order and stability to the urban community.

The shift from benevolence to moralism unified the humanitarian network. Virtually all agreed to the central proposition that poverty was inevitable and reflected individual moral defects; the poor were victims of their own vices; character deficiency caused economic insufficiency. The presuppositions of the humanitarians, of course, dictated their cures for poverty—education, religion, temperance, and work. Although some occasionally proposed other approaches, most agreed upon high priorities for these four "cures." Such proposals revealed underlying assumptions and purposes, diverted attention from serious social and economic inequities, and prevented real solutions.

IV

POVERTY CURES

11

Education

Among proposals for reducing poverty and eradicating pauperism in New York City, reformers advanced education for poor children with more certitude and optimism than any other. New Yorkers fervently subscribed to the traditional American faith in education as a cure-all for individual imperfections and social ills. Humanitarians of all persuasions found a "powerful lever of reformation" in "the Spirit of Education"—the master reform for improving the quality of urban life amid the social disorder of the metropolis.[1]

Reformers, philanthropists, and municipal officials generally adhered to moralistic preconceptions about society and considered poverty the natural result of individual vices and shortcomings. Individual moral reformation, therefore, became the objective of free schools, almshouse schools, charity schools, and Sunday schools. Schooling in principles of morality and training in habits of industry and sobriety served as an important agent of social control. Since the city's growing population of European and native newcomers had little feeling for traditional values and little regard for accustomed behavior, education became a form of "social in-

surance." In this sense, those who promoted education for the poor
became the "moral stewards" of preindustrial New York City.[2]

Humanitarians and reformers, public officials and legislators,
newspaper editors and correspondents emphasized education as
moral training and social control in their public pronouncements
and personal correspondence. As early as 1737 the idea that "a more
regular Education" would improve the morals of poor children
found its way into the press. During the short time the *Gazette of
the United States* published in New York City, it championed
public schools as "the best way of preventing the existence of the
poor." In 1803 a special common council committee found a
fertile source of crime and depravity in the lack of schools for the
poor, and asserted that almshouse schools would foster "principles
of religion and morality" and fit pauper children for useful callings.
In an 1805 petition to the state legislature, the Free School Society
cited consequences of neglected education in New York City:
"ignorance and vice, and all those manifold evils resulting from
every species of immorality, by which public hospitals and almshouses, are filled with objects of disease and poverty, and society
burthened with taxes for their support." Similarly, an 1817 writer
in the New York *Commercial Advertiser* argued that "the best
and cheapest mode of freeing society from the enormous taxes
to support the poor, for clearing our streets of beggars, and for
averting all the evils which befall society, is to *educate* the rising
generation." New York Secretary of State John Van Ness Yates,
in his 1824 report on the poor laws, characterized schools for the
poor as "so many moral engines at work for the extirpation of crime
and pauperism." [3]

New York humanitarians filled their correspondence, speeches,
sermons, and other writings with these views of education as
moral indoctrination. In 1791 the Reverend John Rodgers of
the Brick Presbyterian Church praised religious charity schools
as important dispensers of "sentiments of Piety & Habits of
Morality." In his annual messages of 1802 and 1803, New York
Governor George Clinton advocated public education primarily
to promote morality, virtue, and religion; only secondarily did he

associate diffusion of knowledge with preservation of liberty and good government. In an 1823 letter to charity reformer John Griscom, Presbyterian clergyman Philip Lindsley summarized the moralistic position, asserting that "Education is doubtless destined . . . to be the main instrument by which extreme poverty & grovelling vice, & high-handed crime are to be banished from society." If poor children received proper training in "habits of industry, economy, & virtue," Lindsley wrote, there would be little occasion for "state prisons, penitentiaries, hospitals, alms-houses, Bridewells, poor houses & poor rates—& the thousands of benevolent institutions, & associations for the mere purpose of alleviating & nursing actual misery." Such ideas motivated New York's moral reformers and shaped the educational response to poverty in the urban community.[4]

Several New York City churches first sponsored organized efforts to apply education to poverty, vice, immorality, and ignorance. During the colonial period a few religious charity schools provided primary education for black, Indian, and poor white children. These schools proliferated rapidly following the American Revolution. In 1784 the Episcopal Charity School enrolled 104 poor children from the congregations of Trinity Church, St. Paul's Chapel, and St. George's Chapel. During 1789 several Dutch Reformed churches opened a charity school for thirty indigent pupils; its students totaled one hundred by 1809. The First Presbyterian Church established a charity school in 1790 and the Methodists followed by 1796. Within a few years after 1800 other schools had been opened by Roman Catholics, German Lutherans, English Lutherans, Scotch Presbyterians, Jews, Baptists, Moravians, Christ's Episcopal Church, and the German Reformed Church. By 1825 New York City contained fourteen separate sectarian schools with a total enrollment of 3,371 poor children. Baptists, Catholics, and Methodists conducted the largest schools.[5]

These charity schools held separate classes daily for boys and girls, who received religious and moral exhortation along with lessons in reading, writing, arithmetic, and, for girls, sewing.

When the children reached a suitable age, the schools found positions for them as servants and apprentices. Since most pupils came from indigent or working-class families, the schools supplied the prescribed uniform clothing as well as education without cost to parents. Although the legislature authorized small cash appropriations to the religious schools from the state's common school fund, annual charity sermons in each of the churches provided most of the financial support. Each winter the children of the schools sang hymns and sat in neat, orderly rows before congregations, while ministers appealed for funds.[6]

Benevolent churchgoers generously supported the charity schools, for these educational institutions conformed to the humanitarian rationale of the day. Preachers and writers justified education for the poor with arguments drawn from Enlightenment rationalism and Christian evangelicalism. But New Yorkers saw no contradiction in simultaneously promoting charity schools as a means of creating a virtuous, safe, and law-abiding lower class. The children were "snatched as Brands out of the Burning," instructed in "moral duties," taught habits of industry and sobriety, and prevented from becoming "Nuisances to Society." For the moral stewards of the metropolis, charity schools served as agents of social control as well as dispensers of religious benevolence.[7]

Similar manifestations of dual philanthropic motivations can be found in the African Free School founded in 1787 by the New York Society for Promoting the Manumission of Slaves (commonly called the Manumission Society). Although the school began with only twelve students, by 1796 some 140 boys and girls filled two separate classrooms; in 1823, according to the annual report of the state school superintendent, the African Free Schools enrolled 866 black children between the ages of five and fifteen. In addition to the usual religious and moral indoctrination, boys studied arithmetic, reading, and writing, while girls learned knitting and needlework as well. After a suitable amount of schooling —enough to qualify them as "safe and useful members of society" —the school bound out young blacks as sailors, apprentices, and domestic servants. The Manumission Society aimed its educational program primarily at the free Negro community of the city, but payment of a small tuition fee enabled white families to send slave children to the school as well.[8]

The utility of the African Free School in rescuing poor black children "from the complicated Evils that belong to their Situation" did not pass unnoticed. Humanitarians supported the institution enthusiastically, while the common council commended the school's trustees and teachers for their "Public Spirit & useful labours" in educating the "neglected and despised descendents of Africa." When the Manumission Society petitioned for financial aid in 1813 to expand its school program, the common council responded with the donation of a building lot near City Hall, despite objections of forty-five of the area's white residents that the "noise, confusion, and uproar" of "lower class" blacks would ruin the neighborhood. That enough other New Yorkers saw sufficient advantage in education for blacks is indicated in the establishment of seven African schools throughout the city by 1834, when the Public School Society assumed responsibility for their operation.[9]

The moral mission of the African Free School brought much of its support. The school's general pattern of religious and moral suasion reflected the protective philanthropy characteristic of the early nineteenth century. Readings from the scriptures began each school day; lessons based on religious stories and memorization of a nondenominational catechism composed much of the curriculum. In a contemporary history of the African Free Schools, Charles C. Andrews revealed the school's priorities during the twenty-three years he served as head teacher: "a proper regard for the morals of his pupils, constitutes one of the most important branches of an instructor's business." Education made poor black children "quiet and orderly citizens"; it snatched them from "ignorance, superstition, credulity, and crime." Parental indoctrination was attempted as well, for children brought home booklets containing "useful hints" on proper behavior—regular church attendance, daily Bible reading, and the importance of honesty, sobriety, cleanliness, and industrious habits. Manumission Society "visitors" similarly urged moral reformation on their regular rounds among black families. Essentially, the secular schools of the Manumission Society supplied its charges with a nonsectarian religious education.[10]

Although a number of religious and secular groups sponsored schools for the poor, free public education (except for a primary school in the almshouse) did not exist in preindustrial New York City. However, the state legislature recognized the importance of schools and passed legislation to promote their establishment. The first general education law, enacted in 1795, provided for five annual appropriations of £20,000 to encourage public schools throughout the state. The law called for division of school money among counties on a quota basis (determined by the number of assembly voters in each county) and stipulated that counties raise an additional sum equal to one-half of their annual appropriation for similar purposes. The sum allocated to New York City and County amounted to £1,888, while the common council raised another £944 by a local tax.

In the absence of public schools in the city, difficulties arose over disposal of common school funds. A special provision of the 1795 law which applied only to New York City authorized distribution of these funds among religious charity schools. But the common council in September 1796 determined to establish a public school system and petitioned the legislature for authorization. For this reason the council dispersed only the £944 sum raised by municipal taxation among five church schools and the African Free School sponsored by the New York Manumission Society, while retaining the state's appropriation of £1,888. The legislature supported the idea of municipal schools and amended the common school act in 1797 to permit the common council to keep five-sixths of its share of the annual school fund for the proposed system. The remainder would be allocated among religious charity schools and the African Free School in sums large enough to pay only teacher salaries.[11]

The common council's effort to establish a city school system faltered and, by 1801, failed. One important reason for lack of success, in addition to municipal procrastination, was the legislative decision of 1801 to abandon annual education appropriations. (However, the legislature continued to build a common school fund with proceeds from public lotteries and interest from invested land-sale receipts.) The legislature not only failed to renew the common school act of 1795, but directed the common council to divide all unappropriated school funds equally among the charity schools, now ten in number, and the Manumission Society's school. Since undistributed school money held by the municipality at the time of the new law totaled $17,223, each of the eleven private schools received $1,565. To assure permanent income, the law required each school to invest its portion of the school fund, using only the interest for educational costs. The trustees of each institution made annual reports to the common council on the state of the school and the investment.[12]

At the end of the first decade of the nineteenth century, rising demands for a statewide educational system from New England migrants to upstate New York brought appointment of a special legislative commission on common schools in 1811. Headed by Quaker philanthropist John Murray, Jr., the commission prepared a report which advocated a state school system "to disseminate religion, morality and learning." The idea of education as a technique of fostering moral conformity predominated throughout the report. Although the commissioners listed maintenance of free political institutions among the advantages of universal education, they emphasized that "morality and religion are the foundation of all that is truly great and good, and are consequently of primary importance." Schooling would fill "little minds" with "great moral and religious truths," inspire virtue, and dispel vicious and immoral habits. Modern shibboleths notwithstanding, the commission recommended daily Bible reading in all common schools to secure these benevolent objectives.[13]

These pious arguments convinced the lawmakers. Two new education statutes implemented the commissioners' report. A law of 1812 established school districts in all areas of the state except New York City and allocated state funds for local schools.

Since numerous private and religious schools already functioned in New York City, the legislature made separate provisions for education in the metropolis. Rather than create new common schools where none existed, the education law of 1813 reinstituted the former system of annual appropriations to sectarian and other schools in the city. Once again the common council, through five appointive school commissioners, supervised division of common school funds. The number of students determined the size of each school's allocation. Thus, in 1824 some twenty-two institutions with 10,383 enrolled students divided $14,173 at the rate of $1.36

Table 6

COMMON SCHOOL FUND DISTRIBUTION FOR NEW YORK CITY, 1824

School	No. of Students	Amount
Free School Society	5,209	$ 7,110.28
Bethel Baptist Church	1,616	2,206.75
African Free Schools	843	1,150.69
Female Association	543	741.19
St. Patrick's Church	406	554.19
Methodist Episcopal Church	369	503.69
St. Peter's Church	313	427.25
Protestant Episcopal Church	250	341.25
Orphan Asylum Society	151	206.11
Grace Church	128	174.72
Reformed Dutch Church	100	136.50
Economical School	93	126.95
Hamilton Free School	85	116.02
First Congregational Church	68	92.82
Society of Mechanics and Tradesmen	52	70.98
St. Michael's Church	39	53.23
Roman Catholic Benevolent Society	36	49.14
German Lutheran Church	24	32.76
Scotch Presbyterian Church	23	31.40
First Baptist Church	18	24.57
Christ Church	12	16.38
First Presbyterian Church	5	6.83
	10,383	$14,173.50

Source: *Commercial Advertiser* (New York), January 27, 1825.

per pupil. The New York Free School Society, with 5,209 students, received the largest portion of the school money, as it did each year. A controversy between the Free School Society and the charity schools in the early 1820's led to passage in 1824 of a new school law for New York City, which authorized the common council to terminate assistance to religious charity schools. Thereafter, only secular schools in the city—most of them belonging to the Free School Society and its successor, the Public School Society—received financial aid from the state.[14]

The Free School Society made the most ambitious attempt to educate and improve the morals of indigent children in New York City. Founded in 1805 by leading humanitarians of the city—among them Mayor De Witt Clinton, Thomas Eddy, John Murray, Jr., and Leonard Bleecker—the new organization aimed its program at poor white youths not enrolled in any of the religious charity schools. As society members surveyed the urban community in 1805, they observed vice and immorality rampant among the poor. The "laboring class" had become "less industrious, less moral, and less careful to lay up the fruit of their earnings." Clearly, such conditions resulted from the "want of a virtuous education." [15]

The society's early success stemmed largely from generous municipal and state patronage. De Witt Clinton, president of the society for more than two decades, as well as mayor of the city for ten years and governor of the state for another ten, lobbied vigorously for the society and kept its petitions and memorials continuously before aldermen and legislators. On several occasions the common council provided public buildings for classrooms and cash appropriations for upkeep and repairs. Similarly, the state legislature assisted the society with two grants of $4,000 and an annuity of $1,000 (later increased to $1,500) from the liquor tax collected in New York City. Furthermore, after the common school legislation of 1813 the Free School Society, because it had more students than any other institution, received the largest annual share of the common school money for New York City.[16]

With these funds the Free School Society rapidly expanded

education for the poor. Introduction of the Lancasterian system of monitorial instruction, which utilized older and more advanced students as assistant teachers to instruct younger pupils, minimized operating expenses. Thus, with only a few teachers to pay, the society used most of its financial resources for educational materials and school construction. With adequate space, supplies, and staff, enrollment grew rapidly, as did the society's objectives. In 1814 the society provided free schooling to 1,100 children from lower-class families; by 1825, with two schools under construction, more than 5,200 boys and girls filled five other buildings. In addition, the society worked closely with the trustees of the African Free School and with the Female Association, a group of Quaker ladies teaching some 760 girls by 1822. In 1823 the Free School Society assumed direction of the almshouse schools at Bellevue. Indeed, by 1820, and in the absence of a public school system, the society aimed for a monopoly on free elementary education in New York City.[17]

During the 1820's the Free School Society came close to achieving its objective, but only after dealing a heavy blow to the religious charity schools. From the society's point of view, the only real impediment to the goal of a uniform, Protestant, nonsectarian education for all poor children in the city lay in the denominational schools. The school law of 1813, of course, had provided state support for these institutions, a measure the Free School Society opposed as a stimulus to new church schools. The original legislation made appropriations only for teacher salaries, but an amendment of 1817 exempted the Free School Society from this stipulation. Another amendment in 1822 permitted the Bethel Baptist Church to use portions of its common school money for new buildings. Within two years the Bethel Charity School enrolled 1,616 students—making it second in size to the Free School Society—and reported ambitious plans for further expansion to outlying areas of the city. The Free School Society objected to the competition and quickly applied its weighty influence on common council and state legislature. Petitions and lobbying succeeded in 1824, when new legislation abolished the board of school commissioners in New York City and once again authorized the common council to distribute state school money. Yielding to free school pressures, the council in turn prohibited further allocations to religious charity schools. The Free School Society marked its success by inviting admission applications from all charity school students and, in a symbolic move, changing its name to the Public School Society.[18]

The conflict with the Baptists reflected the interdenominational spirit which motivated most reformers and dominated the humanitarian movement in New York City. Sectarian rivalries, the Free School Society contended, would compromise the effectiveness of moral training and undermine educational efforts among the poor. Only a uniform, nonsectarian system could uplift the lower classes and establish moral conformity.

Education as social control clearly became a central argument in the society's rationale. Schooling for poor children—those who normally became "the burden and pests of society"—would eliminate vice, pauperism, and the "Standing Corps of the base and profligate" among the rising generation. Early instruction, the society asserted in its first public statement in 1805, established "fixed habits of industry, decency, and order." Ignorance among the poor brought only "moral debasement," De Witt Clinton declared in an 1809 address before the society; education for the poor brought "industry, good morals, good order, and rational religion." An 1822 petition to the common council typified the society's position:

> If we would lessen taxes by preventing pauperism; if we would lessen public burdens by diminishing crimes and offenses; if we would render the City more wealthy by increasing individual exertion and enterprize; if we would give greater peace and security to our citizens and render property more sacred; if we would give a broader basis and render firmer the foundations of our political and civil institutions—we shall encourage early education among the poor, inculcate virtuous maxims in the young mind as its powers are unfolded, and teach the principles of self-respect—industry, sobriety, enterprize and usefulness will follow.

Education for the poor represented positive humanitarianism but manifested at the same time the idea of philanthropy as social protection—protection of the community against undesirable and unrestrained behavior and protection of established order against social disturbance.[19]

Throughout the preindustrial period the Free School Society remained one of the most important "engines" of moral reform in New York. The society's schools used moral coercion and religious proselytizing to achieve social order in the urban community. Much of the curriculum centered on religious and moral themes. Bible readings opened a school day filled with scripture lessons and recitations from a nonsectarian catechism. School children also pored over a number of secular schoolbooks which elaborated and reinforced "the great and generally acknowledged principles of Christianity." For a time students even memorized passages from temperance tracts. All students met at their classrooms on Sunday mornings, then marched in orderly fashion under the watchful eyes of monitors to their respective churches. A manual for parents emphasized the importance of a religious home life, church attendance, good manners, and habits of industry and frugality, cleanliness and sobriety.[20]

The New York free schools also adopted unique discipline methods to exact submission and proper conduct. With standard corporal punishment disallowed, Lancasterian schoolmasters used a variety of unusual techniques: six-pound logs, which, when placed on the shoulders of an offending child, bound him to his seat; arm shackles, which locked students at their desks; leg shackles, which made walking almost impossible; a small closet with barred windows for solitary detention; a cagelike arrangement, in which serious transgressors were suspended from the ceiling in full view of jeering classmates. By contrast, masters rewarded good behavior with prizes and honors. Such methods of punishment and reward forced or induced children to conformity, subordination, and submission to authority. Free-school discipline, in other words, reinforced the moral indoctrination of classroom lessons. Both discipline and lessons consciously fostered social control.[21]

Sunday schools for New York City's slum dwellers—both children and adults—formed another vital concern of the moral reformers. Drawing upon the heightened evangelical fervor of the time, such schools sprouted in every ward with remarkable rapidity beginning in 1816. In February of that year New York import merchants Divie Bethune and Eleazer Lord, following the example of religious humanitarians in England and Philadelphia, sponsored a public meeting to generate interest and enthusiasm in the Sunday school idea. The New York Sunday School Union Society which resulted further reflected the interdenominational character of urban reform. Sunday schools caught on quickly and firmly in every congregation. Within six months 250 volunteer teachers had captured more than 2,500 boys and male adults for the Christian cause in twenty-four Sunday schools. By 1820, lay evangelicals had opened thirty-seven schools, while the Female Sunday School Union Society had established another thirty-seven for girls. Episcopalians remained aloof from the interdenominational effort, yet succumbed to evangelical urgency by forming their own Protestant Episcopal Sunday School Society. By 1823 the three societies together enrolled more than 7,000 students.[22]

Religious education became an influential element in the moral attack on New York's poor. The first public pronouncement of the Sunday School Union Society in 1816 set forth the dual purpose of the group: "to arrest the progress of vice, and to promote the moral and religious instruction of the depraved and uneducated part of the community." Each Sunday morning "visitors" gathered poor children and illiterate adults from the city's streets and slums. In classrooms filled to overflowing, teachers sermonized and students learned to read and memorize scripture. Reflecting its approach to pauperism, the Female Sunday School Union Society, in its ninth annual report in 1825, emphasized what seemed its main accomplishment during the preceding year: 3,052 students had memorized 125,030 catechism answers, 144,685 answers to

McDowell's *Questions,* 189,181 scripture verses, and 26,500 hymn verses. Sunday school fervor carried beyond the Sabbath as well, for visitors canvassed lower-class neighborhoods during the week, reinforcing moral lessons taught in the schools.[23]

Few New Yorkers, pious or otherwise, challenged the importance or effectiveness of the Sunday school crusade; most gave unlimited praise and many considerable financial support. At the societies' anniversaries, with school flags and banners held high, Sunday school scholars and teachers paraded through the city in orderly, submissive rows—a public display which reformers always found "truly astonishing" or "deeply affecting," and which never failed to renew evangelical spirit and purpose. Immediately after these parades, society directors packed middle-class church-goers into pews for a round of congratulatory addresses, spirited sermons, and pleas for money. Some evangelical promoters emphasized resulting social improvement in the slums. According to Eleazer Lord, writing in the *Christian Herald* in 1816, Sunday school visitors soon cleared city streets formerly crowded with idle and vicious children profaning the Sabbath; now, he said, such children went to school or stayed at home "to avoid the visitors." Even "Bancker-Street Sabbath-breakers of the vilest class," another reformer wrote, had become "decent in their dress, orderly in their behavior, industrious in their calling, *and punctual at school and church!*" By 1823 Sunday schools had inspired such optimism that one advocate urged visitors to "scour out every haunt of wretchedness," and churchmen to "build up one hundred more schools." More than any other technique of moral reform, "the mighty machinery of Sunday schools" drew continued and substantial support from the urban community.[24]

Yet New York's Sunday school enthusiasts often found their task difficult and discouraging. For example, many children seemed unwilling students. Rudeness, insubordination, irregular attendance, and fighting in the schools disturbed many middle-class, volunteer teachers; indeed, one said, such unruly behavior and the "squalid, filthy appearance" of most students rendered the work "disgusting." Others emphasized need for "order and discipline" in the schools if society could expect any lasting moral improvement. Thus New York's *American Sunday School Teachers' Magazine* devoted many pages to hints on discipline and lists of suggested rules. Although some evangelicals advocated "the rod of correction," many Sunday school superintendents found corporal punishment degrading and self-defeating. "You are forbidden to carry a rod or stick in the school," ran one set of instructions to teachers; "neither to kick or pinch the children; nor to pull their ears or their hair." Thus, conversion and moral improvement depended upon effective use of religious tracts, scripture lessons, and evangelizing techniques in the classroom.[25]

Sunday school promoters clearly envisioned schools as agents of social control. "Are you friends to *social order*," asked a writer in *The Evangelical Guardian* in 1818? "Engage in Sunday schools, that you may be instrumental in teaching the rising generation how to preserve that order." Instructions issued to teachers in May 1816 made the same general point: "while you instill in their young minds the duty of contentment in the stations allotted to them by Providence, you will of course embrace the occasion to point out to them the self-degradation which attend idleness and vice; and the certain rewards which await industry and a virtuous life." Religious education would make the poor conscious of "the responsibilities from which none are free"; it would qualify them "for the limited sphere in which they are called to act"; it would make them "props of enlightened governments"; it was a sure means of "preventing Vice and Pauperism"; it would "preserve and advance social order, peace, and happiness"; it secured society from "the depredations of the thief, and the violence of the robber." "Who must be told," asserted the editor of the *American Sunday School Teachers' Magazine* in 1824, "that an attendance at Sunday schools will give their children habits of order, submission, industry, and thoughts which they never had before." The Sunday school movement drew upon humanitarian fervor and attempted to spread morality through the urban community as a method of social control.[26]

A number of other private secular schools established instruc-

tional programs with similar religious goals. The SRPW emphasized religious and moral instruction in its schools. The Economical
School, founded in 1809 to instruct children of French refugees
and other indigent foreigners, listed propagation of morality and
religion as its primary objective. So also did the Female Association,
the General Society of Mechanics and Tradesmen, the Orphan
Asylum Society, the New York High School Society, and the Infant
School Society—each of which supported schools for the poor. Indeed, few secular schools failed to emphasize religious and moral
instruction.[27]

In serving numerous functions, education enlisted many arguments in its support. Most early reformers and school spokesmen
recognized the importance of an educated electorate in a presumably democratic society. Most acknowledged that compassion and
humanity, the spirit of Christian benevolence, required efforts to
bring "the sunshine of mental and moral illumination" to the poor.
But few failed to emphasize the social dividends such a policy
would pay. Through education, the indigent could "be excited to
emulate the cleanliness, decorum, and mental improvement of
those in better circumstances." Education-minded reformers, Protestant evangelicals, and assorted urban boosters expended much
of their energy and money in classroom proselytizing, for they considered moral education of the poor an effective method of maintaining social control amid threatened urban disorder. For most
middle-class New Yorkers moral training of the people became
"an act of self-preservation." [28]

New York's moral reformers thought of education as the cure for
all the social ills of mankind, and especially for vices they observed
among the poor in their own city. Poverty, immorality, drunkenness, crime, indolence, dependency—all could be erased by the
magic influence of education. Virtually all educational institutions
of the city—public and private, religious and secular—subscribed
to the doctrine of individual improvement. All aimed at inculcation
of accepted behavior and values and creation of a sober and contented, hard-working and law-abiding lower class. All provided

a religious education, albeit a Protestant one in most. All postulated the necessity of moral stewardship.

As prime instruments for dissemination of societal traditions and values, schools in preindustrial New York City provided formal indoctrination in middle-class morality. By demanding ethical conformity, by providing models of decency and decorum, by imposing values upon the lower classes from above, they became protectors of the social order. Evangelical enthusiasts made schools dispensers of an official orthodoxy, a kind of protective, Protestant piety. Religious-oriented reformers brought the Calvinistic work ethic into the classroom. Humanitarians used philanthropic impulses to defend their traditional, structured community. Moral training for the poor represented one important response to urban poverty in a period of social change and economic transition.

12

Religion

If New York reformers promoted education for the poor with energy and enthusiasm, they also worked actively to evangelize the city's new slums and tenements. In the first half of the nineteenth century, strong currents of revivalism and reform swept American Protestantism. Much of the new "missionizing electricity," as Perry Miller called it, obviously grew from sincere religious conviction and evangelical fervor. But much reflected the efforts of pious, middle-class churchgoers and preachers of all denominations to restore order and stability to a society confused and shaken by urban growth and economic transformation. This dualism in evangelical motivation clearly marked the urban missionary movement in New York City in the early nineteenth century. Dedicated to rescuing the irreligious masses for Christ, city missionaries also applied a kind of moral therapy to urban social problems.[1]

The campaign to evangelize the city began slowly at first, for the earliest missionary societies devoted attention to religious deficiencies on the American frontier or the Christian void in Asia and Africa. But by the end of the first decade of the nineteenth century, preachers and reformers noted inconsistency in converting heathens abroad while ignoring heathens at home—the impious, unchurched poor and impoverished Catholic immigrants of the cities. Typically, the Reverend Philip Milledoler, an evangelical Presbyterian preacher, argued in 1812 that "the soul of a pauper in the alms-house of New York, is as valuable as the soul of an Indian on the banks of the Ganges." By the 1820's city missionaries and ward "visitors" saturated the slums of New York, distributing Bibles and tracts, preaching and praying with the poor in their homes, conducting Sunday schools and weekday gospel lectures, converting, exhorting, and evangelizing.[2]

The urban missionary movement stemmed from the altered character of American Protestantism in the post-Revolutionary period. The orthodox Calvinism of colonial years had asserted the total depravity of man in a predetermined and sinful world. But the new, liberal theology of the Second Great Awakening rejected rigid predestination and postulated an achievable salvation for all men. Derived largely from the preachings and writings of New England divines Samuel Hopkins and Nathaniel W. Taylor, the appealing ideas of man's free will, God's free grace, and open salvation infused Protestantism with new vitality. The modified Calvinism of Presbyterian and Congregational liberals declared that Christ died not for the elect alone, but for all men. Taylorism proclaimed repentance as the key to salvation. The Hopkinsian system called upon all Christians to practice universal or "disinterested benevolence"—dedication to human improvement in imitation of divine example. These new theological currents implied that religious activism and missionary zeal might reap innumerable converts, that evangelical pietism might regenerate the whole of society, might indeed bring the millennium. Pious men everywhere transcended interest in their own souls in an aggressive concern for the salvation of others.

Widespread acceptance of the new theology in the early decades of the nineteenth century promoted benevolent efforts to improve and purify the human condition. Evangelical enthusiasm sustained a host of sectarian and interdenominational institutions designed to hasten the millennium. Missionary groups, Bible and tract societies, Sunday schools, temperance and education associations, societies for the suppression of vice and immorality—all worked energetically to dispel the "darkness of heathenism." The "varied schemes of Christian philanthropy" sought to irrigate the "moral desert" of the world, hoped to "fertilize a thirsty soil." Taken together, a multitude of evangelical and moral reform societies helped put Christianity, said New York Episcopalian minister John McVickar, "on its march to universal empire." [3]

That society needed moral improvement became an axiom of the day. "Who does not know," asked the Reverend John Stanford in 1825, "that iniquity has too long run down our streets like water; and that the floods of the ungodly . . . have frequently overflowed the safety and peace of our city?" Amidst the wickedness of the city, the Reverend Ward Stafford wrote in 1817, one could observe "Satan's invisible car, constantly rolling and crunching thousands beneath its weight, and causing our streets to flow with the blood of souls." The Female Missionary Society for the Poor of New York City put the impelling question: "are there not some among the destitute of our own city for whom Christ died?"; some souls "who must yet be gathered in?" Such concerns prompted the evangelical crusade. The movement to reclaim "suffering humanity" in the rising cities and immigrant slums of the new nation claimed the energy and attention of urban missionaries, especially in the decade following the War of 1812. With its thousands of impious, intemperate, and ignorant poor, the city became the "new missionary field." [4]

Divine benevolence, however, represented but one side of an ambivalent attitude toward the urban poor. Religious commitment and pietist perfectionism did not erase the moralistic conceptions New Yorkers held about poverty and its origins. "Almost all the sufferings of the poor in this, and other cities," early urban missionary Ward Stafford wrote in 1817, "are the immediate effect of ignorance or vice." If the poor became that way because of individual shortcomings and moral failings, "let there be a great effort to change the moral character of mankind, to remove the cause of their sufferings." If irreligion headed the list of causes of dependency, the solution, according to the Reverend John H. Rice, appeared simple enough: "as far as the people are brought under the influence of an enlightened evangelical ministry, the evils of pauperism are removed." In 1820, with similar logic, the New-York Bible Society advocated gospel distribution as "the most efficacious" means for the prevention of pauperism.[5]

Many New Yorkers unquestionably advocated religion for the poor to maintain social stability during a period of rapid urban growth. The crusade to stamp the city slums with the Christian imprint, with piety, morality, and right conduct, partially reflected an attempt to buttress the established order. The evangelical emphasis on salvation implied a submission to divine will on earth in return for heaven hereafter. The "doctrine of devout contentment" embellished the sermons of city missionaries and the preachments of ward visitors. As was true of education for the poor, the desire for social control of the lower classes accompanied the increasing evidence of enthusiastic religion in the city. The dual philanthropic motivations of "compassion and protection" clearly characterized the urban evangelical campaign. The religious institutions spawned in New York City reflected these ambiguities in the urban missionary movement.[6]

Surprisingly, the municipal government played an important part in fostering city missions as the nineteenth century began. The city fathers, for example, displayed an unusual concern for the spiritual welfare of public paupers and as early as 1785 authorized Protestant clergymen to preach in the almshouse. Such services were held irregularly until the formation in 1812 of the first city mission organization—the Society for Supporting the Gospel among the Poor of the City of New-York (SSGP). This association, established primarily to conduct religious services for the poor in public institutions such as the almshouse, bridewell, city hospital, and state prison, received generous financial support from the common council after 1814 in the form of annual salary grants to the Reverend John Stanford, the official SSGP preacher.[7]

The SSGP grew out of earlier visits to the public institutions made by Stanford and by the Reverend Ezra Stiles Ely. An English Baptist who migrated to America in 1786, Stanford taught for a short time in Norfolk, Virginia, and held a pastorate in Providence, Rhode Island, before his arrival in New York City in 1789. Although he had no regular pulpit in New York, he conducted a private school, instructed theological students, wrote and distributed religious tracts, and preached frequently in the city and elsewhere. With several friends in 1794 he formed a short-lived Society for Promoting Christian Knowledge and Piety among the Poor—the city's earliest tract society. In 1807 Stanford began to preach in the almshouse. His missionary associate, Ely, was a young Presbyterian evangelical who attended the almshouse and hospital regularly beginning in 1810. Ely kept a journal of his activities—a "record of wretchedness," as he labeled it—and called for the establishment of a permanent fund to support a chaplain for paupers. True Christians, he asserted in an 1810 sermon, should "tax their luxuries," abstain from accustomed pleasures, and put their money into a campaign to bring the gospel to the poor.[8]

The early efforts of Stanford and Ely bore fruition in December 1812, when a number of New York's leading citizens, including lay evangelicals Leonard Bleecker, Divie Bethune, John R. Murray, and John Caldwell, buttressed with common council support, formed the interdenominational SSGP. Stanford and Ely received joint appointments as the first city missionaries. When Ely accepted a call to preach in Rhode Island in June 1813, SSGP duties devolved upon Stanford alone, a missionary labor he continued until his death in 1834 at the age of eighty-one.[9]

An extremely methodical and orderly individual, Stanford reported annually to the common council and kept a diary of his ministerial activities, meticulously recording sermons delivered and deathbed conversions among the paupers. After 1813 his weekly schedule included almost daily visits to the city institutions. On Tuesdays he attended the several wards of the New York Hospital and delivered three sermons. Wednesdays brought him to the state prison and the orphan asylum, where he preached a "baby discourse" and examined waifs and delinquents in the catechism. On Thursdays he exhorted prisoners in the debtor's jail and the bridewell. On Fridays he visited sick patients at the Bellevue alms-

house, preached twice and then again in the penitentiary, after
which he catechized pauper children in the almshouse schools.
With what must have been superhuman effort for an elderly man,
Stanford ministered to all his charges on the Sabbath, delivering
individual sermons in the penetentiary, the state prison, and the
New York Hospital, and two more in the almshouse chapel. He
also instructed reformed prostitutes in the Madgalen Society asylum until the organization dissolved in 1818. After 1825 Stanford's
itinerary included regular calls at the newly established House of
Refuge for juvenile delinquents, an institution he had advocated
as early as 1812. The elderly evangelical Baptist preacher delivered
an average of forty sermons each month and an astounding total of
5,622 between 1813 and 1825. In addition he assisted with the education of the almshouse children, formed a pauper "singing school,"
wrote a catechism for the schools of the almshouse, penitentiary,
and state prison, convinced the common council of the need for a
chapel in the new Bellevue almshouse, and participated in a variety
of reform causes in the city. He undoubtedly earned his $800 salary
from the SSGP and the additional stipend of $250 to $500 provided
annually by the common council.[10]

Such municipal assistance for religious proselytizing among public paupers did not stem from aldermanic zeal alone. "Places of
Worship," a common council committee reported in 1817, are
"highly beneficial not only to the morals, but to the industry of
the Lower Classes of the Community." Few New Yorkers disagreed, but one who did objected more to the expense than the
technique. In an 1824 petition to the council, a man named John
Edwards asserted that many clergymen would gladly preach by
turns in the city institutions without remuneration. In reference
to Stanford's municipal income, Edwards wrote: "I firmly believe
it would be far more acceptable to God and all good and wise men
had you laid out 300 dollars in fat geese and turkeys and given
them to the poor who have seen better days and they would prefer
it at any time to 300 dollars worth of wind." Needless to say,
councilmen preferred an almshouse full of docile converts to less
restrained paupers with full stomachs.[11]

The formation of a number of Bible and tract societies by 1816 provided added stimulus to the city mission movement and carried the evangelical impulse from the almshouse to the slums of the city. The Bible society fad began in 1809 with the formation of three separate groups: the New-York Bible Society, the Young Men's Bible Society of New York City, both interdenominational, and the New-York Bible and Common Prayer Book Society, an Episcopal organization. The religious impulse quickened in 1812 when Bible society promoters channeled their excess fervor into the New-York Religious Tract Society, a new organization designed to supply city and frontier with religious books and pamphlets. Episcopalians remained aloof from interdenominational societies but nevertheless established by 1814 their own New-York Protestant Episcopal Tract Society which zealously engaged in evangelical work in the city.[12]

The revival spirit hit a peak in 1816 when delegates from a number of state and local groups met in New York to establish the nonsectarian American Bible Society. Headquartered in the metropolis, the new national organization resolved to fight "heathenism" at home and abroad with centralized dissemination of the gospels. Sponsoring local auxiliaries as fund-raising agencies to purchase and distribute the Bibles it published, the American Bible Society soon presided over a vast "moral machinery" for the regeneration of American society.[13]

New York City soon sprouted a number of new Bible auxiliaries for local purposes. These included the New-York Auxiliary Bible Society (1813), the New-York Female Auxiliary Bible Society (1816), the Auxiliary New-York Bible and Common Prayer Book Society (1816), a Marine Bible Society (1817), an African Bible Society (1817), and even a Female Juvenile Auxiliary Bible Society (1816). Each of these new groups, together with the earlier societies, made special efforts to bring salvation to slum dwellers, to convert the city's "moral wilderness into the gardens of the Lord." [14]

The societies deluged New York City with a flood of paper and print. Auxiliary members distributed copies of the Bible and tracts to almshouse paupers and hospital patients, to profligate seamen in taverns and boarding houses, to prisoners in jail and prostitutes on the street, to downtrodden blacks and Irish in growing ghettos, to scholars in free schools, charity schools, African schools, Sunday schools, and the orphan asylum. Charitable societies applied for and received them for their pensioners. Translations into French, German, Spanish, and Welch made their way into immigrant households. Typically, in 1821 the New-York Bible Society supplied the urban poor with 27,277 Bibles and 2,247 testaments. By the 1820's the New-York Religious Tract Society printed and distributed 200,000 tracts annually. The general attempt to use religious literature in the struggle against immorality in the city became an important early characteristic of the urban missionary movement.[15]

Many auxiliaries adopted the district visitation plan to systematically saturate the city with the word of God. In 1821, for example, the New-York Bible Society joined the Society for the Prevention of Pauperism in such a plan for district visiting to seek out the poor for relief and moral reform. The Marine Bible Society divided the waterfront into nine sections and selected members to make calls on seamen in each. Other groups appointed "Branch Societies" for each of the city's wards. By 1824 the Female Auxiliary Bible Society had sixty volunteer visitors in fourteen wards. Their duties included not only Bible distribution but exhortation of the poor as well—"to impress upon their minds the importance of reading the Scriptures, and of regular attendance upon some place of Divine Worship." [16]

The central task of Bible distribution brought many middle-class New Yorkers into contact with the poor for the first time. Female visitors in the sixth ward reported in 1824 that they had "never witnessed such utter ignorance and moral depravity." In the outer wards of the city Irish immigrants and free blacks lived in deplorable conditions in filthy, damp cellars and crowded, shabby tenements. Their poverty seemed "so hopeless as to render casual charities of no avail, and their moral degradation such as to discourage an attempt to raise them." These and similar impressions, drawn from personal visitation in the slums, helped shape and solidify the reformers' general attitudes toward the poor and the causes of pauperism.[17]

Bible and tract distributors treated indigence and immorality as two sides of the same general problem and, almost without exception, laid both to lack of religious conviction and the tendency of weak character to succumb to the temptations of vice. When the New-York Bible Society in 1820 asked why the city, its streets, courts, and public institutions, overflowed with vicious and dissolute criminals, beggars, and paupers, the answer seemed logical —"it is because Bibles are not sufficiently distributed among them." The society asserted as an indisputable fact, "that in every country, in proportion as the Bible has been circulated amongst the mass of the population, their temporal condition has been improved; and that in those places in which the Bible is most freely read by the poorer class, that class is best able to provide for itself, and is least a charge to the State." Money only partially relieved beggars and paupers, the tract society announced in 1821; most "would be more benefited by a donation in Tracts." The New-York Bible Society's 1820 report cited the beneficial effects of Sunday schools in improving the temporal and spiritual condition of the poor and then declared: "who can doubt that these benefits have arisen, partially at least, through the instrumentality of the Scriptures, when it appears . . . that above fifty thousand verses are committed to memory every three months." The city mission movement began on a wave of pious optimism, a certainty that evangelical religion would make it possible for the poor to reform themselves and rise above secular troubles.[18]

New York's reformers looked upon their self-assigned task as one of reshaping the character and morals of the lower classes. They thought of the Bible as one essential tool in this refashioning process. Bible reading made men virtuous and useful, sober and industrious; it stimulated "steady habits and correct moral deportment"; it produced "admirers of social order"; it strengthened "the fabric of civil society." Indeed, the very act of Bible distribution revealed the moralistic objective. Most societies began by giving Bibles gratuitously, but by 1820 many demanded a small fee from the poor

to guard against any "abuses" and stimulate "a sense of independence." Bible distributors presumed that such payments benefited
the poor "by raising the standard of their moral feeling." "It is an
established fact," one society asserted positively, "that Bibles that
are purchased are not only more valued, but more read." Thus,
ward visitors often collected weekly or monthly assessments on
their regular rounds. The societies envisioned that in this way
thousands of the poor would "bring their contributions into the
Treasury of the Lord, who might otherwise expend the same sums
in idle or vicious indulgences." The process of general distribution
became one of careful dispensation. The Female Auxiliary Bible
Society assured readers of its tenth annual report in 1826 that the
new method produced "habits which may prove useful to the poor
in many ways." The report did not elaborate. The reformers' conception of poverty dictated that to get something for nothing,
whether it be charity or Bibles, destroyed character. Such ideas
became increasingly evident among municipal officials and humanitarian leaders in the years after 1815.[19]

In the same vein, Bible men emphasized the idea that the pious
and contented poor were close to God. Convinced that the Bible
provided "the cheering prospect of another and a better world,"
its distributors hoped to make poverty, unemployment, and intolerable living conditions acceptable. Persuaded that the Bible
served as "the passport to eternal life," they also offered it to the
poor as a "balm for present consolation." Certain that religious
instruction made the poor "happy in their various stations in life,"
they expected slum dwellers to be docile and contented rather
than disorderly and resentful. The promise of a better deal in the
hereafter became an integral part of the evangelical argument.[20]

The strong pressures for social control which so clearly characterized educational programs for the poor marked the urban Bible
campaign as well. In 1820 an Episcopalian Bible auxiliary stated
one important evangelical objective as "lives well ordered and
passions well regulated." Elias Boudinot of New Jersey, first president of the American Bible Society, alluded to ideas of social control in his speech at the organization's fifth anniversary meeting in

1821: "The union of religious interests effected by the Bible Society secures us from a multitude of evils, that are increasing with fearful luxuriance, in every Soil unacquainted with the blessing of the gospel." A number of society reports and anniversary addresses promoted Bible distribution as essential for "the safety of our own government." Many crimes and vicious acts could not be prevented by civil legislation, the Reverend Robert McLeod of New York told the American Bible Society in 1822; only "that which awes the conscience"—the principles of the gospel—could avert and prevent such evil courses. More specifically, the Marine Bible Society emphasized the social and commercial dividends which might be expected when God-fearing sailors manned ship crews—fewer ships wrecked, cargoes destroyed, and lives lost as a result of superstition, drunkenness, insubordination, and misconduct. In all of these ways a doctrine of moral stewardship accompanied and increasingly compromised the evangelical fervor of the urban religious revival.[21]

Similar attitudes marked the massive efforts at tract distribution in New York City. Organized in 1812, the New-York Religious Tract Society quickly assumed a prominent place in the urban missionary movement. The society printed short religious pamphlets of four to twelve pages, some directed to adults and others to children; each contained pointed moral lessons. Tract titles often revealed evangelical purposes: *Sin No Trifle; The Praying Negro; The Duties and Encouragements of the Poor; A Warning to Gamblers and Swearers; Destructive Consequences of Dissipation and Luxury; The Evils of Drunkenness; Early Piety; Good Examples for Good Children; Happy Poverty.* Most of the tracts were reprints of British publications, but some came from the pens of New Yorkers John Stanford, Gardiner Spring, and Divie Bethune. By 1825 the New York group had issued 192 different adult tracts and 75 children's books; between 1812 and 1825 the society and its female auxiliary distributed more than 2.3 million such publications.[22]

Concern for the moral and spiritual welfare of the poor marked the activities of the New-York Religious Tract Society. Although some religious literature found its way to the frontiers, the squalid slums and waterfront areas of New York City became a special missionary ground. Ward visitors sought out sinners in their "lurking places." Ships and steamboats in the harbor and sailors' boarding houses in adjacent alleys did not escape the "pious exertions" of tract distributors. Some brought tracts into the prisons, the hospital, and the almshouse; others distributed them in free schools and Sunday schools; still others gave them to door-to-door beggars in place of alms. The Female Auxiliary Religious Tract Society hired peddlers to hawk them about the streets and in the public markets. Whatever the method, the purpose remained the same: to halt the course of sinners "hastening down to the pit"; to reform criminals, drunkards, Sabbath-breakers, and "back-sliders"; to bring the wicked and impious poor into the "sheep-fold of the great Shepherd." [23]

Tract readers could hardly escape the moral message. Much of the religious literature railed against "the fiery stream of intoxicating liquors." Some tracts cautioned against such "pernicious" and "criminal" entertainments as the theater. Others emphasized obedience, honesty, cleanliness, self-denial, and industrious habits. Although most tracts focused on a single theme, some were more ambitious. For example, in a single tract entitled *A Dialogue Between Two Seamen After a Storm* the society warned against drunkenness, Sabbath-breaking, promiscuity, and profanity, advocated Bible reading between watches at sea, and urged sailors to become Christian missionaries on foreign voyages. Some publications, such as *An Alphabet of Lessons for Children,* contained not only the usual moral injunctions but appropriate illustrations designed to drive home the point.[24]

The concept of "happy poverty" supplied the tract society with one major theme. Economic realities brought only misery to the lower classes, but many tracts suggested that the poor became rich through faith. The Reverend Leigh Richmond, author of a popular tract titled *The Dairyman's Daughter,* wrote that only among the working poor could one find religion "in its purest character." Poverty, self-denial, and humility preserved believers from "the allurements of luxury." They lacked earthly wealth, to be sure, but the faithful poor had none of "the cares, the anxieties, nor the AWFUL RESPONSIBILITY of riches." These ideas emerged in a typical tract, *The Happy Man; or, The Life of William Kelly*. The pamphlet presented the story of an apprentice tailor addicted to idleness, drunkenness, and vicious habits. Converted in a moment of despair, Kelly thereafter "applied himself diligently to his trade," lived frugally on bread and water, shared his meager income with other poor tenement dwellers, and "made it a constant rule never to get anything without paying for it." Despite frugal habits and continual application to labor, Kelly seems never to have risen above his poverty (a point not emphasized by the tract). Yet once converted, he remained "one of the most cheerful and most contented of human creatures." [25]

Such stories reveal much about evangelical motives. The urban tract campaign became for many a method of buttressing existing social order. Pious promoters saw in tract distribution an effective means of eradicating vice "in its most odious forms," of preserving society from "fraud, and drunkenness, and murder." Religion helped protect republican institutions, became a form of "glorious patriotism." It made the working class and the poor "peaceable" and docile. It forced them to recognize, one tract asserted in an obvious reference to bread riots in England, "that *destroying* provisions is not the way to *lower* their price." Several speakers at anniversary meetings of the tract society pointed to the French Revolution as a result of the moral breakdown of a nation. Tract societies and other "engines" of religious reform, the Reverend Alexander McClelland told assembled evangelicals at the fifth annual tract meeting in 1817, would preserve the United States from such "vice, anarchy, and violence." Indeed, he said, a tract in every home would be the surest guardian of "civil privileges" and "political happiness," the best safeguard against revolution. Such sentiments proved convincing to many pious New Yorkers, who in 1825 joined with tract distributors in Boston to form the American Tract Society, a new national organization for evangelical purposes.[26]

In addition to Bible and tract societies, revivalism in New York also produced some genuine city missions. New Yorkers continued to express their pietism in institutional ways, as a number of urban missionary societies emerged during the second decade of the nineteenth century. The actions and ideas of the city mission groups conformed to the same general pattern of pious paternalism and moral stewardship which marked other associations concerned about the temporal and spiritual welfare of New York City's poor.

The first effort to sponsor religious services in the city slums came in 1814 with the formation of the interdenominational Benevolent Christian Society. In that year several clergymen, led by the Reverend Josiah B. Andrews, a Presbyterian from Connecticut, and the Reverend Timothy Alden, a Congregationalist from Massachusetts (both recently arrived in the city and both without churches), decided to carry the gospel message to the unchurched. The benevolent ministers maintained that excessive pew rents in established churches effectively excluded large numbers of lower-class people from regular Sabbath services. In a November 1814 petition to the common council, Andrews and Alden stated the willingness of a number of clergymen to preach to the poor, provided the municipality supplied a building for the purpose. The city's aldermen noted the "novel" nature of the preachers' request, but the conviction that "public good will result from the proposed arrangement" brought swift council approval on December 5, 1814. The common council, presided over by Mayor De Witt Clinton, applied to the Free School Society (whose president was Clinton) for use of one of their schoolrooms. The society granted the request, the municipality agreed to provide winter fuel, and clergymen began preaching on December 18, 1814. Indicative of the broadening concerns of the urban missionary movement, the Benevolent Christian Society also persuaded the New York Medical and Surgical Society to provide free medical care for the new parishioners.[27]

The revival spirit which prevailed after the War of 1812 carried the evangelical impulse to greatly enlarged boundaries. The formation of three new urban missionary societies in 1816 injected new energy into the spiritual attack on pauperism. Two of these new groups—the Female Missionary Society for the Poor of the City of New-York and the Young Men's Missionary Society of New-York (YMMS)—began earlier as money-raising auxiliaries to the New-York Missionary Society (founded in 1796 to evangelize Indians on New York frontiers). Drawing pietist inspiration from the simultaneous formation in 1816 of the American Bible Society and the New York Sunday schools, both groups severed connections with the parent society and abandoned passive supporting roles for active missionary work. The third new organization, the New-York Evangelical Missionary Society of Young Men (EMSYM) sprang from a doctrinal dispute among members of the YMMS within a year of its founding. By a substantial majority, the YMMS had rejected as a missionary the Reverend Samuel H. Cox, a young and newly ordained Presbyterian minister and a liberal on such crucial theological matters as original sin, total depravity, atonement, and justification. The Reverend Gardiner Spring, Cox's mentor and the ideological leader of New York's liberal Presbyterians, then led about one-third of the membership in a secession movement which resulted in formation of the new evangelical society.[28]

The missionary efforts of the three societies followed a similar pattern. Each group sent ministers and laymen throughout the city on evangelical errands; each sponsored "free" churches in poor neighborhoods; each worked energetically to bring salvation and moral order to the slums. For example, the Female Missionary Society established a "mission church" in the black ghetto around Bancker Street and hired city missionaries to evangelize that "seat of Satan." Similarly, the YMMS early resolved on a mission station in New York City (although most of its missionaries labored among white settlers on the frontier of New York and Pennsylvania and in the Middle West). Beginning in the fall of 1817 the Reverend John E. Miller, a Presbyterian of the anti-Spring faction, served the society as an itinerant minister in the slums, visited and prayed with the poor in their homes, distributed Bibles and tracts, and preached in Sunday schools and "wherever he could gather a company of sinners." Within a year the society had built a church and raised a small congregation in one of the city's poorest neighborhoods, the immigrant ghetto near Corlear's Hook on the East River. Until the early 1820's, when an exhausted treasury forced abandonment of the mission church, the YMMS employed a succession of young preachers as urban evangelicals.[29]

From the beginning the EMSYM had a more dynamic urban missionary program. Although it, too, sent itinerant preachers and Bible distributors to the frontier, the society seemed most concerned with the estimated 50,000 "heathens" in New York City. From two mission stations—one in Corlear's Hook and the other near Bancker Street—the EMSYM assaulted the "moral wilderness." The weekly labors of the Reverend Elihu W. Baldwin in Corlear's Hook typified urban evangelism: he conducted three Sunday services in his mission church, instructed more than one hundred children in a Sunday school, spent half of each weekday in family visitations, gave Bible lectures and held prayer meetings nightly, and in general worked mightily to "purify the pollution" of the city. The Reverend Samuel E. Cornish, a black preacher recruited from Philadelphia, engaged in similar tasks in the Bancker Street area. Both congregations eventually became self-sufficient and independent Presbyterian churches.[30]

Evangelical concern for irreligious, disorderly, and "vastly wicked" sailors generated a powerful marine missionary thrust after 1815. The Reverend Ward Stafford, preacher at large of the Female Missionary Society, advocated gospel work among seamen as early as 1817 in an important document entitled *New Missionary Field*. In a series of articles in the *Christian Herald and Seaman's Magazine*, one writer noted with obvious distress that sinful sailors laughed at religion, profaned the Sabbath, supported "grogshops," brothels, and gambling dens along the waterfront, and in general had "a most ruinous effect on the morals of our cities." Such "streams of vice" could be halted, such "sinks of pollution" bottled up, these writers argued, only by zealous missionary activity. Thus Stafford and others helped organize the Marine Bible Society in 1817. Stafford also played a central role in the formation in 1818 of the New-York Marine Missionary Society and of the Port of New-York Society for Promoting the

Gospel among Seamen. Both groups worked closely, employed Stafford and other evangelical preachers as marine missionaries, and in 1819 erected and supported the interdenominational Mariner's Church near the East River docks on Cherry Street. In 1821 the New-York Bethel Union joined the waterfront crusade, organizing nightly prayer meetings on wharved ships ("Floating Chapels") and in sailors' boarding houses. The missionaries and concerned members of these seamen's societies engaged in typical evangelical tasks—friendly visiting, Bible and tract distribution, and Sunday school instruction. Indeed, in every way, their pious purposes and social attitudes matched those of other urban missionary groups.[31]

Whatever their special interests and whatever their doctrinal differences, the missionary societies basically agreed on social questions. Each group supported the view that pauperism might be prevented, even eradicated, by religion; each subscribed to prevailing doctrines of moral stewardship and social control. In a sermon on the first anniversary of the YMMS in 1817, the Reverend Alexander McClelland emphasized the importance of churches in maintaining "a well-ordered civil policy." Religious conviction, he claimed, produced "conformity with certain established regulations" and "obedience to certain constituted authorities"; it nourished such desirable traits as "meekness," "docility," and "correct and sobered habits"; above all, it prevented "the horrors of a degenerate democracy." The impious and "besotted" poor, a speaker told the EMSYM in 1817, had no God but "their own brutal propensities" and seemed "little elevated above the beasts"—views which mirrored middle-class attitudes and fears. In 1821 the Female Missionary Society presented what appeared convincing evidence of the success of the Bancker Street mission: "the fact, that the torch of an incendiary has not been applied to that building—that standing reprover of their sins." In generating support for Samuel Cornish's church, the *Christian Herald* noted that in addition to saving the souls of "vile and contemptible" blacks, the new mission would "prevent them from being enemies to good order." The waterfront evangelicals conformed to the

ambivalent standards of the urban missionary movement as well.
In pronouncing the objectives of the Bethel Union in 1822, the
Reverend James Milnor of St. George's Episcopal Church spoke
for most city evangelicals: "in the forecastle of every ship Christian hymns will occupy the place of lewd ballads, religious tracts
that of profane jest-books." Each of the seamen's societies sought
to bring salvation to sinful sailors, but also to promote "peaceful
habits," particularly "sobriety, honesty, and order." [32]

In many ways, Ward Stafford's *New Missionary Field* contained
the most elaborate statement of the urban evangelical creed. A
fifty-five page social and religious survey of the New York slums,
this report to the Female Missionary Society revealed "heathenism" at home and helped divert evangelical energy from foreign
to domestic missionary work. With powerful phraseology Stafford
described the "pollution" of the city and called for immediate and
vigorous effort to improve "the moral state of the people." The
techniques he advocated—Bible and tract distribution, friendly
visiting, free churches, Sunday schools, the waterfront crusade—
were the same ones soon implemented by the city missionary
societies. Stafford's report reflected perfectly the ambiguity of the
new urban movement: real religious conviction and a fervent concern for saving souls, yet an intense moralism on social questions,
a clear and often-stated belief in the necessity for moral stewardship and social control of New York City's engorged population
of lower-class people. The removal by evangelical means of such
urban vices as intemperance, idleness, prostitution, and Sabbath-
breaking, would bring salvation to the poor, eliminate dependency,
and improve social order.[33]

Stafford's report was widely distributed and had an immediate
impact, perhaps because it stated clearly what most middle-class
churchgoers already accepted and believed. Governor De Witt
Clinton, for one, congratulated Stafford for his judicious and persuasive views on pauperism and vice—ideas, he said, which suggested "with great justice and truth" proper preventives and remedies. Many other pious New Yorkers imbibed the report's principles and accepted its call for action. The urban missionary socie-

ties sprouted to implement its suggestions. By the early 1820's the evangelical movement Stafford stimulated in New York reached high tide with formation of the United Domestic Missionary Society (UDMS). In 1822 leaders of the YMMS and the EMSYM overcame theological differences and united, along with eight other state missionary groups, to create the new society. Other local mission societies became UDMS auxiliaries, while the new parent group assumed responsibilities for five missionaries laboring in New York City. By mid-decade the trend toward national evangelical institutions had surfaced once again, for in 1826 the UDMS took the lead in formation of the American Home Missionary Society.[34]

Religious moralism spawned other groups in New York City. The Sunday school crusade sprang from evangelical motives. Other groups were less powerful but no less fervent. As early as 1815 the metropolis could claim a Society for the Prevention of Vice and Immorality, a group devoted to legislative lobbying for moral reform. Each major denomination formed education societies to support ministerial training for "poor and pious youth"; ladies' groups in every congregation—"female cent societies," as they were called—organized savings funds for such purposes. In addition, the religious zeal which created the urban missionary societies, which indeed built a nationwide evangelical system, spilled over into noninstitutional directions. The list of religious periodicals published in New York City is impressive. Journals such as the *New-York Missionary Magazine,* the *Evangelical Guardian and Review,* the *Christian Herald and Seaman's Magazine,* the *Gospel Herald,* and a number of denominational publications all reflected the urgency and the moralism of the urban religious revival. So also did a strong campaign to preserve the Sabbath, "one of the most efficient expedients," said the Reverend Gardiner Spring, "for the prevention of pauperism." [35]

The missionary movement in New York typified reaction to disturbing changes in the social and economic makeup of the city. In the quarter-century after 1800 the urban community passed through an important transitional stage. No longer a small, stable, well-regulated town, the metropolis by 1820 contained a large population of poor, low-paid immigrant workers and native transients. Home industries began to challenge entrenched mercantile interests, new business concerns to rival old merchant families. The influence of established institutions of social control wavered and faltered. Through their presumed habits of intemperance, idleness, and impiety, the poor threatened social order. Thus religion became an instrument in the more general attack on pauperism and dependency, a protective device against urban disorder. Evangelical preachers and civic leaders turned the missionary impulse to the defense of established order. By emphasizing "pious poverty," they hoped simultaneously to pacify and save the burgeoning lower class. The double-barreled motives of the urban missionary movement seemed to most evangelicals a natural kind of dualism. Only religious conviction and benevolent moralism together, they implied again and again, could bring a stable, safe, and well-ordered millennium.

13

Temperance

The process of urbanization in New York City seemed to intensify observable social ills, particularly the prevalence of drunkenness and alcoholism. The upper class normally confined drinking to home and club, but slums bred "tippling houses" and "grog shops" on every block. Official reports laid idleness, extravagance, crime, and every species of vice to drinking habits of laborers and immigrants. By easy and seemingly logical steps, New Yorkers concluded that drink brought pauperism. Thus, a general effort to curb lower-class drinking marked the early war on poverty. The humanitarian reformers who sponsored charitable societies, education for the poor, and the urban missionary movement headed the temperance campaign as well. Through individual moral reform, heavy liquor taxes, and licensing reforms, they hoped to restrict dependency, reduce poor-relief expenditures, and restore a measure of social order to the changing community.

A general addiction to alcohol characterized American society in the eighteenth and nineteenth centuries. The Puritan ethic condemned excessive use of alcohol in the seventeenth century, but moral controls had broken down by 1700. As rum making, distilling, and brewing became important economic activities, drinking habits hardened. In every colonial city and town taverns served as social and political centers. Local officials tried to control and regulate alcohol consumption through taxes and tavern licenses, but these efforts often proved ineffective. Numbers of illicit, unlicensed liquor shops and taverns sprang up in every colonial urban center, contributing to worsening social problems. Some colonists, mainly government officials and clergymen, protested the rising incidence of alcoholism. Cadwallader Colden, a future lieutenant governor of New York, attacked "excessive drinking" as destructive of "body & soul" as early as 1726; strong liquors, Colden contended, undermined morals, sapped the industry of laboring men, and ruined the country's economy. However, the arguments of Colden and others had little impact on a society which viewed liquor as an indispensable commodity. By 1773 New York City contained 396 licensed taverns and an undetermined number of illegal "grogeries." [1]

Alcohol addiction intensified in post-Revolutionary years. In 1792, according to Treasury Secretary Alexander Hamilton, annual consumption of liquor averaged two and one half gallons per person. By 1823 a Boston newspaper estimated that average Americans drank seven and one half gallons each year. European travelers frequently commented on the drinking habits of Americans. "Intemperance is everywhere a prevailing vice," wrote English visitor John Duncan in 1818. "Under the denominations of *anti-fogmatics, mint julep*, and *gin sling*, copious libations are poured out on the alters of Bacchus," Britisher Adam Hodgson observed in 1824. Others noted more alcoholism in the United States than in any other country. "The evil is manifested in almost every walk of life, contaminates all it touches," another English traveler, Basil Hall, asserted in the 1820's. Native Americans made similar observations. Federalist merchant John Pintard reported in 1821, for example, that "grovelling drunkenness increases among the lower vulgar [class] owing to the reduced prices of ardent spirits." An 1814 temperance address typically described the pervasive influence of the whiskey jug: "Success *deserves* a treat, and disappointment *needs* it. The *busy* drink, because they are busy; the *idle* because they have nothing else to do. The farmer must drink, because his work is hard; the mechanic because his employment is sedentary and dull. It is warm, men drink to be cool; it is cool, they drink to be warm." [2]

In New York City, the national evil of alcoholism seemed well entrenched by the nineteenth century. In 1789 the editor of the *Daily Advertiser* commented critically on the "disproportionate number" of taverns and demanded legislative remedy. Observers noted little improvement over the next several decades. In 1810 the Humane Society reported more than 1,600 licensed taverns in New York City; in addition, more than 1,800 retail liquor permits had been issued. (Because many taverns also had retail permits, the Humane Society's statistics tended to magnify an admittedly serious problem.) Illegal liquor shops or "groceries" dotted the slums and the waterfront. Peddlers and hawkers sold whiskey and rum in the streets as cheaply as twenty-five cents a gallon. Prisoners in jail and paupers in the almshouse found easy access to the "streams of liquid fire." Employers customarily supplied liquor to laborers on the job, master craftsmen plied their apprentices in the shop. Rich men and poor men alike used liquor at family meals. Firemen drank at fires, watchmen on the watch. Men drank at elections, weddings, and funerals. On holidays such as the Fourth of July, liquor shops set up in tents and stalls around City Hall supplied boisterous and milling crowds. On such occasions, "drunkenness thickens upon the public eye," the editor of the *Christian Herald* wrote in 1822; the revelry of drunkards saddened and disgusted "the few sober and honest people" and made "the watching angels weep." [3]

Reformers advanced a number of reasons for such unwholesome drinking habits. Many pointed to the impious and immoral tendencies of New York City's newcomers, particularly impoverished Irish immigrants who increasingly became a large and visible ingredient of the population after 1800. Some blamed farmers for turning grain into alcohol for cash sale in urban markets. Others accused distillers, retailers, and tavern keepers—"lovers of filthy lucre"— who played upon human weakness, tempted the poor to addiction, and "fattened on the spoils and misfortunes of their fellow men." Few temperance reformers failed to mention the excessive number of liquor shops and taverns, legal and illegal, in New York and other cities. Some also criticized politicians and legislators who permitted such conditions by avoiding reformed licensing procedures and high taxes on alcohol. More realistically, perhaps, one temperance preacher found "too much capital vested" in the liquor business to make any legislation practical or effective. According to this analysis, the only solution lay in religious and moral reformation. Yet a few suggested that religious leaders had immorally neglected to demand abstinence or temperance from congregations. Some pamphleteers noted that many clergymen themselves used liquor immoderately or had become addicted to the "sparkling poison." Indeed, one of the most powerful early temperance leaders, Lyman Beecher, began his crusade against drink after attending a meeting of clergymen which "looked and smelled like the bar of a very active grog-shop." Thus humanitarians found a number of convincing explanations for an intemperate society.[4]

Whatever the reasons, the results of excessive and widespread alcohol addiction seemed obvious to reformers and moralists. Temperance advocates argued with conviction that drinking undermined morality and thus destroyed a main prop of the social order. Liberty and popular government, the Humane Society claimed in 1810, could not survive "the corruption of the lower classes." Drink promoted iniquity and debauchery, brought the "lowest moral degradation," and advanced "satan's kingdom," an anonymous pamphleteer wrote in 1811. "No one vice is destructive of so many virtues," New Yorker Thomas Herttell contended in 1819. In 1813 the Reverend Alexander Gunn sermonized against the "shocking and disgusting spectacle" of public intoxication; taverns and liquor shops, he said, served as "hot-beds of rebellion" and drunkards destroyed "peace and prosperity" as well as public morals. Clearly, a concern for moral conformity and social order marked the polemics of most temperance reformers.[5]

Humanitarians commonly associated excessive drinking with a variety of health hazards. Dr. Benjamin Rush of Philadelphia first popularized the medical argument for temperance. In 1784 Rush published a pamphlet, *An Inquiry into the Effects of Ardent Spirits*

upon the Human Body and Mind, which advanced scientific and
medical evidence to prove the destructive nature of alcohol. Re-
printed in many editions over the next half century, Rush's pamphlet listed the medical effects of immoderate drinking as epi-
lepsy, palsy, apoplexy, gout, diabetes, madness, obstructions of the
liver, jaundice, "dropsy of the belly and limbs," and eruptions or
"rum buds" on the body. Rush's arguments seemed convincing and
New Yorkers elaborated upon them with vigor and creativity. The
Reverend John Stanford, for instance, found a major cause of
insanity in "the baneful practice of relaxing the nervous system"
with ardent spirits. "Wine often turns the good-natured man into
an idiot" wrote the editor of *Forlorn Hope* in 1800. Another editor
attributed the yellow fever epidemic of 1822 to "midnight revels
and drunkenness," particularly on the Sabbath. Writing in the
Commercial Advertiser in 1820, "Observator" described all liquors
as "poisonous," even when used in moderation. According to the
Humane Society, drinking killed "more victims than all the other
causes of premature mortality." Smoking and tobacco chewing
had similar destructive effects, claimed Dr. David Hosack, because these habits frequently led to intemperate drinking. Most
temperance reformers accepted and used the medical evidence
put forth by Rush and others.[6]

Philanthropists and public officials found even greater unanimity
on another point—the close relationship between drinking and
dependency. Few contradicted the contention that intemperance
brought poverty and pauperism. Virtually every investigation of
New York's poor came to this conclusion. The Humane Society's
special report of 1809 described intemperate drinking as the source
of misery and poverty for "most of the labouring poor." A common council committee in 1812 blamed drunkenness for "the
present state of the Alms house, and the calls for charity." The
1817 *ad hoc* relief committee, as previously noted, traced seven-
eighths of New York's pauperism to "the free and inordinate use
of *spirituous liquors.*" A legislative committee in 1819 labeled intemperance a primary cause of dependency and recommended
poor-law revisions to eliminate "unworthy" paupers from welfare

rolls. In his 1824 report on the poor laws, Secretary of State Yates agreed that alcoholism produced "more than two-thirds" of New York's paupers. In the late 1820's the New York City Temperance Society reported that three-fourths of the poor owed their condition to "strong drink." With few exceptions, private societies and government officials at every level accepted and acted upon these views, especially as the humanitarian rationale shifted from benevolence to moralism.[7]

The same arguments linking drinking and poverty embellished sermons, addresses, and innumerable humanitarian publications. Going beyond his medical evidence, Benjamin Rush called intemperance "the certain forerunner of poverty." Few temperance preachers failed to describe the poverty and misery which drunkards could expect. Indeed, alcoholism not only impoverished man but, in the words of the Reverend Nathanial S. Prime, reduced him "to the level of a worm." "Most of those who do not enjoy the necessaries of life," an anonymous polemicist wrote in 1811, "owe their uncomfortable situation, in some way or another, to the habitual use of strong drink." Nine-tenths of poverty stemmed from intemperance, "Philadelphus" contended in 1821. Furthermore, the habit carried beyond a single generation, for every drunkard seemed to produce "a tribe of idle, thriftless, beggarly children" who began life with "a bottle at their mouths." For New York's moral reformers, drink appeared the main source of lower-class dependency and temperance a sure poverty cure.[8]

Benevolent leaders further contended that intemperance drained tax resources, diverted assistance from the "deserving" poor, filled the streets with vagrants, and populated prisons, hospitals, and almshouses. Lyman Beecher, a Long Island and Connecticut preacher and an early temperance mainstay, spoke for a whole generation of humanitarian moralists in his popular sermons on intemperance:

> In every city and town the poor-tax, created chiefly by intemperance, is augmenting. The receptacles for the poor are becoming too strait for their accommodation. We must pull them down and build greater to provide accommodations for the vo-

taries of inebriation; for the frequency of going upon the town
has taken away the reluctance of pride, and destroyed the motives to providence which the fear of poverty and suffering once
supplied. The prospect of a destitute old age, or of a suffering
family, no longer troubles the vicious portion of our community.
They drink up their daily earnings and bless God for the poorhouse, and begin to look upon it as, of right, the drunkard's
home, and contrive to arrive thither as early as idleness and
excess will given them a passport to this sinecure of vice. Thus
is the insatiable destroyer of industry marching through the
land, rearing poor-houses, and augmenting taxation.

Beecher's pointed moralism reflected general attitudes toward
poverty and accepted the presumed link between alcoholism and
pauperism.[9]

The views of Beecher and other temperance advocates had
important implications for social welfare and urban reform. The
new moralism of the nineteenth century attributed pauperism to
individual moral defects. In the eyes of middle-class reformers
the poor became personally responsible not only for their poverty
but for their drunken habits as well. Expanding upon the new
moralistic rationale, humanitarians argued that charity not only
destroyed character but encouraged lower-class alcoholism. Cash
relief constituted the worst form of charity, William Coleman
of the *Evening Post* wrote in 1809, "since nine times out of ten . . .
the money is laid out in dram shops." The Humane Society erected
its soup house partially to prevent debtors from selling the society's
food donations for liquor. Similarly, Bible societies slowed gratuitous distribution of religious publications when they found sailors
exchanging Bibles for whiskey and rum. In 1817 the common council committee on charity called relief agencies "a great and leading
cause of Pauperism" which induced the poor "to neglect all provision for the future, by dissipating what they earn, beyond their
present necessities, in tippling and idleness." Most humanitarian
leaders eventually came to believe that less charity meant more
temperance.[10]

The joint attack on alcohol and pauperism began slowly and
moved through several stages. The earliest temperance advocates

simply counseled moderation in drinking or censured only whiskey and rum but not wine, cider, or beer. Later reformers urged
voluntary abstinence from all alcoholic beverages. Many temperance men soon recognized, however, that exhortation had
little impact on slum-dwelling, working-class drinkers. Middle-class
churchmen might convince middle-class churchgoers, but failed to
reach unchurched laborers, Catholic immigrants, and the poor.
Thus restrictive legislation seemed to many the only solution to
the dual problem of drinking and dependency.

Liquor controls through legislation, of course, began in the
colonial period. Provincial and municipal authorities levied alcohol taxes, demanded licenses and fees for taverns and inns, prevented liquor sales to slaves and servants, closed taverns on Sun-
days, and imposed other restrictions on innkeepers. State and local governments implemented similar laws and ordinances after
the American Revolution. Yet a number of defects remained. Until
the 1820's, for example, New York City's mayor possessed sole
authority over tavern permits. License fees ranged from five to
fifty-five dollars, of which the unsalaried mayor kept almost half.
Tavern license fees thus became one of the perquisites of office
and an important source of mayoral income. A single commissioner
of excise issued permits for retail liquor shops. Reformers argued
that such procedures, completely dominated by two men, encouraged discrimination among applicants and insufficiently safe-
guarded public interests.[11]

Considerable evidence suggested the ineffectiveness of municipal liquor controls. Temperance reformers unanimously condemned the excessive number of tavern licenses and retail permits issued each year. The number of taverns, Thomas Herttell
wrote in 1819, seemed "limited only by the number of persons
desirous to keep them." According to "Observer" in the *Evening
Post* in March 1816, the plans of benevolent societies for moral
improvement of the poor would remain "partial expedients" as
long as the public tolerated "upwards of *Fifteen Hundred* sources
of *Drunkenness, Disease, Poverty, Felony* and *Murder*." New York
bulged with humanitarian organizations, but where, he queried,

"is the society pledged to the annihilation of the fifteen hundred grog shops of our city?" Municipal authorities appeared unable to maintain the orderly conduct required of officially approved taverns. The Humane Society described even licensed alehouses and inns as "perpetual scenes of riot and disorder." Some claimed that children might often be found drinking in such "detestable holes." Like "swine in the filthy mire," drunkards reeled through the streets with impunity. Government made few efforts to shut down unlicensed liquor shops. Such conditions reflected the breakdown of municipal controls under new pressures of urbanization.[12]

Numerous temperance reformers, however, demanded governmental action. Indeed, they sought action at every level of government. They constantly pressured for licensing reforms—severe restrictions on the number of tavern and liquor permits, higher license fees, stricter supervision of licensees, and broadening of the permit-granting apparatus to eliminate monopoly powers of the mayor and excise commissioner. Other proposals received wide support as well. The Reverend Alexander Gunn advocated stronger municipal ordinances against public intoxication. To eliminate alcohol purchases on credit, delegates of New York's "moral societies" meeting in Albany in 1819 demanded state legislation to prevent tavern keepers and liquor dealers from recovering debts. Many reformers sought higher state taxes on distilled alcohol. The New York College of Physicians petitioned Congress for high tariffs on imported liquors. The Society for the Prevention of Pauperism demanded heavy federal taxes on distilleries. When moderation and voluntary abstinence produced no immediate results, many humanitarians and reformers turned to government.[13]

The campaign for governmental intervention had mixed results. Early efforts of the Humane Society persuaded the state legislature to prohibit liquor sales to debtors and prisoners. The common council awakened slowly to temperance demands. In 1811, almost two years after the Humane Society's initial report on urban alcoholism, the council purchased two thousand copies of Benjamin Rush's pamphlet on the "destructive effects of intemperate drinking" for distribution in the slums. Although an urban reformer, De Witt Clinton did little to advance temperance during his ten years as mayor, especially when compared with his efforts for other humanitarian causes. Between 1818 and 1821 Mayor Cadwallader D. Colden, a descendant of the eighteenth-century lieutenant governor, added official sanction to the anti-alcohol movement and secured a moderate licensing reform. Suppression of taverns and "dram shops," Colden explained in 1819, "would do more to lessen idleness, prevent poverty, and to suppress vice" than any other governmental action. Mayor Stephen Allen, Colden's successor, found the "real" cause of pauperism in "the inordinate use of Ardent Spirits" and thus urged stronger municipal restrictions and higher license fees. Writing to state legislator John Morss in 1823, Allen contended that since liquor drained citizens' pocketbooks "by creating pauperism and crime," justice demanded "that the business which causes the evil and is the means of the public expense, ought to return to the treasury some portion of it, by and through the medium of the price paid for a License." By the 1820's a few municipal authorities had become concerned enough about lower-class drinking to recommend stricter controls.[14]

Despite support from both Colden and Allen, municipal temperance reforms proved meager. Licensing changes in 1819 and 1821 had little impact on urban drinking habits. The ordinance of 1821, for example, raised minimum license fees to fifteen dollars, but reduced the maximum fee from fifty-five to thirty dollars. In addition, a board of license commissioners, composed of the mayor and two aldermen, replaced the single excise commissioner and the mayor who had issued permits separately in previous years. Finally, the new law made "good moral character" the eligibility requirement for liquor-license holders. Zealous temperance men hardly found such "reforms" satisfactory and some turned to demands for total prohibition of alcohol by law.[15]

Advocates of legal action attributed ineffective governmental reforms to an irresponsive political atmosphere. In the complicated morass of New York city and state politics, office holders approached touchy issues with caution. At both the state and municipal level, politicians clearly hesitated to take on powerful business interests. Distillers, brewers, retail liquor merchants, and tavern owners represented an important economic and political force. Whiskey and rum manufacturing was big business in an urban processing center like New York City; every tavern served also as a political forum. Lawmakers thus tred gingerly when it came to temperance reform. The city council in particular hedged on tough liquor controls. All councilmen agreed, of course, on the necessity to close down illegal liquor shops, but few seemed willing to risk political futures by attacking established tavern keepers and licensed grocers—"a very numerous and respectable class of our fellow citizens," the common council said in 1821, "whose interests ought not and must not be injured." Grocers and tavern owners organized and used propaganda effectively, publicly contradicting reports of citizen committees and charitable societies linking drink to crime and pauperism. Many reformers eventually went beyond temperance programs to attack politicos, men "borne away too much by the tide of party to feel the weight of moral subjects." [16]

A split among temperance reformers posed equally serious difficulties. Although many saw solutions to alcoholism and its excesses in governmental action, others objected and urged individual moral reformation as the only answer. "The laws, though well meant, can do but little, in a matter of this kind," one pamphleteer argued in 1811; "it is the *manners* and *good sense* of the people alone, that can furnish the remedy." Another polemicist contended that the licensing system encouraged proliferation of taverns and grog shops, thus casting "multitudes of bacchanalians" on the public charity. In this sense, the fee system drained more money from the municipal treasury than it added. Thomas Herttell opposed both licensing and liquor taxes, since government became dependent on an immoral income. Curtailing the number of taverns would have little effect, he maintained, because the "*habit* of intemperance" would remain undiminished. Lyman Beecher typified the purist strain of temperance reform, labeling alcoholism "a moral *miasma*." For many humanitarians temperance meant abstinence, a matter not for legislation but for "self-government." The division among anti-alcohol advocates, which hardened in the 1820's with the formation of a number of temperance societies (including the New York City Temperance Society), diluted reform efforts.[17]

Despite differing views on strategy and method, humanitarians agreed on the necessity for reform. Alcoholism seemed an endemic characteristic of urban workers and urban paupers. Reformers argued with apparent logic that excessive drinking destroyed incentive to work and brought crime and social disorder. Like schools for the poor and the urban missionary movement, temperance represented an effort to impose decent, middle-class habits and acceptable, middle-class values upon immigrants and workers whose habits and values had been shaped in a different environment. The temperance movement further reflected attempts of like-minded moralists to prop up a social order which seemed to be eroding before important social and economic changes. Through temperance, as a recent student of the phenomenon has written, "a declining social elite" sought to preserve its power and prestige while making lower-class Americans "into a clean, sober, godly, and decorous people." Without exception the reformers also accepted the presumed link between drinking and dependency. Thus temperance became a method of destroying pauperism. Certain that alcohol produced paupers and vagrants in great numbers, optimistic moralists fought "demon rum" and promoted temperance as a sure poverty cure.[18]

14

Work

In addition to education, religion, and temperance, most humanitarians also offered work as a poverty cure. As already suggested, New Yorkers generally attributed dependency to character defects. Beyond immorality, drunkenness, and impiety, moralists argued that slum dwellers and alms seekers remained idle and thus poor because of an aversion to work. The idea of stimulating industrious habits among the poor seemed a certain solution for idleness and pauperism. The few who recognized unemployment as an important source of dependency also promoted work as the cure. For different reasons, therefore, New York's benevolent network agreed on the necessity of putting the poor to work.

Schemes for private work relief abounded in early New York City. In his Report on Manufacturers, for instance, Alexander Hamilton urged employment for the poor in place of alms. To implement his ideas, Hamilton helped organize the New York Manufacturing Society in 1789. Designed to stimulate American manufacturing as well as provide work for the "honest poor," the society established cotton and linen factories and hired numerous laborers and young apprentices. Supporters approached the new scheme with great optimism. One advocate expected that respectable citizens would no longer have their "feelings" constantly "shocked with haggard looks, pitious solicitations, or the moving tale." Work, another wrote, would make the poor "useful to themselves and society." The expectations of humanitarian capitalists, however, proved illusory. Organized on a corporate basis, the society failed as an investment and disbanded in 1793.[1]

The Society for the Promotion of Industry sponsored a second important private work-relief plan. Organized in 1814 by women from the SRPW and the Orphan Asylum Society, the new society aimed at reducing pauperism by employing poor women during winter months when relief costs mounted. Aided by a $750 donation from the common council, the society established a "house of industry," which during the winter of 1814–1815 employed more than 500 women workers at tailoring, sewing, spinning, and knitting. A committee placed other women as domestic servants throughout the city. Community leaders and urban reformers gave the society immediate support. Most expected the new workhouse to stimulate "virtuous industry," reduce relief costs, eliminate begging, and "foster self-respect in the honest poor." But once again achievement failed to match benevolent ambitions. Despite annual common council appropriations ranging from $400 to $1,000, the society had difficulty securing other donations. Each year found the organization "richer in experience and poorer in funds." Aside from a government contract to supply a naval squadron with uniforms and blankets, the society sold very few of its finished textile products. Furthermore, the minuscule wages paid women workers, about twenty-five cents a day, hardly fostered economic independence. This combination of reasons forced permanent closing of the house of industry early in 1820.[2]

Many humanitarians advocated a variety of public work projects. Some proposed employment programs in the jail and debtor's prison, while others urged public jobs during hard times to prevent crime. Eighteenth-century England had experimented with "houses of industry" to reduce pauperism, and some New Yorkers popularized such institutions—combined workhouses and religious reformatories which presumably rescued immoral idlers from "the high way to destruction." Writing in the *Commerical Advertiser* in 1809, "Humanitas" recommended compulsory public workshops for beggars, drunkards, and prostitutes. In February 1817 "Rumford" suggested a "public laboratory" not only to provide jobs for unemployed workers, but to compel "slothful" vagrants to earn wages. In an underpopulated and developing nation such as the United States, "Rumford" argued, every worker could be "usefully employed"; it required only governmental guidance and direction. Writing to former mayor De Witt Clinton in February 1818, former mayor Marinus Willett urged "an entire change" in municipal welfare programs and suggested public employment rather than pauper-producing charity. In August 1820, a grand jury of the court of general sessions endorsed a city workhouse "to encourage industry and decent habits among the lower orders." These and similar proposals seemed logical to moral reformers but depended upon municipal implementation.[3]

Municipal officials attempted an ambitious employment scheme in 1816 with completion of the new Bellevue almshouse. Employable paupers, of course, had always been made to work in the almshouse, but such labor had rarely turned a profit. In a special report to the common council in 1814, city comptroller Thomas Mercein noted the progressive rise in almshouse expenditures and suggested a comprehensive work program for the new Bellevue establishment. With new machinery, particularly in textiles, Mercein urged that the "sluggish & hitherto dormant capital of human strength & talent" of almshouse tenants and bridewell vagrants be made productive. Paupers might be enabled to supply many of their own needs, especially clothing, blankets, and shoes. The common council implemented Mercein's plan, and within a year the comptroller reported that increased self-sufficiency brought considerable reduction in almshouse expenses. Officials later expanded the manufacturing program from textiles to other products. With a pin factory established in 1821, for example, the almshouse superintendent sought to maximize pauper labor by employing children and elderly and infirm dependents. Occasionally, as during epidemics and the embargo crisis, city government also instituted some temporary programs of public work relief for the outdoor poor. But these city work programs hardly represented the major thrust of the municipal war on poverty.[4]

Despite numerous plans for public and private work relief, few efforts proved successful. Much of the difficulty rested in a confusion of aims. Authorities originally proposed almshouse factories to reduce poor-relief costs rather than to cure unemployment. By the 1820's institutional work seemed designed more as punishment, a deterrent to welfare. In December 1821 a common council committee confidently reported that forced labor in the almshouse would encourage paupers to seek "a course of voluntary industry of their own choice to a systematic Service under the Overseers in the Poorhouse." The installation of a "tread-mill" (a mechanical contraption utilizing human power to move heavy grindstones) at Bellevue in 1822 reflected similar attitudes. By 1830 some aldermen not only urged the common council to "turn to *some advantage* the labour of the more feeble," but argued that work improved health and character. Thus municipal officials generally postulated work as a solution to pauperism, but ironically few related dependency to urban unemployment.[5]

Private humanitarians and benevolent societies subscribed to equally moralistic conceptions. "Man is naturally idle," the Reverend Ward Stafford wrote in 1817. But "let it be known," he contended "that death or extreme suffering will be the consequence of idleness, or profligacy, and the number of the idle and the profligate will soon be diminished." Most other charity reformers agreed. The Puritan work ethic survived undiluted into the nineteenth century. Work preserved "the morality of the poor," stimulated self-reliance, brought good health, reduced welfare expenses, and added to national prosperity. As moralism supplanted benevolence as a prevailing humanitarian motive, work became a means of building character and preventing the much-feared "impositions." [6]

Not many New Yorkers traced pauperism to unemployment. Among the few who did, however, was Edward Livingston, a prominent member of a politically powerful New York family and mayor of the city from 1801 to 1803. In January 1803, apparently influenced by the writings of Jeremy Bentham and Alexander Hamilton, Mayor Livingston proposed a comprehensive plan for employing the urban poor. The forces generated by the Livingston scheme bared political passions as well as humanitarian moralism, providing insights into social welfare in the preindustrial city.[7]

Livingston had risen rapidly as a politician and lawmaker. He had been elected to the House of Representatives from New York City in 1794 and reelected in 1796 and 1798. He declined to run for a fourth term in 1800, but Republican success in the presidential election of that year led to his appointment as federal district attorney for New York. Shortly thereafter, on August 11, 1801, the state's Republican-dominated Council of Appointment selected him as mayor of New York City, an office he held concurrently with the federal position.

The mayoralty presented Livingston with opportunities to support local reform causes, especially revisions in poor-law administration and in the penal system—subjects which had concerned him at least since 1795 when he had presented a bill in Congress for reformed criminal legislation. Although warned by his brother, the famous Chancellor Robert R. Livingston, on his assumption of office to "receive with great caution every new proposition of improvement," Livingston remained undeterred and supported a variety of humanitarian schemes despite Federalist origins. In October 1801 an important reform of the city's almshouse administration was implemented, an improvement devised under Federalist Mayor Richard Varick in 1800. Livingston supported new state legislation of 1802, originally suggested by Federalist merchant and Quaker reformer Thomas Eddy, which authorized New York City to construct a penitentiary on a plan embodying reformed techniques of prison discipline such as solitary confinement. By 1803 Livingston seemed a dynamic but humane urban reformer, a man who often placed civic betterment above partisan loyalties.[8]

Livingston recognized unemployment as a major source of urban poverty. He envisioned a joint effort by municipal authorities and urban craftsmen to provide day laborers, immigrants, women, and other unskilled workers with training and jobs. At the same time, implementation of such a plan might eliminate crimes induced by the desperation of poverty. Most significant, the mayor's proposal for public employment of the poor advanced a poverty solution unencumbered by prevailing attitudes of benevolent moralism.

Livingston embodied his plan in a letter of January 1, 1803, to James Warner, president of the General Society of Mechanics and Tradesmen of the City of New York (commonly known as the Mechanics Society). Calling attention to the plight of the poor, many of whom sought work unsuccessfully, the mayor first urged the Mechanics Society to join with municipal government in establishment and supervision of public workshops in trades such as shoemaking and hat manufacturing. Second, Livingston suggested that carpenters, masons, and other tradesmen hire poor, unskilled, and unemployed laborers when they needed extra helpers. Implementation of such a dual plan, Livingston argued, would create enough new jobs to put the employable poor to work. The common council would supply necessary capital for initiation of the project, while committees from the Mechanics Society would manage each of the workshops and train unskilled workmen. For those so employed, the mayor recommended a special wage scale calculated to protect master craftsmen as well as journeymen and apprentices. Livingston aimed the plan primarily at those temporarily unemployed because of economic fluctuations and those unable to obtain work during normal times, such as unskilled day laborers, recently arrived immigrants, and discharged or pardoned convicts. In a wing of the almshouse, women and children, widows and orphans, might be trained in suitable trades as well.

The proposal, Livingston asserted, was realistic, humane, and benevolent. He optimistically expected the workshop plan to effectively eradicate mendicity, alleviate poverty, and reduce crime. Each applicant for public or private charity "would if capable of labour be directed at once where to find it—if unable to provide for himself, be maintained in the alms house—or if reduced by vice and idleness, have these habits punished or removed in the house of correction." Although the project would be costly, municipal expenditures for the almshouse and outdoor relief would simultaneously be lessened. Furthermore, the reformation of discharged criminals and convicts would be speeded by constant application to industry and labor. Livingston argued that these numerous beneficial results would be obtained if the Mechanics Society joined with municipal authorities in carrying out the proposed scheme.[9]

Founded in 1785 and incorporated in 1792, the Mechanics Society provided focus for social and political activities of New York City's skilled workmen, a numerous and influential segment of the electorate. Urban artisans and craftsmen had contributed important support for the goals of the American Revolution and effectively promoted ratification of the federal Constitution. By 1789 the Federalist party enjoyed a near monopoly on the political sympathies of the "mechanical interest." But as partisan spirit developed and intensified during the 1790's, and as divisive issues such as foreign policy and liberalization of voting qualifications created political controversy, New York City's mechanics gradually turned Republican. At the time of Jefferson's election to the presidency in 1801, most artisans, craftsmen, and tradesmen in the city had been drawn safely within the Republican fold.

Mayor Livingston officially presented his letter to the Mechanics Society on January 4, 1803, at the organization's anniversary meeting in the newly completed Mechanic Hall on Broadway. The mayor himself attended the banquet and delivered a toast to "the Mechanics of New York—may industry and skill, patriotism and integrity, continue to be their characteristic." Obviously, Livingston patronized the mechanics, who constituted a large portion of his political following, and he expected support for the humane plan he outlined.[10]

But at a regular business meeting held the next day, the Mechanics Society found the proposal "inexpedient." One day after receipt of the mayor's letter, therefore, with only a minimum of consideration and debate, the Mechanics Society rejected the workhouse plan. A committee of five tradesmen immediately began preparing a formal response to Livingston's communication. Meeting on February 2, 1803, the society approved the committee's draft reply and forwarded a copy to Mayor Livingston.[11]

The society's reply set forth a series of objections to the proposed workshops: participation in the scheme contravened the society's charter; the plan seemed an "engine of oppression" tending toward monopoly; it appeared injurious and degrading to honest and industrious workmen; it threatened to undermine the "spirit of industry and enterprise" among apprentices by making the skills and techniques of craftsmanship available to all; the lower wage rate for those employed under the plan "would strike at the very vitals of the mechanic interest" by creating ruinous competition. In general, the evils produced by the contemplated plan would be greater than those removed by its operation. And finally, the mechanics subscribed to a Malthusian view of society—the idea that poverty was natural and ineradicable and that "the industrious poor will always be employed, in proportion to the quantum of business there is to be done." Little could be gained, the mechanics argued, by interfering with the operation of natural economic principles in an attempt to create useless and unnecessary employment.[12]

Livingston must have suspected the hostile reaction among the mechanics long before formal receipt of their answer. In a move calculated to muster popular support for the employment scheme, the mayor's letter to the Mechanics Society appeared in several of the city's daily newspapers between January 18 and January 24, receiving generally favorable editorial comment. The *Daily Advertiser*, for example, expected unanimous support of New Yorkers for the humanitarian proposal, which promised to "lessen the wants and importunate claims of the needy, and diminish the taxes for the maintenance of paupers and vagrants." The editor suggested formation of a special organization to implement the plan should it be rejected by the Mechanics Society.[13]

To counter the propaganda created by publication of Livingston's letter, and to parry the expected charges of inhumanity and disregard for public interest, the Mechanics Society decided to put the reasons for rejection of the work relief project before the public. On February 2, 1803, the society resolved that "if the Mayor don't publish the answer of this Society within one week," the secretary should arrange for its publication in all the newspapers which had carried the chief magistrate's original communication. Within three weeks, eight editors honored the mechanics' request for equal time.[14]

Advocates of the workshop plan continued to promote the idea of municipal employment for the poor, even as the mechanics renounced support. Some justified the Livingston proposal with Enlightenment doctrines of rationality and progress. Writing in the *Mercantile Advertiser*, "Cornplanter" maintained that civilized nations responsibly eliminated avoidable social evils such as poverty, and he suggested the irrationality of unemployment in a flourishing country during a period of prosperity. He argued that work relief seemed a practical and feasible method of assisting the poor—one which would encourage individual industry and self-sufficiency as well as "augment the wealth of the nation." Instead of exporting the natural products of America's farms, mines, and forests in exchange for foreign manufactures, this same correspondent suggested processing and manufacturing these raw materials in the United States, thus creating work for the poor and the unemployed.[15]

The inspectors of the state prison in New York City, headed by several prominent reformers, supported the workhouse project in their annual report to the state legislature in February 1803. The report advocated prevention rather than punishment as the key to wise and effective penal legislation. The good order of any community depended upon "a regular and virtuous course of industry, amongst the indigent classes." To secure this end, the inspectors recommended the establishment, under patronage of the legislature, of a society "for the purpose of *employing* the laboring poor" in New York City.[16]

Others supported the Livingston plan as well. On February 14, 1803, the common council appointed a committee of three to consider the project. The committee, composed of city recorder John B. Prevost and aldermen Joshua Barker and Robert Bogardus, brought in a favorable report the following week, along with the draft of a petition to the state legislature requesting financial aid for the plan. By this time, however, the mechanics made their opposition to the workhouse idea public, and a majority of the aldermen, exercising classic political caution, voted ten to five to postpone consideration of the committee's report until the ensuing December. This move effectively killed municipal backing for the mayor's work-relief reform.[17]

Livingston refused to be discouraged by the negative reply of the Mechanics Society or by defeat in the common council. Assisted by other "friends of the poor," the mayor immediately circulated a legislative petition among the citizenry. This petition, which first appeared in the press on March 5, 1803, detailed New York City's unemployment problem and noted both heavy demands for poor relief among able-bodied, employable paupers and the high crime rate among the poor. The petitioners requested legislative assistance in financing and organizing public workshops, now to be directed by "discreet citizens" rather than the common council and the Mechanics Society as originally proposed. They sought legislation creating a board of directors vested with power to erect workshops and purchase materials for employing the poor. The petition estimated that an annual revenue of $12,000 for ten to fifteen years would permit successful initiation of the project. The petitioners suggested auction taxes in New York City as the source of funds.[18]

Within a few days eighty-five prominent citizens, headed by Livingston and Samuel Osgood, former Postmaster-General of the United States, signed the legislative petition. Supporters promptly sent the document off to Albany, where it was read in the assembly on March 11, 1803, and referred to a committee of three. Eight days later, on March 19, the committee reported favorably upon the Livingston plan, calling it "benevolent" and "beneficial." The assembly accepted the committee's report, but decided to postpone consideration of the subject to the next session because of the plan's "novel nature, and the great press of business at present before the Legislature." Thus, although Livingston did not achieve immediate implementation of his proposal, the door remained open for its future adoption.[19]

But if supporters of the mayor's program seemed active, opponents voiced objections even more vociferously. Laborers and workmen in general joined with the Mechanics Society in an early display of labor unity and strength. A meeting of mechanics and craftsmen on March 18, 1803, resolved that institutions designed to alleviate sufferings of the poor deserved aid and encouragement, but that honest workers had an equal duty "to oppose with manly firmness any attempts to injure or degrade the situation of the industrious part of the citizens of these United States." Other mechanics suggested that the municipal corporation might better employ the able-bodied poor on the roads and similar public projects, rather than create a state monopoly which would "bear down the fair prices of the industrious Mechanic." [20]

The city's newspapers supplied the prime vehicle for attacks on the workhouse plan. Editors James Cheetham of the Republican-oriented *American Citizen* and William Coleman of the Federalist *New-York Evening Post,* usually at loggerheads on all issues, joined in denouncing the mayor's house of industry, while managing at the same time to criticize and castigate each other. Similarly, correspondents filled the columns of these journals with critical comments. "Q," for example, condemned the project as "visionary, expensive, and useless," designed solely "to give celebrity to the present Mayoralty." Furthermore, public workshops would invite the "unworthy and dissolute" from other towns and cities to migrate to New York, where they would be assured employment. Public provisions for idlers and vagabonds were not necessary or even desirable, "Q" argued, for able and willing laborers, even those without skills, could easily find jobs at high wages. "The idle and the dissolute may be without employment and sometimes without bread," he wrote, "but is it incumbent on the public to countenance their idleness or reward their crimes by expensive establishments exclusively for their benefit? Certainly not." Denying Enlightenment thinking, critics thought of poverty and misery as natural products of urban society and predicted certain failure for any reform efforts.[21]

The mechanics also applied for legislative support in an effort to safeguard workingmen's interests. In answer to the petition of Livingston, Osgood, and other work relief advocates, the city's workers sent an opposing petition to Albany. The mechanics' statement emphasized the futility, the useless and inessential character, of the proposed workshops and the encouragement which their completion would give to urban crime. "Where is the repentent convict . . . and where the industrious poor man who cannot earn their livelihood?," queried the mechanics. The project was monopolistic in its tendencies, "a kind of entering wedge" to destroy the freedom and independence of honest, frugal, and industrious workmen. The petition was read and approved at a meeting of mechanics on March 18, signed by committees of craftsmen from each of the city's seven wards, and sent to the state capital, although the assembly did not receive it before the favorable committee report on Livingston's plan on March 19, 1803.[22]

Publication of the exchange of correspondence between the mayor and the mechanics and succeeding newspaper commentary and criticism had roused the antagonisms and animosities of New Yorkers. What had begun as a serious and well-intentioned suggestion for social improvement became a matter of heated public controversy. Political repercussions were readily observable. The city's mechanics, largely a Republican group, had squared off against leading Republican politicians. This development held special significance in view of the rapidly approaching statewide election, scheduled for the end of April. Not suprisingly, the workhouse scheme became the central issue in that election in New York City.

Federalist politicians and publicists seized the opportunity to split feuding Republican factions by supporting the mechanics against the Livingston group, hoping thereby to reap a harvest of labor votes in the coming election. The key individual contest in the election pitted Republican John Broome against an old Federalist leader, Egbert Benson, for the office of state senator from New York's southern district. Broome had signed the legislative petition requesting consideration for Mayor Livingston's work-relief plan. The Federalists, therefore, promoted their candidate as the mechanics' friend, while the Republicans tried to explain Broome's supposed hostility to urban craftsmen.

The weight of opinion wielded by the Mechanics Society represented a powerful political force. As the election campaign got under way, and as the drift of events became obvious, Republican politicians moved rapidly to disassociate themselves from the Livingston proposal. Many who had originally championed the plan and signed the mayor's petition now renounced support and claimed they had been misled by promoters of the project. Samuel Osgood, one of the first to reverse his position, begged the mechanics, as editor Coleman of the *Evening Post* put it, "to forget and forgive, and be friends." At the same time a group of young Republican lawyers and political hopefuls joined in a petition to the legislature backing the mechanics' demands. Among those who succumbed to the mechanical interest were Broome and De Witt Clinton, then a United States Senator from New York and soon mayor of New York City. Some mechanics, however, went unconvinced; one spokesman sardonically expressed regret that Republican concern for laborers had not manifested itself a little sooner. But supporters of work relief, such as "Civis" in the *Daily Advertiser,* criticized those who renounced the mayor's project "from mistaken motives of popularity." [23]

The newspaper war continued throughout the campaign. The *New-York Evening Post* provided the engine for Federalist electioneering propaganda. In a fervent editorial on March 19, Coleman promised the mechanics his complete support in opposing the "nefarious" schemes of the mayor and his friends. Coleman also pointed out the political motivations which brought disavowal of the work-relief project by anti-Livingston Republicans such as Broome and Clinton. A correspondent who called himself "A Mechanic" asserted the need for understanding and unanimity among artisans and merchants, who formed a significant por-

tion of Federalist political support in the city. This Federalist
mechanic recommended that both groups "study their true interests," and, "without reference to party," elect as legislators men
opposed to "destructive measures" such as public workshops. "The
most weighty reason why we should prefer Mr. Benson to Mr.
Broome," another "Mechanic" wrote, "is, that the latter has affixed
his signature to the petition for *Public Workshops*." Rhetorically,
he queried, "should we vote for a man who has thus signed the
death-warrant" of all mechanics in the metropolis? [24]

Republican politicians concentrated their polemics in the columns of the *American Citizen*, while editor Cheetham directed his
barbs at the Federalists in an attempt to retain mechanic support
for candidate Broome. In a typical display of spleen, Cheetham
accused Coleman of hypocrisy in professing friendship for laboring men. Countering Federalist charges, the *Citizen* called the
workhouse scheme a "federal trick," proposed by Federalists who
had deceived Mayor Livingston and other Republican supporters
with humanitarian pronouncements. To substantiate these charges,
Cheetham printed names of the eighty-five signers of the original
petition, only twelve of whom were admitted as Republicans.
Broome, the editor asserted, had been one of those so misled. The
Morning Chronicle, organ of the Burrite faction, similarly defended the honorable and benevolent motives of Republican advocates of the workshop plan, whose "conduct in abandoning the
design, when it was found to clash with the mechanic interest,
shews their attachment to that numerous and important class of
citizens." [25]

The election was held on April 28, 1803. Federalist Egbert Benson received a 74-vote majority in New York City, 1,198 to 1,124,
but a heavy Republican ballot in Suffolk, Westchester, and other
counties of the southern district elected John Broome to the state
senate seat. Federalist strategy had succeeded in attracting a sufficient number of mechanic votes to give their senatorial candidate
a slight edge in New York City. But the workhouse project remained a local issue capitalized by city Federalist politicians and
publicists. The Federalist appeal did not impress the rest of the

southern district, largely an agricultural section, nor did the issue affect the assembly contests. All nine Republican candidates for the assembly from New York City swept into office with large majorities. The voters elected Mechanics Society leaders James Warner and Peter H. Wendover to the assembly, while rejecting Federalist candidate Jacob Sherred, a former president of the society. Thus, although the work-relief issue hardly affected the outcome of the election, Livingston's plan induced a significant defection of mechanic voters to the Federalist senatorial candidate, more as a sign of displeasure with Broome than approval for Benson.[26]

In New York at the end of the eighteenth century, as Staughton Lynd and Alfred Young have recently asserted, "the demands of the mechanics formed the stuff of politics." New York's artisans and tradesmen remained a powerful force in urban politics as the nineteenth century began. Through united action they succeeded in defeating Mayor Livingston's relief program, although Republican amity was temporarily shattered as a result. The Federalist party—"a party in search of an issue" in the years after the Jeffersonian victory of 1800—seized the opportunity presented by the miscalculations of New York Republicans in 1803 to appeal for renewed support of workingmen at the polls. The effort succeeded to the extent that mechanics abandoned Republican leaders who appeared hostile to the interests of the city's skilled workmen.[27]

Conceived in enlightened humanitarianism, Mayor Livingston's workhouse proposal was an important, farsighted, even modern, attempt to deal with urban poverty. Ignoring contemporary moral opinions about the poor, Livingston recognized that immigrants and other unskilled workers needed jobs rather than alms. Borrowing from Hamilton and Bentham, the mayor projected a major municipal work-relief program long before government at any level was prepared to accept such responsibilities. But the project would have been costly and presented the mechanics with the very real threat of low-priced competition. Political considerations prevented rational discussion of the workshop plan. Further, the outcome of the controversy reflected the ambiguities of benevolent moralism. Humanitarians urged work on the poor to punish vice, strengthen character, or build self-reliance. Aside from Edward Livingston, few envisioned work relief as anything more than a moral purgative. Livingston's resignation as mayor in August 1803 amid charges of corruption struck down any hopes for immediate welfare reform. Poverty and pauperism remained significant social problems as urbanization progressed throughout the nineteenth century. And plans for improvement and reform were smothered as New Yorkers continued to moralize about the poor.[28]

V

HUMANITARIAN RESPONSE TO URBANIZATION

15

The Society for the Prevention
of Pauperism

More than any other group, the New York Society for the Prevention of Pauperism (SPP) characterized the anti-poverty campaign of the early nineteenth century. As previously noted, heavy immigration, rapid urbanization, and industrial beginnings intensified urban problems and loosened the social and personal ties which had preserved order in the eighteenth-century city. Pauperism and associated lower-class "vices" stimulated middle-class apprehension and concern. Numerous voluntary associations with humanitarian purposes sought to improve the caliber of urban life and restore order to an increasingly chaotic society. Simultaneously, motivation for humanitarian work moved markedly from benevolence to moralism. The demand for social control of a rapidly growing population of newcomers and an ideology of moral stewardship increasingly compromised reformist fervor. Civic leaders sought effective ways to eliminate pauperism and dependency while reducing relief costs. In its attitudes, assumptions, and activities, the New York SPP typified the new humanitarianism and the course of philanthropic reform in the preindustrial city of the nineteenth century.

Three prominent urban reformers and civic leaders—Thomas

Eddy, John Pintard, and John Griscom—organized the SPP in 1817. The career of each not only reflected business-oriented, middle-class humanitarianism, but illustrated important links in the network of urban benevolence as well. Born in Philadephia in 1758 of a prominent family of Tory sympathizers, Eddy settled in New York after the Revolution and soon became a successful insurance broker and a Federalist. He was a substantial stockholder in the Western Inland Lock Navigation Company and an early proponent of the Erie Canal, serving for a time as a member of the state's board of canal commissioners. As a Quaker philanthropist, Eddy promoted a variety of humanitarian causes—antislavery, abolition of imprisonment for debt, public education, improved care for the insane, prison reform, and missionary activity among Indians. Before becoming involved in the SPP, he founded the Bloomingdale Insane Asylum, served as superintendent of Newgate state prison in New York City and as a commissioner of the city's almshouse, and actively participated in the affairs of the Manumission Society, the Free School Society, the Humane Society, the New York Hospital, the Magdalen Society, the Fuel Association, the Society for the Suppression of Vice and Immorality, the Society for the Promotion of Industry, and the American Bible Society.

John Pintard's career paralleled that of Eddy. A native New Yorker, Pintard was born in 1759 and raised by his merchant uncle, Lewis Pintard. A patriot during the Revolution and a Federalist after, he followed his uncle's path into mercantile activity, becoming by 1792 one of the most prosperous of New York's importers of East India goods. However, speculative activity and association with such manipulators as William Duer brought financial ruin during the 1790's and even a term in debtor's prison. After regaining freedom, Pintard's interests carried him in three directions. He set his business career on a more conservative course after 1800, becoming an officer or director of the Mutual Fire Assurance Company, the New York and Brooklyn Steamboat Ferry Company, several banks, and a rejuvenated Chamber of Commerce. His duties as a state legislator, city councilman, clerk of the municipal corporation, and city inspector marked him as a dedicated public servant. And Pintard's interest in community affairs spanned a host of civic organizations: the Academy of Fine Arts, the Literary and Philosophical Society, the New-York Society Library, the New-York Historical Society, the Humane Society, the Free School Society, the Society for the Promotion of Industry, the Sailor's Snug Harbor, the New-York Bible Society, and the American Bible Society, in addition to the SPP and the institutions it spawned.

Unlike his two friends, John Griscom arrived in New York City in the Jeffersonian period. A teacher, chemist, and Quaker, Griscom was born of a New Jersey artisan family in 1774 and for several years conducted the Friends' Academy in Burlington. In 1807 a group of New York Quakers induced him to settle as a schoolmaster in their city; after 1813 Griscom also lectured on chemistry at Columbia College. His religious, educational, and scientific interests brought him into association with leading humanitarians, and Griscom rose very quickly to an influential position within the urban leadership group. Indeed, Griscom provided the SPP with intellectual direction and organizational energy.

Local reactions to the magnitude of the post-1815 relief crisis prompted appearance of the new philanthropic organization in 1817. Paternalistic civic leaders condemned the relief system which seemed to perpetuate poverty; the social and political elite occasionally matched humanitarian concern for the poor with an undisguised contempt for the lower classes, particularly impoverished immigrants. Typically, John Griscom declared in February 1817 that charity and alms created pauperism among the lower classes by stifling industry, initiative, and self-reliance; he contended that only societies which supplied employment to the poor deserved public support. Writing in 1817, Pintard objected to subsidizing "indigent foreigners" who worked at high wages in summer but, through extravagance and imprudence, became municipal charges by winter. He rejected permitting poor immigrants to starve as inhumane and unthinkable, but supporting them in idleness encouraged "growth of an oppressive evil." De Witt Clinton, now

governor, noted in his first annual address to the legislature in
January 1818 that increasing taxes to support New York City's
poor seriously threatened property values and business prosperity;
destructive pauperism might be removed "by rendering it a greater
evil to live by charity than by industry . . . and by adopting a
system of coercive labor." In an 1817 letter to Clinton, Thomas
Eddy asserted that public and private charity supported some
15,000 New Yorkers, about one-sixth of the city's population. "I
am tired assisting them in their distress," Eddy wrote. "It appears
to me more wise, to fix on every possible plan to *prevent* their
poverty and misery by means of employment . . . and to do all
in our power to discourage the use of spirituous liquors, which is
in fact *the true source of all the Evils* attending the poor." Each
of these New Yorkers implied that the problem of poverty and
relief could be solved only by determining and then eliminating
the causes of pauperism.[1]

During 1817 the urban leadership made several ineffectual attempts to illuminate these causes. In February a citizens relief
committee, originally formed to solicit and distribute contributions
to the poor, selected a subcommittee to investigate pauperism; as
previously noted, this effort resulted only in a legislative petition
for liquor-licensing reforms. In May a special committee of the
common council, appointed to prevent repetition of the relief crisis
of previous winters, identified lax enforcement of state poor laws
and indiscriminate charity as prime causes of urban indigence and
dependency. During August Zachariah Lewis, editor of the *Commercial Advertiser*, publicized the activities of the Pennsylvania
Society for the Promotion of Public Economy, which had investigated the nature of poverty in Philadelphia, pointed out defects
in the existing system of public charity, and proposed some radical
alternatives. Editor Lewis suggested that New Yorkers might well
emulate Philadelphia's reformers.[2]

At about the same time, Griscom, Pintard, and Eddy met in-
formally on several occasions to discuss pauperism and possible
methods of prevention. A general meeting of interested citizens
on December 16, 1817, sponsored by the three friends and chaired

by banker Matthew Clarkson, resulted in formation of the SPP. The new society first appointed a committee headed by Griscom to draw up a constitution and make a report on pauperism in the city. That evening Pintard wrote his daughter that "a wide survey is about being taken of the state of pauperism in our city. To see if we cannot check in some degree the growth of the present system of relieving the poor." [3]

At a second meeting on March 8, 1818, the society selected officers and managers, adopted the proposed constitution, and accepted the Griscom committee report. Although Clarkson became the SPP's first president, Griscom clearly emerged as the association's ideological leader. The Quaker educator did not envision the SPP as a relief-giving agency but merely as an investigatory body. He listed determining reasons for pauperism and indigence and proposing measures to eliminate such causes as the organization's most important objectives. Article two of the SPP's constitution established its purpose in detail:

> To investigate the circumstances and habits of the poor; to devise means for improving their situation, both in a physical and moral point of view; to suggest plans for calling into exercise their own endeavours, and afford the means for giving them increased effect; to hold out inducements to economy and saving from the fruits of their own industry, in the seasons of greater abundance; to discountenance, and as far as possible, prevent mendicity and street begging; and in fine, to do every thing which may tend to meliorate their condition, by stimulating their industry, and exciting their own energies.

Beyond helping the poor to help themselves, the reformers generally agreed that existing programs of public relief and private charity were not only inadequate, but irrational as well. Without radical changes in the system, without renewed insistence on self-reliance and morality, "helplessness and poverty would continue to multiply." The SPP, the reformers hoped, could indicate the kinds of reforms needed.[4]

Griscom's *Report of a Committee on the Subject of Pauperism* articulated the rationale of the SPP and new philanthropic atti-

tudes toward urban poverty and pauperism. In essence, the report
stated that any realistic, workable system of charity had to combine relief of unavoidable indigence with prevention of "artificial"
dependency. But according to Griscom, nine-tenths of New York's
poor fell into the latter category. The report then identified nine
prominent causes for such pauperism: (1) ignorance, especially
among the foreign poor; (2) idleness; (3) intemperance, "the
crying and increasing sin of the nation"; (4) extravagance among
the lower classes; (5) imprudent and hasty marriages; (6) lotteries and gambling; (7) pawnbrokers, who encouraged theft; (8)
houses of prostitution, "sinks of iniquity" where all "base-born
passions are engendered"; (9) and finally, the charitable institutions and societies of the city, which, despite Christian motives
and philanthropic zeal, encouraged laziness, fostered reliance on
benevolence, and could never "effect the removal of poverty, nor
lessen its general amount." This attitude—that most indigence was
"artificial" and resulted from individual vices and moral deficiencies—characterized the SPP from beginning to end and determined
its course of action.[5]

The program outlined by the Griscom committee amounted to
an all-inclusive attack on the supposed causes of pauperism. (Indeed, William Coleman of the *New-York Evening Post* criticized
the organization for attempting too much at once.) The committee recommended division of the city into small districts and appointment of "visitors" from the society to guide, counsel, advise,
and exhort the poor in each. It suggested the establishment of
savings banks, workhouses, churches, and Sunday schools, especially in poverty-stricken sections of the city. It demanded fundamental changes in the state poor laws so that public relief would
only be granted, after thorough investigation, to aged, sick, or
otherwise helpless and unemployable individuals. It cited the need
for new municipal regulations to prohibit street begging and improve liquor-licensing procedures. It also proposed to channel all
public and private charity into a single fund for systematic distribution.[6]

During 1818 the SPP put the Griscom committee blueprint into operation. Among its first actions the society appointed ward visitors to simultaneously counsel the poor and conduct a scientific social survey. The duties of visitors closely resembled the activities of volunteer charity organizers of the late nineteenth century and professional social workers of the twentieth:

> To become acquainted with the inhabitants of the district, to visit frequently the families of those who are in indigent circumstances, to advise them with respect to their business, the education of their children, the economy of their houses, to administer encouragement or admonition, as they may find occasion; and in general, by preserving an open, candid, and friendly intercourse with them, to gain their confidence, and by suitable and well timed counsel, to excite them to such a course of conduct as will best promote their physical and moral welfare.

In this project the SPP worked closely with the New-York Bible Society and the Sunday School Union Society, both of which sponsored ward visiting. Visitors kept record books which listed families in their districts and appropriate information about each— name and age of family heads, occupation and character, church membership, size of family, number of blacks, number not vaccinated, number of deaf, dumb, or blind, number unable to care for themselves, and whether the family possessed a Bible. At the same time, visitors distributed Bibles and tracts, enrolled children in nearby Sunday schools, recruited Sunday school teachers, and directed those in need of employment or special care to the proper places. Although the SPP approached ward visiting with great optimism, early efforts revealed that "the fruits of such experiments were not sufficient to invite a second attempt." The society never completed its social survey, but some of the impressionistic evidence assembled by ward visitors seemed to buttress SPP reports and recommendations.[7]

In addition to working with poor people individually, the SPP established nine standing committees, one for each of the supposed causes of pauperism. These committees gathered information and statistics and recommended specific corrective measures.

The committee on ignorance, for example, reported in 1819 that elementary schools in the city accommodated little more than half of 21,000 eligible children. Committee members obviously equated education with moral instruction, for they investigated school and church attendance simultaneously, estimating that nonchurchgoers exceeded 75,000 persons (more than three-fifths of the city's population). For these nineteenth-century moralists, the way to reduce poverty-spawning ignorance seemed simple and apparent; the city required more schools and churches to preach religion and righteous conduct to the poor. Editor Theodore Dwight of the *New-York Daily Advertiser*, a strong supporter of the SPP, even urged the municipal government to donate vacant lots and supply funds for church construction in low-income areas, as "no species of ignorance is so dangerous or mischievous as that which relates to moral and religious obligation and duty." [8]

Other committees reported with equivalent moralism. Investigating "the most prolific cause of pauperism," the committee on intemperance found one of every seventeen houses in New York City licensed to sell liquor. It asserted the absolute need for legislation to limit the number of taverns and retail liquor shops and for stricter supervision of licensees. Mayor Cadwallader D. Colden, who later became president of the SPP, agreed with the committee's assessment of the liquor problem and fought successfully for moderate municipal licensing reforms. Colden's successor, Stephen Allen, similarly supported tougher liquor controls. But sustaining state-wide legislative reforms did not follow and, in the opinion of the SPP, little hope existed of significantly reducing intemperance without cooperative efforts by state legislature and city council. [9]

The committee on idleness and sources of employment first suggested public employment as the most effective method of "dispensing charity." It praised the house of industry established in 1814 by the New York Society for the Promotion of Industry, and recommended establishment of similar workhouses under supervision of the almshouse commissioners. Other jobs listed for the able-bodied poor included public employment on the streets and in construction of new municipal buildings. To finance such a program of public works, the committee proposed legislative appropriations and a theater tax. But by 1821 the SPP had moved to a harsher, less humanitarian position. In that year a new committee disavowed the workhouse idea, unless as a temporary expedient, on the grounds that "if the public should undertake to provide employment for the poor, they would no longer take the pains to find it for themselves." [10]

Another important committee, that on charity, censured benevolent societies. It alleged that since the poor had been taught to rely on charity, the detrimental effects of dependency more than offset any beneficial results of public assistance and private almsgiving. The SPP recognized relief of helpless and impotent unemployables as a laudable humanitarian endeavor, but wished to avoid the socially undesirable consequences of charity. Thus to prevent the usual "impositions" it recommended that charitable societies in the city work closely with the society's ward visitors, who knew the needs and character of the poor at firsthand. Of door-to-door beggars, the SPP advised householders to require some kind of work "to make them earn what they receive." [11]

Other committees reported on pawnbrokers, lotteries, gambling, and prostitution. The society also investigated immigration, juvenile delinquency, and criminal court procedures as reformers associated these ingredients of urban society with poverty and pauperism. Along the same lines, the SPP published in 1822 a lengthy report on American penitentiary systems and recommended such supposed reforms as solitary confinement, separate juvenile reformatories, rigid prison discipline, and sparse use of pardoning powers. [12]

The state poor laws provided another target for the New York reformers. The SPP asserted in its fifth annual report that public poor relief should be provided only on a most discriminating basis after careful investigation of each applicant. Essentially, it recommended the abolition of most public assistance. Many felt, as did Theodore Sedgwick of Albany, who addressed the annual meeting of the society in February 1823, that "the effectual way to make poor people, was, to provide for poor people." The employ-able poor had to rely on their own exertions, for "as long as the public is willing to support them, they will find it most agreeable to live upon the public." Lack of a job was not sufficient excuse for idleness; rarely could one find "an industrious and virtuous person wanting the necessaries or the comforts of life." The SPP's reports and proposals created public awareness of pauperism in the city and contributed to widespread demand for welfare re-form. But the poor-law revision of 1824, the first important change since 1788, ignored the society's recommendations. Instead, the new statute established the county poorhouse system and actually extended public assistance by abolishing settlement and removal provisions of earlier laws.[13]

Throughout its short existence the SPP attempted to help the poor to help themselves. The establishment of two new institutions —a savings bank and a fuel fund—reflected these efforts to impose new values upon the lower classes. Leading members of the SPP agreed that lack of foresight and frugality among the poor gen-erated dependency and resulted in heavy relief costs, especially during winter months. Poor people, wrote John Pintard, "are like the Indians, who think when Spring comes that there will be no more winter, and are improvident until the cold pinches wh. awakens their sensibilities when too late." The savings bank and the fuel fund could counteract this tendency by encouraging habits of industry and economy, thrift and self-reliance.[14]

The idea of a savings bank had been suggested as early as 1809, when Pintard advanced such a scheme. Several years later, in November 1816, a citizens meeting adopted a constitution for a bank, but the institution did not open until 1819, when the SPP became its sponsor. That most of the original directors of the sav-ings bank (Griscom, Pintard, Eddy, Clinton, and other prom-inent persons) composed the leadership of the SPP was no co-incidence. The conditions revealed by the Griscom report and news of successful savings institutions in Europe and other American cities, especially Boston, Philadelphia, and Baltimore, also stimulated the society's interest in the bank.[15]

Furthermore, the savings bank idea corresponded with the society's analysis of pauperism. Men became indigent because of personal shortcomings such as intemperance, idleness, immorality, and irreligion. Only individual efforts at improvement would enable such paupers to overcome their vices; the savings bank would stimulate such exertions. "There are few spectacles more truly gratifying," the bank directors asserted in 1819, "or more honorable to human nature, than a poor man, surmounting, by his own exertions, the difficulties of his situation, and training up his family in the ways of honor and virtue, of industry and independence." The myth of an open and mobile society, strongly tinged with sentiments of moral uplift, supplied the rationale which motivated New York City's humanitarians.[16]

Early in 1819 the state chartered the new bank, the common council provided accommodations in a municipal building, and business began on July 3 with Pintard as president. The institution accepted initial deposits as small as one dollar and paid 5 per cent interest on accounts of more than five dollars. Deposits on opening day totaled $2,807; within six months 1,527 persons entrusted $153,378 to the benevolent bankers; and by January 1821, some 2,015 additional savings accounts had been opened, overall deposits amounting to $342,085. Established largely by laborers and artisans, most of these accounts held less than ten dollars. The savings bank, therefore, seemed an immediate success, and the common council praised the new facility as a "great and lasting blessing" to the community.[17]

The SPP organized a second self-help institution to finance winter fuel purchases for the poor. The scarcity and high cost of firewood during cold seasons created annual hardship for New York's poor, and a large portion of public relief took the form of wood. Like the savings bank, the fuel fund was a product of the inventive mind of John Pintard, who had proposed a plan for a nonprofit municipal fuel supply as early as 1804. But Pintard's first project did not succeed and several similar schemes, including the short-lived Fuel Association, also failed. Unusually severe weather during the winter of 1820–1821, however, drew renewed attention to the problem and resulted in numerous charity collections to heat the homes of the needy. These benevolent efforts generated some adverse reactions on the theory that the poor should have made their own provisions for winter firewood. "A.B.," for instance, suggested in the *New-York Evening Post* that "a little restriction in the consumption of *internal fuel*" would enable the poor to lay aside sufficient funds for winter use.[18]

Stimulated by such complaints and by the earlier proposals of Pintard and others, the SPP inaugurated the new project in May 1821. A separate board of managers administered the fund, which accepted weekly deposits as small as twenty-five cents from poor subscribers. The managers purchased firewood during the summer at low prices, and members drew upon their investment during the winter, when fuel became scarce and expensive. But despite optimistic assessments of first year results, relatively few poor families joined the fuel fund and the society abandoned the project in 1822.[19]

In addition to such self-help schemes as savings banks and fuel funds, the SPP engaged in a variety of other activities designed to restore health and order to the urban community. Reports from standing and special committees occupied biweekly meetings. Numerous petitions and memorials directed to city council and state legislature revealed a multifaceted moralism. They dealt with a wide range of subjects: marriage laws; theater and gambling taxes; tavern and liquor licenses; restriction of billiard tables and the sale of playing cards; revision of poor law and penal code; defects in prison construction and criminal court procedure; and immigration restriction. Lobbyists sent to Albany "nursed" the society's petitions with varying degrees of success.[20]

On another plane of activity, the SPP corresponded with humanitarians in other cities on poverty and unemployment, relief and reform. A joint campaign with the Baltimore Society for the Prevention of Pauperism (organized in 1820 on the New York model) sought federal liquor taxes to curb lower-class drinking habits. Delegates attended annual conventions of the state's "Moral Societies" in Albany. An apprentices' library, founded in 1820 in cooperation with the Mechanics Society of New York City, reflected concern for educating young workingmen and unskilled laborers. At the same time, the SPP accumulated an extensive library of its own, composed largely of books and pamphlets on political economy, poverty, and related subjects donated by Griscom, Pintard, and Eddy. The society also published booklets for the poor on household economy, accompanied by appropriate excerpts from Benjamin Franklin's *Poor Richard*.[21]

In all its enterprises, the SPP worked closely with municipal government. When requested, city officials promptly supplied facts and statistics about poor relief, immigration, crime, taverns, and municipal expenses. Mayors Colden and Allen supported antipauperism goals, cooperated in furnishing information, and both became leading members of the society. A committee of four aldermen conferred with the organization periodically, and municipal authorities attended SPP meetings and received copies of reports and other publications. Although the council did not always agree with SPP proposals or enact requested reforms, the common desire to rid the city of pauperism while reducing excessive poor rates created an obvious bond of understanding.[22]

European precedent and example supplied many of the ideas propagated and implemented by the New York reformers. They modeled their district visitation plan, for example, upon similar schemes adopted in Munich by American expatriate Benjamin Thompson, Count Rumford, and in Glasgow by Scottish clergyman Dr. Thomas Chalmers. Intellectual and philanthropic currents between Europe and America were strong. As early as 1799 Pintard read the works of Rumford with sympathy and approval. John Griscom, who traveled in Britain and Europe in 1818–1819, evaluated Chalmers' plan for the "moral superintendence of neighborhoods" as the most effective method ever devised to eliminate poverty. More important, London reformer Patrick Colquhoun directly influenced the New York urban leadership by corresponding with Thomas Eddy for two decades and furnishing a philosophical framework for SPP activities.[23]

In London Colquhoun proposed tavern restrictions, censured

indiscriminate charity, castigated the poor laws, and attributed rapid growth of England's pauper and criminal element to "a general inattention to the religious education and moral habits of the children of the lower classes." From Colquhoun's major work, *A Treatise on Indigence*, published in 1806, New Yorkers borrowed much. In Malthusian fashion, the British reformer considered poverty a natural, necessary, and ineradicable ingredient of society; indigence, however, implied destitution and dependency, an absence of means of subsistence and support. The problem, therefore, became one of restoring indigent persons to a subsistence level and preventing those in the normal state of poverty from falling into indigence. These ideas embellished reports of the SPP. Colquhoun's list of the causes of indigence matched that prepared by the Griscom committee. His remedies for pauperism included religious and moral education, occupational training, savings banks, temperance, frugality, and industriousness—all widely propagated by the New York SPP.[24]

The Colquhoun-Eddy correspondence provides an illuminating case study of the transit of humanitarian ideas and reform techniques from Europe to America. Between 1800 and 1818, Colquhoun supplied his American counterpart with an unending stream of British publications: tracts on education and poor relief; works on public health, police, prisons, and public houses; plans for savings banks and soup houses; the writings of Jeremy Bentham; pamphlets on "supplying the poor and preventing idleness and vagrancy"; and annual reports of Colquhoun's London Society for Bettering the Condition of the Poor. These works ultimately found their way into the library of the New York SPP, where they furnished inspiration and example in the struggle against paperism and moral evil.[25]

By its surveys and reports, by its proposals and savings institutions, the SPP hoped to attract public attention to the increase of pauperism in New York City and create popular demand for municipal and state reforms. The appearance of enterprise, commerce, and industry in the urban community disguised, to a great extent, the existence of widespread dependency. A campaign to enlighten and arouse the citizenry, therefore, became essential; thus in 1822 the SPP established a special committee "to inform & instruct the Public mind upon the causes & cure of pauperism." [26]

But continual efforts to enlist public opinion behind reform proposals met repeated frustration, disappointment, and defeat. The press occasionally pointed out SPP failures. The editor of the *Christian Herald,* for one, criticized the SPP in March 1821, for "a great deal of unproductive speechifying" and very few positive results. William Coleman of the *Evening Post* castigated the SPP in August 1821 for failing to carry out its objectives. Rather than diminishing, pauperism seemed on the increase. The reports of the society breathed "zeal, ardor and resolution" but no tangible results followed. "Is this the way to prevent moral evils?" Coleman asked, clearly equating pauperism with immorality. "Will an annual report, or a public meeting once in twelve months, arouse the attention and command the zeal and confidence of a great and slumbering metropolis, in plans of reform?" [27]

Defenders of the SPP replied immediately, asserting that the organization did not propose to end poverty directly by providing relief or employment, but merely hoped to delineate causes of pauperism and suggest preventive measures. This it had done. Implementation of these measures depended upon the alacrity and compliance of municipal authorities and state legislators; but both, SPP supporters said, had shown "total aversion" to significant reforms. Too deeply entrenched and "far too sturdy in its character," pauperism could never be eliminated by private or local efforts alone. Only government, the society maintained in report after report, possessed sufficient power and authority to implement solutions successfully. [28]

Yet the SPP failed to secure requisite legislative reforms. Petitions to the common council and the state legislature advocating strong controls on tavern and liquor licensing met repeated rejections. The 1824 poor-law revision ignored entirely the society's recommendation to do away with the existing relief system. City authorities refused to act on proposals for municipal workhouses and other public employment for the able-bodied poor. The suggestions embodied in the penitentiary report were not implemented. Although a few minor reforms became law—such as municipal regulation of pawnbrokers and lotteries—much more frequently the SPP went down to legislative defeat.

In 1823, as a result of the failure of municipal and legislative reform, the society's managers adopted new approaches to urban poverty. John Griscom, an educator himself, focused SPP attention on education and job training. Many SPP members had worked with the Free School Society and with Sunday schools, and most shared the optimism of educators that moral training in schools would cure pauperism. One New Yorker, an associate of SPP leaders but not a member of the organization, made related suggestions. Almshouse chaplain John Stanford urged establishment of an asylum for delinquent and abandoned children who formed the "*Core* of pauperism." Until such children could be removed from the streets, instructed in moral and religious principles, and apprenticed in respectable trades, Stanford asserted, "Societies for the cure or prevention of Pauperism, may hold their meetings, & publish their annual Reports, without any other benefit than what would accrue to the paper mill and the printing press." These and similar observations helped the SPP redirect its attack on pauperism.[29]

A committee of the SPP had already noted a positive relationship between juvenile delinquency and pauperism. The idea of eradicating indigence and vice by reforming and educating the beggars, vagrants, and delinquents of the rising generation seemed convincing. Beginning in 1823, under the guiding influence of Griscom, the society developed a new, double-barreled program —the organization of infant schools and high schools to supplement the elementary education supplied by the New York Free School Society and religious charity schools; and second, the establishment of a "House of Refuge" for juvenile delinquents.[30]

The second half of the program was implemented first. Griscom headed a committee to report on the proposed reformatory. His plan for a juvenile asylum, patterned on that of the London Philanthropic Society which he had visited in 1818, received a favorable response at the annual SPP meeting in December 1823. Delinquent children, the report maintained, despite being raised in iniquitous environments, could be educated and reformed, "carefully instructed in the nature of their moral and religious obligations," and restored to society as useful citizens. Griscom's new plan inspired such optimism that the SPP abandoned its original objectives and adopted a new name—the Society for the Reformation of Juvenile Delinquents.[31]

The transformed group put its plans rapidly into effect. The common council endorsed the organization and donated a lot at the site of the present Madison Square Park, while the federal government sold the United States arsenal located on the property to the new society for $6,000. A public subscription raised $16,000 for the asylum, and the legislature granted a charter of incorporation and five-year annuity of $2,000 as well. The House of Refuge, which opened on January 1, 1825, became an immediate success, if the testimony of Governor Clinton, District Attorney Hugh Maxwell, and John Stanford can be believed. Within ten years 1,120 boys and girls had been admitted to the institution; allegedly, most were reformed and bound out to suitable trades— the boys usually in farming and whaling and the girls in domestic occupations. Civic leaders in Boston and Philadelphia, supplied with information by Griscom, emulated New York's example by establishing juvenile reformatories in their own cities.[32]

New educational institutions in New York City also absorbed the considerable energies of former SPP leaders. Griscom played a central role in organizing the city's first high school in 1825. Here again New Yorkers borrowed from European practice, for Griscom modeled the new school on the Scottish system which had been described to him by his friend, Professor James Pillans of the University of Edinburgh. As early as 1821 Griscom had met with Pintard, Colden, and others to discuss this project. The New-York High School Society resulted from these preliminary meetings. Designed only for boys, the school opened on March 1, 1825; to accommodate girls, a second high school began in February 1826. Griscom also helped found an Infant School Society shortly thereafter. Thus the experience of the SPP in investigating poverty in the city and failure in the legislative arena led to emphasis on improvement of youth through education, moral and religious exhortation, occupational and apprenticeship training, and reformation of juvenile delinquents. As the SPP expired in 1823, several praiseworthy institutions emerged on a new and reinvigorated wave of moralism and reform sentiment.[33]

Reacting to urban changes, SPP leaders attempted to face indigence and dependency in their city realistically, systematically, even scientifically. Griscom, Pintard, Eddy, and other SPP leaders had been raised intellectually on the classical liberalism of Malthus, Ricardo, and Colquhoun. Idleness, intemperance, immorality, irreligion, ignorance—they enumerated these as the most prolific sources of pauperism. Such vices could be exterminated, the SPP asserted over and over again, only by calling opposing virtues into play—"by inculcating religion, morality, sobriety, and industry, and by diffusing useful knowledge among the indigent and laboring people." Few considered that the social and economic conditions of the urban environment might be responsible for pauperism and the vices observable among the poor. In rejecting the rational humanism and Christian charity which had characterized benevolence in an earlier generation, SPP reformers preached a doctrine of moral stewardship. The SPP clearly revealed the humanitarian response to urbanization—middle-class moralists struggling to control the vices of newcomers and restore stability to an increasingly disordered society.[34]

16

Social Welfare and Humanitarianism in Urban America

By 1825 the pattern and practice of social welfare and humanitarianism in preindustrial New York City had clearly emerged. English tradition and colonial law had firmly established society's obligation to care for its helpless members. During post-Revolutionary years, New York City authorities met state welfare requirements by constructing almshouses and helping the outdoor poor during emergencies. Private philanthropy, as Merle Curti has suggested, showed "a special inventiveness and creativity in meeting individual and social needs largely neglected or inadequately provided by government." Thus a multitude of charitable societies sprouted to bring relief and moral reform to the urban poor. With varying degrees of effectiveness and commitment, welfare officials and charity leaders fought poverty and pauperism with public and private resources.[1]

By the mid-1820's New York City had passed beyond the preindustrial period. As industry increasingly rivaled commerce, as factories replaced small workshops, the city grew in size and importance. But business prosperity and commercial success, as reflected in the Erie Canal celebration of 1825, did not simultaneously promote municipal consciousness and civic betterment. With rising

immigration, urban population became more ethnically hetero-
geneous. Urban growth brought new social problems and intensified old ones. All the unsavory characteristics of city life—crime,
filth, disease, prostitution, alcoholism, pauperism—prospered in
New York City and seemed to affirm the validity of Jeffersonian
anti-urbanism. The well-ordered, closely regulated town of the
eighteenth century did not survive the transition to industrialism.
Although a small group of civic leaders emphasized urban improvement, the well-entrenched tradition of "privatism" shaped most
responses to city problems by the early nineteenth century.

Such changing economic and social patterns reflected the dynamic nature of urbanism in post-Revolutionary and early national
years. By the 1820's humanitarian attitudes and social-welfare practices clearly had shifted in response to new urban pressures. Despite failures and lapses in other areas, city government expanded
relief programs during economic crises and achieved a measure of
sophistication in social-welfare institutions. The 1824 poor-law reform abolishing residency requirements for relief revealed an important new trend, a recognition that such medieval techniques
served few positive purposes in a modernizing, mobile society. The
simultaneous effort to abolish outdoor relief indicated, however,
that municipal officials had succumbed to the new benevolent moralism.

In many ways, voluntary philanthropic associations experienced
metamorphosis by the 1820's. With the deaths of John Murray, Jr.,
in 1817, Divie Bethune in 1824, Thomas Eddy and Matthew Clarkson in 1827, and De Witt Clinton in 1828, and with others (Leonard
Bleecker, John Pintard, and John Griscom) abandoning central
roles, humanitarian leadership passed into new hands—activists
such as the Tappan brothers who turned philanthropy toward
anti-slavery goals. Individual groups changed in other ways, too.
For example, reformed debtor legislation made the Humane Society's original purpose obsolete, moving the organization to more
general humanitarian objectives. Municipal suspension of financial
aid to religious schools boosted the Free School Society, which in
1825 established wide, new goals as the Public School Society.

Moral reformers began to build high schools and infant schools for the poor during the same decade. The urban missionary movement reached a peak by the mid-twenties. Reflecting on frustration and failure, the Society for the Prevention of Pauperism transformed itself into the Society for the Reformation of Juvenile Delinquents in 1823. Most apparent, by the 1820's the humanitarian network accepted unquestioningly the proposition that immorality caused pauperism. Just as clearly, the moralists argued almost unanimously that the middle-class values of honesty, sobriety, industriousness, self-reliance, and religious conviction would end working-class poverty.

These social-welfare patterns revealed much about urban society in the early nineteenth century. Among the consequences of New York's rapid urbanization, none seemed more threatening to social stability, more disturbing to community order, than the rising incidence of poverty and economic dependency. Public officials and private philanthropists, civic leaders and city boosters all sought "cures," or at least temporary expedients, for indigence and pauperism. Yet the general conviction that dependency stemmed from character defects dictated the nature of the humanitarian response. Aldermen, almshouse commissioners, and almshouse superintendents fulfilled minimum welfare requirements, but consistently emphasized removal of ineligible paupers and reduction of relief expenditures. They particularly guarded against assistance to "unworthy" dependents and thus tried to end outdoor relief in the 1820's. Similarly, private charities increasingly moved from benevolence to moralism as the nineteenth century progressed. The societies carefully dispensed relief to "deserving" applicants, always accompanied by appropriate moral messages. Many associations firmly advocated exhortation, indoctrination, and religious conversion as the best possible cures for pauperism. For most humanitarians, moral stewardship seemed a way of aiding the poor and simultaneously preserving social order.

Given the prevailing moralistic views of society, few New Yorkers accepted alternative explanations for urban poverty. Most ignored the social and economic inequities of the urbanizing, industrializing, capitalistic environment. Economic stagnation due to business fluctuations, embargoes, and war periodically brought unemployment to working-class men, women, and children. Yellow fever epidemics, which occurred regularly in the early years of the period, forced middle-class flight from the city and suspension of normal business activity, leaving low-paid workers in disease-infected districts without jobs or food. Heavy fuel costs each winter drained workers' savings and required massive relief. Severe cold weather also reduced employment for unskilled, outdoor workers—cartmen, fishermen, dock workers, construction laborers, and others. The constant injection of large numbers of penniless immigrants and native rural migrants without skills depressed wage levels and increased dependency for those without regular jobs. The economic need of many other city residents, of course, stemmed from age, injury, sickness, or the absence of breadwinners. Despite the obvious relationship between heavy relief costs and such economic factors as depression and unemployment, New Yorkers continued to castigate the "unworthy" poor, guard against "promiscuous charity," and emphasize moral reform. Clearly, adherence to moral platitudes and the constant, paternalistic effort to propagate middle-class values masked economic realities for most municipal officials and charity leaders.[2]

Although it is always dangerous to generalize from a single case study, it seems clear that other urban centers duplicated New York City's brand of humanitarianism. Indeed, the seaport cities developed along remarkably parallel lines. The dynamics of urban growth may have differed in each case, but cities like Boston, Philadelphia, and Baltimore experienced all of New York's problems. Economic depressions, business fluctuations, unemployment, low wages for unskilled workers, heavy immigration, epidemics, winter relief demands, pauperism—these conditions affected all the port towns. Municipal and civic leaders responded in similar fashion everywhere; that is, the almshouse and the voluntary association became characteristic nineteenth-century urban institutions.

Moral reform also characterized philanthropy in every city and town. The principles and programs of such groups as the Society for the Prevention of Pauperism, preindustrial New York's typical anti-poverty effort, were duplicated in other major cities. The Pennsylvania Society for the Promotion of Public Economy, established in Philadelphia in 1817, has already been mentioned. This organization followed a path closely resembling that of New York's moral reformers. The Philadelphia society attempted a scientific survey of poverty and adopted the district visitation plan, while committees reported on poor laws, public prisons, domestic economy, public schools, and the suppression of vice and immorality. Believing their city "an emporium of beggars," Philadelphia reformers eventually focused on moral and religious education as the best method of striking at "the roots of poverty and vice." The same trend could be observed in the activities of the Society for Bettering the Condition of the Poor, formed in 1829 under the sponsorship of the Philadelphia publisher, political economist, and charity reformer, Mathew Carey. A comparable response to urban poverty emerged in Baltimore, the nation's third largest city, where humanitarians established a Society for the Prevention of Pauperism in 1820 with a program clearly based on the experience of the New York SPP. In Boston a Society for the Moral and Religious Instruction of the Poor functioned during the 1820's, and city missionary Joseph Tuckerman helped organize a Society for the Prevention of Pauperism in 1835. The motivations of Boston and Baltimore philanthropists matched those of New York reformers. Few disagreed with the analysis of poverty made by Boston's Unitarian minister, William Ellery Channing, in 1835: "the condition of the poor deserves sympathy; but let us not, by exaggeration of its pains, turn away our minds from the great inward sources of their misery." Charity leaders throughout the United States responded to urban poverty and lower-class pauperism in exactly the same way. Attributing poverty to the poor themselves, most humanitarians had moved by 1825 from benevolence to moralism.[3]

New York's social-welfare history leads to other conclusions as well. If moral reform typified philanthropy in the early nineteenth century, it also prevailed in later urban humanitarian organizations.

The New York Association for Improving the Condition of the Poor (AICP), for example, hardly improved upon the SPP analysis of pauperism. Founded in 1843 by Robert M. Hartley, the AICP focused on indolence, improvidence and intemperance as responsible for lower-class dependency and applied most of its energy to improving the moral condition of the poor. Similarly, the early anti-pauperism campaign anticipated the charity organization movement of the late nineteenth century. The New York Charity Organization Society (COS), established in 1882, emphasized co-ordination of welfare services, close investigation of relief applicants, friendly visitation through district committees, and moral indoctrination and exhortation as a substitute for alms—all elements of "scientific philanthropy" originally promoted by the SPP and other early humanitarian associations. Although both later groups, particularly the COS, increasingly recognized possible social and economic reasons for pauperism, environmentalism did not capture professional social workers until the twentieth century. Even such a careful late-nineteenth-century student of urban poverty as Jacob Riis, author of *How the Other Half Lives,* described pauperism as "a moral distemper" and labeled the "clothes-line" the real distinction "between pauperism and honest poverty." [4]

Social-welfare and humanitarian patterns in early New York City also provide some interesting and instructive perspectives on modern public-assistance efforts. Like the urban reformers and charity leaders of the nineteenth century, Americans continue to moralize about the poor and ignore more fundamental causes for poverty. Certainly contemporary social critics like Michael Harrington, Richard M. Elman, Daniel P. Moynihan, Richard A. Cloward, and the authors of the *Report of the National Advisory Commission on Civil Disorders* have rejected the deterministic paternalism and harsh moralism propagated by such groups as the SPP and its nineteenth-century successors. But despite the plethora of evidence documenting the extent of poverty in contemporary America and revealing serious inequities in the welfare system, few positive changes are observable. The idea of America as the land of opportunity continues to nurture middle-class moralism. Some sug-

gest that the war on poverty—both the Johnson and the Nixon variety—is ineffective, even irrelevant, because it has emphasized job
training and employment. Most of those who live in poverty, it is
argued, are either too young, too old, or too sick to work. Others
are already employed at below-subsistence wages, or are mothers
with dependent children. Assistance techniques and poverty cures
have hardly improved over two centuries. The bulk of modern welfare programs have been stretched upon a framework fashioned
by nineteenth-century moralism. In post-Revolutionary New York
City contemporary social attitudes impeded real reforms. This
problem seems just as real in mid-twentieth century. The crisis of
urban America demands fresh ideas, new approaches, and more
effective solutions. While the critics argue, while the experts examine, while the politicians talk, while the public condemn the
poor, poverty endures and deepens.

A Note on Sources

The sources upon which this study rests are almost entirely primary in nature. Six months of uninterrupted newspaper research provided a wealth of important and essential information. The most consistently useful newspapers were the *Daily Advertiser* (1786–1805), the *Commercial Advertiser* (1797–1825), and the *New-York Evening Post* (1801–1825). More than fifty other papers yielded less substantial but nevertheless usable data. The best guide to these sources is Clarence S. Brigham, *History and Bibliography of American Newspapers, 1690–1820* (2 vols., Worcester, Mass., 1947). Also useful were some periodicals, especially the *Christian Herald and Seaman's Magazine,* the *Evangelical Guardian,* and the *American Sunday School Teachers' Magazine.*

State documents and municipal records supplied materials for the public-assistance side of New York's social-welfare history. Essential published sources included *Minutes of the Common Council of the City of New York, 1675–1776* (8 vols., New York, 1905); *Minutes of the Common Council of the City of New York, 1784–1831* (21 vols., New York, 1917); *The Colonial Laws of New York* (5 vols., Albany, 1894); *Laws of the State of New York; Journal of the Assembly of the State of New York; Journal of the Senate of the State of New York;* and Charles Z. Lincoln, ed., *Messages from the Governors* (11 vols., Albany, 1909). The manuscript records of city welfare officials are indispensable historical sources. For colonial years, these included

Church Wardens Minutes, 1694–1747, located in the New York Public Library, and Church Wardens Accounts, 1714–1738, deposited in the New-York Historical Society. The New York City Municipal Archives and Records Center contains massive amounts of manuscript materials for social-welfare history in post-Revolutionary years. Most important are the Alms House Records, including minutes and reports of alms-house commissioners, reports and correspondence of almshouse superintendents, and voluminous records on indentured children, transported paupers, outdoor relief, infants at nurse, immigrant ships, and bonding procedures. The City Clerk Documents complement the Alms House Records and reveal common council actions and attitudes on social-welfare problems. This large and unorganized collection contains petitions, reports of common council committees, correspondence of municipal officers, and other valuable material not printed in the published *Minutes of the Common Council*. Other important municipal records are the Minutes of the Commissioners of the Alms House and Bridewell, 1791–1797, in the New York Public Library, and the Minutes of the Committee of Health, 1793–1796, in the New-York Historical Society.

The sources for private humanitarianism are varied and extensive. Every organization issued annual reports for publication either in the newspapers or separately in pamphlet form. Charity sermons, temperance polemics, and religious tracts yield important information on changing attitudes toward poverty and the poor. Many manuscript records of the charities are still extant; the New-York Historical Society, for example, has records and minute books of the Humane Society, the Society for the Prevention of Pauperism, the Society for the Relief of Poor Widows with Small Children, the New York Manufacturing Society, and the New York Asylum for Lying-in Women. Other New York City depositories with institutional records include the General Society of Mechanics and Tradesmen, the New York City Mission Society, the American Bible Society, and the Society of Friends.

The correspondence and writings of city leaders and urban reformers are vital for an understanding of both public welfare and private charity in New York. Major manuscript collections include the De Witt Clinton Papers at Columbia University Library; the John Griscom Correspondence and the Richard Varick Papers at the New York Public Library; and the papers of John Stanford, Stephen Allen, John Pintard, John Rodgers, James Duane, Richard Varick, and John Jay at the New-York Historical Society. Published correspondence and other primary material can be found in such works as Dorothy C. Barck, ed., *Letters from John Pintard to His Daughter Eliza Noel Pintard Davidson, 1816–1833* (4 vols., New-York Historical Society *Collections*, LXX-LXXIII, 1937–

1940); Samuel L. Knapp, *The Life of Thomas Eddy* (New York, 1834); and William W. Campbell, *The Life and Writings of De Witt Clinton* (New York, 1849).

The writings of native and foreign travelers added interesting, occasionally colorful, material. Though some are reliable, others leave distorted impressions and must be used with care. The best guide to travel accounts for New York City is Bayrd Still, *Mirror for Gotham: New York as Seen by Contemporaries from Dutch Days to the Present* (New York, 1956). City directories and locally issued guidebooks also supplied essential materials unobtainable elsewhere.

A number of general studies in the history of philanthropy and social welfare provide insights and perspectives applicable to the New York City experience. Especially useful are Robert Bremner's two books, *From the Depths: The Discovery of Poverty in the United States* (New York, 1956) and *American Philanthropy* (Chicago, 1960), and a number of perceptive articles by Merle Curti: "The History of American Philanthropy as a Field of Research," *American Historical Review*, LXII (January 1957), 352–363; "American Philanthropy and the National Character," *American Quarterly*, X (Winter 1958), 420–437; "Tradition and Innovation in American Philanthropy," *Proceedings of the American Philosophical Society*, 105 (April 1961), 146–156. The Russell Sage Foundation, *Report of the Princeton Conference on the History of Philanthropy in the United States* (New York, 1956) offered orientation and helpful suggestions. Important for an understanding of the English background of social welfare and humanitarianism is Samuel Mencher, *Poor Law to Poverty Program: Economic Security Policy in Britain and the United States* (Pittsburgh, 1967). A recent survey of the American experience is Blanche D. Coll, *Perspectives in Public Welfare: A History* (Washington, 1969).

I have also profited from reading Ralph Pumphrey "Compassion and Protection: Dual Motivations in Social Welfare," *Social Service Review*, XXXIII (March 1959), 21–29; Clifford S. Griffin, *Their Brothers' Keepers: Moral Stewardship in the United States, 1800–1865* (New Brunswick, N. J., 1960); Charles I. Foster, *An Errand of Mercy: The Evangelical United Front, 1790–1837* (Chapel Hill, N. C., 1960); and Benjamin J. Klebaner, "Poverty and Its Relief in American Thought, 1815–61," *Social Service Review*, XXXVIII (December 1963), 382–399. Klebaner's unpublished dissertation, "Public Poor Relief in America, 1790–1860" (Columbia University, 1952), combines detailed information with good insight and extensive bibliography to research materials. Although based only on published sources, David M. Schneider, *The History of Public Welfare in New York State, 1609–1886* (Chicago, 1938) remains useful.

A more complete guide to the sources for this book may be found in the notes, in the bibliography of the dissertation upon which it is based (deposited in the New York University Library), and in my published articles: "Poverty in Early America, a Reappraisal: The Case of Eighteenth-Century New York City," *New York History*, L (January 1969), 5–27; "Education as Social Control in New York City, 1784–1825," *ibid.*, LI (April 1970), 219–237; "The Humane Society and Urban Reform in Early New York, 1787–1831," *New-York Historical Society Quarterly*, LIV (January 1970), 30–52; "Poverty, Politics, and the Mechanics of New York City, 1803," *Labor History*, 12 (Winter 1971); and "Humanitarianism in the Preindustrial City: The New York Society for the Prevention of Pauperism, 1817–1823," *Journal of American History*, LVII (December 1970), 576–599.

LIST OF ABBREVIATIONS USED IN NOTES

ABCPB	Auxiliary New-York Bible and Common Prayer Book Society
ABS	American Bible Society
AHMS	American Home Missionary Society
AICP	New York Association for Improving the Condition of the Poor
COS	New York Charity Organization Society
CUL	Columbia University Library
EMSYM	New-York Evangelical Missionary Society of Young Men
FABS	New-York Female Auxiliary Bible Society
FMS	Female Missionary Society for the Poor of the City of New-York
FSS	New-York Free School Society
HSS	New-York High School Society
Laws	*Laws of the State of New York*
MBS	New-York Marine Bible Society
MCC	*Minutes of the Common Council of the City of New York, 1784–1831* (21 vols., New York, 1917)
NYBS	New-York Bible Society
NYHS	New-York Historical Society
NYMA	New York City Municipal Archives and Records Center
NYPL	New York Public Library
NYTS	New York City Temperance Society
RTS	New-York Religious Tract Society
SPP	New-York Society for the Prevention of Pauperism
SRDD	Society for the Relief of Distressed Debtors
SRPW	Society for the Relief of Poor Widows with Small Children
SSGP	Society for Supporting the Gospel among the Poor in the City of New-York
SSUS	New-York Sunday School Union Society
UDMS	United Domestic Missionary Society
YMBS	Young Men's New-York Bible Society
YMMS	Young Men's Missionary Society of New-York

Notes

CHAPTER 1

1. James G. Wilson, *The Memorial History of the City of New-York* (4 vols., New York, 1892–1893), III, 319–331; Cadwallader D. Colden, *Memoir, Prepared at the Request of a Committee of the Common Council of the City of New York, and Presented to the Mayor of the City, at the Celebration of the Completion of the New York Canals* (New York, 1825), 151–161, 317–329.
2. Robert G. Albion, "New York Port in the New Republic, 1783–1793," *New York History*, XXI (October 1940), 388–403.
3. Myron H. Luke, *The Port of New York, 1800–1810* (New York, 1953); Robert G. Albion, *The Rise of the New York Port, 1815–1860* (New York, 1939); James Hardie, *The Description of the City of New-York* (New York, 1827), 309.
4. Sidney I. Pomerantz, *New York: An American City, 1783–1803* (New York, 1938), 194–199; Allan Pred, "Manufacturing in the American Mercantile City, 1800–1840," *Annals of the Association of American Geographers*, LVI (June 1966), 307–338; David Montgomery, "The Working Classes of the Pre-industrial American City, 1780–1830," *Labor History*, 9 (Winter 1968), 3–22.
5. George Rogers Taylor, "American Urban Growth Preceding the Railway Age," *Journal of Economic History*, XXVII (September 1967), 309–339; David T. Gilchrist, ed., *The Growth of the Seaport Cities, 1790–1825* (Charlottesville, Va., 1967), 25–53; Franklin B. Hough, *Statistics of Population of the City and County of New York* (New York Board of Supervisors, Document No. 13, August 15, 1866), 60.

6. John W. Francis, *Old New York; Or, Reminiscences of the Past Sixty Years* (New York, 1858), 15.

7. Bayrd Still, ed., *Mirror for Gotham: New York as Seen by Contemporaries from Dutch Days to the Present* (New York, 1956), 82; Timothy Dwight, *Travels in New-England and New-York* (4 vols., London, 1823), III, 450; Adam Hodgson, *Letters from North America, Written During a Tour in the United States and Canada* (2 vols., London, 1824), II, 110; "Diary of the Honorable Jonathan Mason," Massachusetts Historical Society *Proceedings*, 2nd series, II (March 1885), 8; De Witt Clinton to John Jacob Astor, December 2, 1824, in Vivian C. Hopkins, ed., "John Jacob Astor and De Witt Clinton: Correspondence from Jan. 25, 1808, to Dec. 23, 1827," *Bulletin of the New York Public Library*, 68 (December 1964), 666; Dorothy C. Barck, ed., *Letters from John Pintard to His Daughter Eliza Noel Pintard Davidson, 1816–1833* (4 vols., New-York Historical Society *Collections*, LXX-LXXIII, 1937–1940), II, 265.

8. On the colonial city, see Arthur E. Peterson and George W. Edwards, *New York as an Eighteenth Century Municipality* (2 vols., New York, 1917); Carl Bridenbaugh, *Cities in the Wilderness: The First Century of Urban Life in America, 1625–1742* (New York, 1938); and Carl Bridenbaugh, *Cities in Revolt: Urban Life in America, 1743–1776* (New York, 1955).

9. *Daily Advertiser* (New York), November 17, 1798, May 30, 1801; Allan Nevins and Milton Halsey Thomas, eds., *The Diary of George Templeton Strong* (4 vols., New York, 1952), I, 110; William Dalton, *Travels in the United States and Part of Upper Canada* (Appleby, 1821), 5.

10. *Daily Advertiser*, September 7, 1798; Nelson Blake, *Water for the Cities* (Syracuse, 1956), 44–62, 100–171.

11. An excellent recent study is John Duffy, *A History of Public Health in New York City, 1625–1866* (New York, 1968).

12. R. Richard Wohl, "Urbanism, Urbanity, and the Historian," *University of Kansas City Review*, XXII (October 1955), 54.

CHAPTER 2

1. The clearest statement of this thesis may be found in Robert E. Brown, "Economic Democracy Before the Constitution," *American Quarterly*, VII (Fall 1955), 257–274.

2. J. P. Brissot de Warville, *New Travels in the United States of America. Performed in 1788* (2nd ed., New York, 1792), 89; Felix de Beaujour, *Sketch of the United States of America, at the Commencement of the Nineteenth Century, from 1800 to 1810*, trans. by William Walton (London, 1814), 150; Charles W. Janson, *The Stranger in America, 1793–1806*, ed. by Carl S. Driver (New York, 1935), 191; *Niles' Weekly Register* (Baltimore),

April 17, 1813; James Boardman, *America, and the Americans* (London, 1833), 11–12.

3. William Cobbett, *A Year's Residence in the United States of America* (London, 1818–1819), 377–380.

4. Dwight, *Travels*, III, 431; SPP, *Second Annual Report* . . . (New York, 1820), 3.

5. *Independent Journal* (New York), February 18, 1784; James Duane to Common Council, February 7, 1784, box 6, James Duane Papers, NYHS; James Duane to Rev. John H. Livingston, February 12, 1784, *ibid.*; *MCC*, I, 49, 115; Richard Varick to James Duane, December 31, 1788, box 7, Duane Papers.

6. Pomerantz, *New York*, 203; *MCC*, II, 124–125, 212; *Minerva* (New York), September 5, 1797.

7. *Daily Advertiser,* November 3, 1798; *New-York Evening Post,* September 30, October 26, 1803, November 14, 1805, March 12, 1817; *Commercial Advertiser* (New York), September 16, 1805; De Witt Clinton to Members of the Assembly from the City and County of New York, January 23, 1805, microfilm reel 5, De Witt Clinton Papers, CUL; *MCC*, IV, 702–704, V, 123–124, 494–495, VIII, 204; Thomas Eddy to De Witt Clinton, February 15, 1817, reel 3, Clinton Papers.

8. *New-York Evening Post,* February 17, 18, March 10, 1817.

9. *MCC*, VII, 424, 742, VIII, 205; Ward Stafford, *New Missionary Field: A Report to the Female Missionary Society for the Poor of the City of New-York, and Its Vicinity* (New York, 1817), 12; *Daily Advertiser,* November 17, 1798; *New-York Evening Post,* January 23, 1805; *Commercial Advertiser,* January 9, 1809. See also James Ford, *et al., Slums and Housing* (2 vols., Cambridge, Mass., 1936), I, 72–121.

10. *Christian Herald and Seaman's Magazine* (New York), VIII (June 16, 1821), 71, IX (February 1, 1823), 553; Account Book of Cash Distributions to the Poor, 1809–1816, entries for January 11, 20, 30, 1810, Volume 0383, Alms House Records, NYMA.

11. *Ibid.,* January 1810; *Longworth's American Almanac, New-York Register, and City Directory, 1810* (New York, 1810).

12. Minutes of the Justices, Church Wardens, and Vestrymen of the City of New York, Charged with the Care of the Poor, 1694–1747, entry for June 3, 1736, NYPL (hereafter cited as Church Wardens Minutes); *New-York Evening Post,* March 12, 1817; SPP, *Report of a Committee on the Subject of Pauperism* (New York, 1818), 4–5.

13. *MCC*, II, 125, V, 628–629, X, 466, XIII, 90–91; Ezra Stiles Ely, *Visits of Mercy* (2 vols., Philadelphia, 1829), I, 153, 215, II, 31–32; Cadwallader D. Colden to Charles G. Haines, December 1, 1819, in SPP, *Second Annual Report,* 64.

14. These various categories of dependents are revealed in the Alms House Records located in NYMA. These manuscripts include alms-

house censuses, reports of the superintendent of the almshouse, minute books of the commissioners of the almshouse and bride-well, nursing accounts, and registers of deaths, apprentice inden-tures, forced removals, and immigrant bonds. On the numbers of indigent immigrants in the almshouse, see *MCC*, IX, 609, X, 398, XI, 154, 414, XIII, 84, 739, XV, 414.

15. *New-York Gazette*, July 2, 1801; *The Medical Repository* (New York), V (1802), 69–70.

16. Account Book of Cash Distributions to the Poor, 1809–1816, Volume 0383, Alms House Records. Innumerable examples of such helpless individuals and families on outdoor relief or assisted by charity may be found throughout the Alms House Records; in New York Asylum for Lying-in Women, Minutes of the Visiting Com-mittee, 1823–1831, NYHS; in SRPW, Minute Books, 1797–1932, NYHS; and in Humane Society of the City of New York, Reports of the Visiting Committee, 1805–1815, NYHS.

17. Petition of Jacob Abrahams, January 17, 1786, Petitions, 1784–1787, City Clerk Documents, NYMA; Minutes of the Commissioners of the Alms House and Bridewell, 1791–1797, 19, NYPL; *MCC*, VI, 578–579, 585, 652, 666.

18. Petition of the French Benevolent Society, February 25, 1811, box 3149, City Clerk Documents; *Commercial Advertiser*, November 19, December 2, 1814, January 27, 1825, January 19, 1826; *New-York Evening Post*, February 18, 1817, January 26, 1825; SRPW, Minute Books, 1797–1932, entry for November 15, 1821.

19. *Daily Advertiser*, January 30, 1788.

20. *Ibid.*, January 30, 1788, January 13, 1791; Ely, *Visits of Mercy*, I, 39–40.

21. *Daily Advertiser*, January 13, 1791; *New-York Evening Post*, Oc-tober 12, 1804, December 9, 1817; *Republican Watch-Tower* (New York), January 23, 1805; *Commercial Advertiser*, August 19, 1817.

22. *Daily Advertiser*, December 9, 1808; *New-York Evening Post*, January 21, 1809; SRPW, Minute Books, 1797–1932, entry for November 16, 1820.

23. *Journal of the Assembly of the State of New York*, 47th session (1824), II, Appendix B, 44.

24. *Commercial Advertiser*, November 1, 1798; Peter Force, ed., *Ameri-can Archives*, 5th series (Washington, 1848), II, 1273.

25. *Commercial Advertiser*, November 28, 1809; *Columbian* (New York), December 30, 1818; Ely, *Visits of Mercy*, I, 65; *MCC*, XII, 158.

26. *Daily Advertiser*, September 6, 1798, September 4, 1799; *New-York Evening Post*, July 30, 1807; *Commercial Advertiser*, October 6, 1812; Petition of Peter Lial, July 17, 1815, box 3175, City Clerk Documents.

27. Presentment of Grand Jury to Court of General Sessions, March

12, 1824, box 3152, *ibid.;* John Stanford, Annual Report on the Bellevue Establishment, 1819, box 2, John Stanford Manuscripts, NYHS.

28. *New-York Evening Post,* June 8, 1804; Register of Persons Transported or Removed, 1808–1811, Volume 089, Alms House Records.

29. *New-York Evening Post,* February 11, 1805; Deposition of Josiah Shippey, Jr., June 24, 1808, box 3172, City Clerk Documents; Minutes of the Commissioners of the Alms House, 1791–1797, 229.

CHAPTER 3

1. W. K. Jordan, "The English Background of Modern Philanthropy," *American Historical Review,* LXVII (January 1961), 404. On British welfare policy and benevolence see David Owen, *English Philanthropy, 1660–1960* (Cambridge, Mass., 1964); Karl de Schweinitz, *England's Road to Social Security* (Philadelphia, 1943); and Samuel Mencher, *Poor Law to Poverty Program* (Pittsburgh, 1967).

2. *The Colonial Laws of New York* (5 vols., Albany, 1894), I, 24–25, 131–133. During the early Dutch period, the settlers of New Amsterdam imitated the charitable practices of Holland—a combination of religious and public relief. In 1661 the first general poor law in New Netherland stipulated poor relief as a governmental responsibility and authorized each town and village to raise and administer a "poor fund." *Laws and Ordinances of New Netherland, 1638–1674* (Albany, 1868), 411–412.

3. Richard B. Morris, ed., *Select Cases of the Mayor's Court of New York City, 1674–1784* (Washington, 1935), 67–71; *Minutes of the Common Council of the City of New York, 1675–1776* (8 vols., New York, 1905), I, 172, 205, 220, 258, 348, 387, II, 68, 330, IV, 309; Church Wardens Minutes, November 17, 1713, October 17, 1721, February 19, 1722, March 1, 1725, March 4, 1728.

4. *Ibid.,* January 24, 1700; Church Wardens Accounts, 1714–1738, box 50, New York City Miscellaneous Manuscripts, NYHS.

5. Church Wardens Minutes, November 24, 1697; Church Wardens Accounts, 1714, 1723–1735.

6. Church Wardens Minutes, September 20, 1700, November 10, 1713, February 2, 1732; *Common Council Minutes,* I, 212, 220, 391, 429, II, 206, III, 52–53, 83; *Colonial Laws,* I, 507–508, II, 56–61; *New-York Gazette,* February 16, 1731; *New-York Weekly Journal,* February 20, May 22, 1738; *Manual of the Corporation of the City of New-York for 1858* (New York, 1858), 570.

7. Church Wardens Minutes, February 15, 1700; *Common Council Minutes,* I, 417, III, 59–60; *New-York Gazette,* February 18, 1734.

8. *Colonial Laws,* II, 617; *Common Council Minutes,* IV, 240–241.

9. *Ibid.,* 305, 307–311; Church Wardens Minutes, April 6, May 4, June 3, 1736, January 7, 1737.

10. *Ibid.*, May 18, 1736, January 26, 1739; *New-York Gazette, or Weekly Post-Boy*, March 30, 1772.

11. *New-York Weekly Journal*, February 14, 1737, January 12, 19, 1741; Address of Lieutenant Governor George Clarke, April 5, 1737, in Charles Z. Lincoln, ed., *Messages from the Governors* (11 vols., Albany, 1909), I, 260; Church Wardens Minutes, February 2, 1732; *New-York Mercury*, November 13, 1752.

12. *New-York Evening Post*, November 9, 1747; *Common Council Minutes*, VI, 167; *New-York Gazette*, January 21, 1760, supplement; *New-York Gazette, or Weekly Post-Boy*, January 30, 1749, March 25, 1762.

13. *Independent Reflector* (New York), December 28, 1752, March 15, 1753.

14. Bridenbaugh, *Cities in Revolt*, 325; *Common Council Minutes*, VI, 403; *Colonial Laws*, V, 659–661; *New-York Gazette, or Weekly Post-Boy*, January 24, 1765, February 11, 1771, March 30, 1772; *New-York Gazette, and Weekly Mercury*, March 15, 1773; Petition of Vestrymen and Church Wardens to Provincial Congress, May 1776, in Force, ed., *American Archives*, 4th series (Washington, 1840), VI, 627.

15. *New-York Gazette, or Weekly Post-Boy*, June 18, 1750, January 13, 1772; *New-York Mercury*, July 23, 1753; *Common Council Minutes*, VI, 297–298, VII, 435, VIII, 75; *Colonial Laws*, V, 513–522; *New-York Gazette*, October 26, 1767; *New-York Journal*, November 12, 1767.

16. *New-York Gazette, or Weekly Post-Boy*, December 6, 1764, February 21, March 14, June 13, 1765; *New-York Journal*, December 31, 1767; *The Committee appointed . . . to consider of the Expediency of entering into Measures to encourage Industry and Frugality, and employ the Poor, Do Report . . .* , January 1768, broadside, NYPL; Force, ed., *American Archives*, 4th series, III, 1424–1426. The manufacturing program of the New York Society continued to function under direction of the Committee of Safety during the first half of 1776. See *American Archives*, 4th series, IV, 437, 1071–1072, 1104. Similar activities were carried out in Boston. See *Proposals for carrying on a Manufacture in the Town of Boston, for Employing the Poor of said Town*, March 1, 1768, broadside, NYPL.

17. *New-York Gazette, or Weekly Post-Boy*, August 19, 1751, May 19, 1763, January 8, 1767; *New-York Journal*, July 23, December 24, 1767, January 7, August 4, 1768; *New-York Mercury*, February 22, 1768; *To the Public. Whoever seriously considers the impoverished State of this City . . .* , January 15, 1770, broadside, NYHS.

18. *New-York Gazette, or Weekly Post-Boy*, July 6, 1752, November 28, 1768, July 5, 1773; *New-York Mercury*, December 30, 1754; *New-York Journal*, December 21, 1769, February 13, 1772; Issac N. P. Stokes, comp., *The Iconography of Manhattan Island* (6 vols., New

NOTES TO PAGES 49 TO 59

York, 1915–1928), IV, 841. On the changing character of Quaker charity, see Sidney V. James, *A People Among Peoples: Quaker Benevolence in Eighteenth-Century America* (Cambridge, Mass., 1963).

19. *Rules and Orders Agreed Upon by the Scots Society in New-York,* February 27, 1744, broadside, NYHS; *Articles and Regulations of the Friendly Society of Tradesmen, House Carpenters, in the City of New-York,* March 10, 1767, broadside, NYPL; *New-York Mercury,* November 13, 1752; *New-York Gazette, or Weekly Post-Boy,* December 31, 1753, August 27, 1761, March 27, 1769; *New-York Gazette, and Weekly Mercury,* December 11, 1769, April 4, 1774; *New-York Journal,* December 29, 1774.

20. *Constitutional Gazette* (New York), February 14, 1776; Force, ed., *American Archives,* 4th series, IV, 437, 1071–1072, 1121–1122, 5th series, I, 1539, 1563, III, 307; *Journals of the Provincial Congress, Provincial Convention, Committee of Safety and Council of Safety of the State of New-York, 1775–1776–1777* (2 vols., Albany, 1842), I, 518, 587, 710, 729, 916; Accounts of the State of New York to Various Persons for the Care of the Poor Refugees from New York City, 1776–86, New York City Miscellaneous Manuscripts, NYHS; *Laws,* 1st session, June 29, 1778, Chapter 38.

21. *Royal Gazette* (New York), December 27, 1777, February 14, 21, 1778; *New-York Gazette, and Weekly Mercury,* January 5, 12, July 20, 1778; New York City Accounts, 1778–1783, NYHS; Oscar T. Barck, *New York City During the War for Independence* (New York, 1931), 93.

CHAPTER 4

1. Edward Robb Ellis, *The Epic of New York City* (New York, 1966), 174; Barck, *New York City,* 207–230; Pomerantz, *New York,* 15–22.

2. *Laws,* 2nd session, October 23, 1799, Chapter 28; *New-York Packet,* November 24, 1783; *Independent New-York Gazette,* December 6, 1783.

3. *New-York Gazetteer,* December 10, 1783; *Independent Journal,* December 22, 1783, February 11, 1784; *MCC,* I, xiv; Pomerantz, *New York,* 25–31.

4. *Laws,* 7th session, April 17, 1784, Chapter 35; *ibid.,* April 20, 1784, Chapter 38.

5. *MCC,* I, 48–51; *Independent Journal,* February 18, 1784.

6. *Laws,* 8th session, March 18, 1785, Chapter 40; *MCC,* I, 140.

7. *Laws,* 7th session, April 17, 1784, Chapter 35.

8. *Ibid.,* 11th session, March 7, 1788, Chapter 62.

9. *Ibid.* The passport system was included in both the last colonial poor law of 1773 and in the law of 1784, but in neither case was its use specifically related to employment needs.

10. *Ibid.*, 20th session, April 3, 1797, Chapter 101; *ibid.*, 22nd session, April 1, 1799, Chapter 80.

11. *MCC*, IX, 410–411, X, 589–590.

12. Lincoln, ed., *Messages from the Governors*, II, 365; *MCC*, II, 416; Jacob de la Montagnie to Richard Varick, January 27, 1798, Richard Varick Papers, NYHS; *Laws*, 21st session, April 4, 1798, Chapter 89.

13. Stephen Allen to Charles Town, March 6, 1824, Letterbook, 1821–1849, Stephen Allen Papers, NYHS; *Laws*, 44th session, March 31, 1821, Chapter 220.

14. *Ibid.*, 24th session, April 8, 1801, Chapter 184; *ibid.*, 32nd session, March 24, 1809, Chapter 90; *ibid.*, 36th session, April 8, 1813, Chapter 78; *ibid.*, 38th session, October 21, 1814, Chapter 13.

15. Lincoln, ed., *Messages from the Governors*, II, 914, 915; *New-York Daily Advertiser*, February 17, 1820.

16. *Assembly Journal*, 47th session (1824), I, 393, 394.

17. *Ibid.*, 395–396; *Laws*, 47th session, November 27, 1824, Chapter 331. For an elaboration of later poor-law changes, see David M. Schneider, *The History of Public Welfare in New York State, 1609–1866* (Chicago, 1938), 233–253 and Martha Branscombe, *The Courts and the Poor Laws in New York State, 1784–1929* (Chicago, 1943), 30–48.

18. *Assembly Journal*, 47th session (1824), I, 389, II, Appendix B, 39–45; *MCC*, XIV, 770, XV, 90, 365–366; *New-York Daily Advertiser*, March 2, 1824; Stephen Allen to Charles Town, February 24, March 6, 1824, Allen Papers.

19. *Assembly Journal*, 47th session (1824), II, Appendix B, 45.

CHAPTER 5

1. *MCC*, I, 48–51.

2. *Ibid.*, 151, 229, 284, 367, 505, 521, 544.

3. *Ibid.*, 664; *Laws*, 11th session, March 7, 1788, Chapter 62.

4. Richard Varick to Jacob de la Montagnie, March 12, 1798, Richard Varick Papers, NYPL.

5. *Laws*, 21st session, April 3, 1798, Chapter 80; *MCC*, II, 436.

6. *Ibid.*, 661–672.

7. *Ibid.*, III, 7–8, 33–34.

8. *Ibid.*, V, 3–4, 16–17, 226, 786–787, VI, 513; Minutes of the Commissioners of the Alms House and Bridewell, 1808–1829, entry for July 27, 1808, Volume 0194, Alms House Records.

9. *Laws*, 11th session, March 7, 1788, Chapter 62; *MCC*, II, 665–672.

10. Minutes of the Commisisoners of the Alms House, 1791–1797, 46–47, 55, 98, 194, 198–199.

11. Minutes of the Commissioners of the Alms House, 1808–1829, entry for March 22, 1808.

12. The occupational breakdown has been achieved by matching the

names of almshouse commissioners against the city directories of the year of appointment.

13. A large number of such petitions may be found in the City Clerk Documents.

14. *MCC*, VI, 572–573, 696, IX, 152, X, 396, XII, 455, XV, 613.

15. Committee of Health, Minutes, 1793–1796, entries for October 8, November 2, 13, 1795, NYHS; James Hardie, *An Account of the Malignant Fever Lately Prevalent in the City of New-York* (New York, 1799), 49–64; *MCC*, III, 675, IV, 698, 702–704; *New-York Evening Post*, January 22, 1805.

16. *Laws*, 2nd session, March 13, 1779, Chapter 34; Hardie, *Account of the Malignant Fever*, 7; *MCC*, III, 7, 33–34.

17. *Ibid.*, II, 661–672; Minutes of the Commissioners of the Alms House, 1808–1829, entry for March 22, 1808.

18. *MCC*, III, 45, 744–745; *New-York Evening Post*, July 17, 18, 1805, August 14, 1806.

19. *MCC*, IV, 344–345, 361; *New-York Evening Post*, November 7, 1805, January 5, 1807; *Commercial Advertiser*, May 7, 8, 1805, February 4, 1807; *American Citizen* (New York), May 8, 1805, November 6, 12, 14, 15, 19, 1806, February 4, 1807. On the libel suit, see William Sampson, *A Faithful Report of the Trial of the Cause of Philip I. Arcularius, and William Coleman, Gent. Etc. Being an Action for a Libel* (New York, 1807).

20. *MCC*, IV, 725, V, 11, 35; *New-York Evening Post*, February 18, 1808.

21. *MCC*, V, 40, 57; Minutes of the Commissioners of the Alms House, 1808–1829, entries for March 2, 22, April 5, 1808.

22. *Ibid.*, entries for May 6, 10, 1808; Deposition of Josiah Shippey, Jr., June 24, 1808, box 3172, City Clerk Documents; Interrogatories presented to Wm. Few Esqr. in behalf of the Commissioners, to be put to the officers of the Alms House, July 18, 1808, box 3172, City Clerk Documents; *MCC*, V, 116.

23. *Ibid.*, 157, 164, 202, 221–222, 226; Minutes of the Commissioners of the Alms House, 1808–1829, entries for June 13, July 27, 1808; Deposition of Josiah Shippey, Jr., June 24, 1808, box 3172, City Clerk Documents.

24. *MCC*, V, 651, 714–727; Report of the Committee on Mooney Investigation, October 30, 1809, box 3172, City Clerk Documents.

25. *MCC*, V, 670–671, 780–781; *New-York Evening Post*, November 14, 15, 16, 17, 1809; *Public Advertiser* (New York), November 15, 18, 1809; *American Citizen*, November 20, 1809; *Commercial Advertiser*, December 13, 1809.

26. *Laws*, 37th session, April 15, 1814, Chapter 176; *ibid.*, 44th session, January 22, 1821, Chapter 13; *Commercial Advertiser*, November 15, 1814; Protest of Minority of the Common Council on the Appointment of the Superintendent of the Alms House, October 31, 1814, box 3165, City Clerk Documents; Resolutions Relative to

Applications to the Legislature, December 26, 1820, box 3165, City Clerk Documents; *MCC*, VII, 660–662, 703–704, VIII, 776, XI, 445, XII, 68.

CHAPTER 6

1. Franklin D. Scott, trans. and ed., *Baron Klinkowstrom's America, 1818–1820* (Evanston, Ill., 1952), 111–112; Anne Royall, *Sketches of History, Life, and Manners, in the United States* (New Haven, 1826), 251.

2. *MCC*, I, 35, 505, II, 124–125, 212.

3. Minutes of the Commissioners of the Alms House, 1791–1797, 7, 43–44, 77, 88, 136, 144, 166, 181; *MCC*, I, 229, 284, 314, 387, 452, 544, 760, II, 52, 185, 191, 192–193.

4. *Laws*, 18th session, April 6, 1795, Chapter 51; *MCC*, II, 60, 239, 343, 358; Minutes of the Commissioners of the Alms House, 1791–1797, 247; *Daily Advertiser*, May 27, 1795.

5. *Commercial Advertiser*, January 25, 1817; *MCC*, VI, 501–502, 561–563, VII, 423.

6. William P. Cutler and Julia P. Cutler, eds., *Life, Journals and Correspondence of Rev. Manasseh Cutler, LL.D.* (2 vols., Cincinnati, 1888), I, 307; *MCC*, II, 100–101, VI, 557, 561–563; Committee of Health, Minutes, 1793–1796, entry for September 10, 1794; *Daily Advertiser*, September 28, 1798.

7. *New-York Evening Post*, August 8, 1811, July 3, 1815; *MCC*, VI, 578, 628, VII, 184–185, 327, VIII, 232–236, 488; Royall, *Sketches*, 251; *Inquirer* (Nantucket, Mass.), December 27, 1824.

8. *MCC*, IX, 481; Royall, *Sketches*, 249; Dwight, *Travels*, III, 438–440; Zerah Hawley, *A Journal of a Tour Through Connecticut, Massachusetts, New-York, the North Part of Pennsylvania and Ohio* (New Haven, 1822), 154.

9. Stokes, comp., *Iconography*, VI, 208–209.

10. *Independent Journal*, March 18, 1786; *Commercial Advertiser*, January, 25, 1817, January 5, 1820; *New-York Evening Post*, January 15, 1825.

11. *MCC*, X, 398. For the almshouse commissioners' reports, see *MCC*, VII, 423, 741, VIII, 204, IX, 609, XI, 153, XII, 414, XIII, 84, 739, XV, 414. See also the manuscript almshouse census reports, volumes 160, 161, 162, 178, 179, 212, Alms House Records.

12. Royall, *Sketches*, 255.

13. *Daily Advertiser*, November 3, 1788; Account of Monies expended by the Commissioners of the Almshouse and Bridewell . . . after the 1st of May 1796, Volume 145, Alms House Records; *MCC*, XI, 476–477.

14. *Ibid.*, VIII, 204–205; *Commercial Advertiser*, June 5, 1817; *New-York Evening Post*, June 3, 1819.

15. Royall, *Sketches*, 249–250; Samuel S. Griscom, Journal of a Tour

Thro N Jersey, Penna and N York with occasional remarks on the People, Literary Characters Ladies Institutions, etc., 1824, 27, NYHS; De Witt Clinton, Diary, 1802–1828, entries for November 19, 20, 1823, NYHS.

16. Royall, *Sketches*, 250; Ely, *Visits of Mercy*, I, 153, II, 49, 71, 76, 95, 121–122; *MCC*, IV, 227, V, 434, X, 466.

17. Ely, *Visits of Mercy*, I, 88, 89, II, 28–29; John Stanford, Annual Report to the Society for Supporting the Gospel among the Poor, December 31, 1823, Stanford Manuscripts.

18. *Ordinances, Rules and Bye-Laws, for the Government of the Alms-House, and House of Employment, of the City of New-York*, June 16, 1784, broadside, NYHS; Minutes of the Commissioners of the Alms House, 1791–1797, 32, 41; *MCC*, II, 662; Minutes of the Commissioners of the Alms House, 1808–1829, entry for April 5, 1808.

19. Ely, *Visits of Mercy*, I, 86–87; *Ordinances, Rules and Bye-Laws; MCC*, II, 126, XII, 149; *New-York Evening Post*, January 23, 1811; *Laws*, 45th session, February 4, 1822, Chapter 13.

20. Minutes of the Commissioners of the Alms House, 1791–1797, 187, 195, 249; *MCC*, I, 302, 734, II, 464, XIII, 173.

21. Minutes of the Commissioners of the Alms House, 1791–1797, 13–14; *MCC*, I, 251, III, 181–182, XIII, 173; *New-York Daily Gazette*, November 12, 1789; *Daily Advertiser*, April 9, 1791; Helen M. Morgan, ed., *A Season in New York, 1801: Letters of Harriet and Maria Trumbull* (Pittsburgh, 1969), 131; *Commercial Advertiser*, April 26, 1806.

22. *MCC*, I, 66, III, 49; Minutes of the Commissioners of the Alms House, 1791–1797, 32, 42, 67–68, 181–182, 212.

23. *MCC*, IX, 77–78, XI, 77; *New-York Evening Post*, August 28, 1806; Felix Pascalis to Common Council, November 31, 1816, box 3175, City Clerk Documents; Report of a Committee Recommending Changes in the Medical Department at Bellevue, March 31, 1817, box 3181, *ibid*.

24. Minutes of the Commissioners of the Alms House, 1791–1797, 21, 202, 255; *MCC*, I, 185, II, 750, III, 9, VIII, 559, IX, 760, X, 7, XIII, 732–733, XV, 56.

25. *Ibid.*, III, 337; Minutes of the Commissioners of the Alms House, 1791–1797, 37.

26. *Ibid.*, 196; *MCC*, XIII, 92, 203–205; Petition of Dunbar Sloan, January 25, 1819, box 3176, City Clerk Documents; John Stanford, Annual Report on the Bellevue Establishment for 1822, December 1, 1822, Stanford Manuscripts.

27. *MCC*, I, 169, II, 662.

28. *New-York Evening Post*, August 16, 1809, May 29, 1817, March 4, 1820; *MCC*, I, 670, II, 180, 451, V, 586, 719–720, VI, 90, IX, 627, XI, 423; Minutes of the Commissioners of the Alms House, 1791–1797, 209, 250; John Pintard to Health Committee, August 1, 1804, box 3172, City Clerk Documents.

CHAPTER 7

1. Minutes of the Commissioners of the Alms House, 1791–1797, 15, 46–47, 53, 98, 100, 191, 194, 195, 238; *MCC*, I, 619, 696; *Daily Advertiser*, February 5, 1796.
2. *New-York Evening Post*, November 17, 1809; *MCC*, IV, 325, 339.
3. *Ibid.*, I, 267, VII, 173; Philip Arcularius to Common Council, October 30, 1805, box 3155, City Clerk Documents; *Columbian*, January 25, 1814. Reporting in 1815 that Mayor Clinton had lent money to an evicted tenant, an anonymous correspondent suggested that "for the good of the community, and especially the poor we thought they ought to know who are their real friends, and who not." *New-York Evening Post*, March 6, 1815. The link between poverty and politics was not new. One newspaper printed reports in April 1772 that two aldermen "had within the space of one month, during the late winter, drawn out of the hands of the Church-wardens £900 under pretence of supplying the needy, the poor, and the indigent; but in truth . . . with intent to secure their elections by bribing the voters with the public money." *New-York Journal*, April 30, 1772.
4. *Commercial Advertiser*, February 7, 1799; *New-York Evening Post*, February 26, 1806.
5. Committee of Health, Minutes, 1793–1796; *MCC*, III, 651, 712.
6. Richard Varick to Matthew Clarkson, October 6, 1795, in *Daily Advertiser*, October 8, 1795; Committee of Health, Minutes, 1793–1796, entries for September 10, 1794, October 5, 8, November 13, 1795, January 28, 1796.
7. Duffy, *History of Public Health in New York City*, 104–105.
8. *Daily Advertiser*, September 28, October 8, 9, November 3, 1798; Hardie, *Account of the Malignant Fever*, 49–64.
9. *Commercial Advertiser*, December 8, 1798, February 12, 1799; *Daily Advertiser*, February 1, 1799.
10. *New-York Evening Post*, September 30, October 26, 1803, November 14, 1805; *Commercial Advertiser*, November 14, 1805; Philip Arcularius to Common Council, October 30, 1805, box 3155, City Clerk Documents; De Witt Clinton to Robert Smith, September 21, 1805, reel 5, Clinton Papers.
11. *Daily Advertiser*, January 13, 1791; *New-York Evening Post*, October 12, 1804.
12. Report of the City Inspector concerning Fuel for the Poor, October 15, 1804, box 3172, City Clerk Documents.
13. *MCC*, III, 675, 676; Petition of the Corporation to the State Legislature, January 23, 1805, reel 5, Clinton Papers; De Witt Clinton to Members of the Assembly from the City and County of New York, January 23, 1805, *ibid.*; *New-York Evening Post*, January 29, 1805; *American Citizen*, February 4, 1805; *Laws*, 28th session, January 30, 1805, Chapter 3.

14. *MCC*, III, 665, 676, 688; *New-York Evening Post*, January 15, 17, 18, 19, 22, 23, 24, 28, February 5, 1805; Horatio Gates to De Witt Clinton, February 6, 1805, reel 1, Clinton Papers.

15. *Mercantile Advertiser* (New York), December 31, 1807; *Commercial Advertiser*, January 6, 20, 1808; *New-York Evening Post*, August 26, 1808. A foreign traveler who commented on the economic results of the embargo in New York City was John Lambert, *Travels Through Canada, and the United States of North America in the Years 1806, 1807, & 1808* (2 vols., London, 1814), II, 64–65, 294–295.

16. *MCC*, IV, 700–701; *New-York Evening Post*, January 9, 1808. See also George Daitsman, "Labor and the 'Welfare State' in Early New York," *Labor History*, IV (Fall 1963), 248–256.

17. *MCC*, IV, 702–704, 713–715, V, 123–124; *Laws*, 31st session, April 6, 1808, Chapter 131; *American Citizen*, May 18, 1808; *Daily Advertiser*, December 9, 1808.

18. *MCC*, V, 364, 423, 430–431, 471; William Mooney to Common Council, January 16, 1809, box 3172, City Clerk Documents; Henry Dearborn to De Witt Clinton, December 14, 1808, box 3180, *ibid.*

19. *MCC*, V, 316, 396, 494; Report of Commissioners of the Alms House, April 3, 1809, box 3172, City Clerk Documents; *New-York Evening Post*, April 5, 1809.

20. *MCC*, V, 494–495; *American Citizen*, May 18, 1808; *Daily Advertiser*, December 21, 1808; *Mercantile Advertiser*, December 31, 1808; *New-York Evening Post*, January 21, February 6, 1809; *Commercial Advertiser*, January 24, 1809.

21. *MCC*, VII, 424, VIII, 82, 204–205, 401–402; Report of Committee of Charity, December 4, 1815, box 3175, City Clerk Documents; *Columbian*, January 25, 1814.

22. George Dangerfield, *The Awakening of American Nationalism, 1815–1828* (New York, 1965), 72–74. See also Murray N. Rothbard, *The Panic of 1819: Reactions and Policies* (New York, 1962), 1–23.

23. *Assembly Journal*, 40th session (1816–1817), 41; *Journal of the Senate of the State of New York*, 40th session (1816–1817), 26, 29; *MCC*, VIII, 682–683, 767; *New-York Evening Post*, November 11, 1816; *Commercial Advertiser*, February 8, 1817.

24. *MCC*, VIII, 681–685, 751, 763, 765–769; *New-York Evening Post*, November 11, 1816; *Commercial Advertiser*, January 25, 1817.

25. *MCC*, XV, 90; *Assembly Journal*, 40th session (1816–1817), 81, 241–243, 245–247.

26. *Commercial Advertiser*, February 8, 1817; *New-York Evening Post*, February 18, March 1, 12, 1817; *MCC*, IX, 361; Memorial of a Committee Appointed by a Meeting of Citizens, March 8, 1817, box 3181, City Clerk Documents.

27. SPP, *Report on Pauperism*, 3.

28. Report of a Special Committee on the Subject of Providing for the Poor, November 17, 1817, box 3181, City Clerk Documents; *MCC*, IX, 143, 159, 162, 360–362; *Commercial Advertiser*, May 22, 1817; *New-York Evening Post*, November 26, 1817.

29. Memorial of a Committee Appointed by a Meeting of Citizens, March 8, 1817, box 3181, City Clerk Documents; *MCC*, IX, 38–39, 62–63; *New-York Evening Post*, March 12, 1817, February 24, March 9, 10, 1818.

CHAPTER 8

1. Merrill Jensen, *The New Nation: A History of the United States during the Confederation, 1781–1789* (New York, 1950), 302–303, 309–310; E. Wilder Spaulding, *New York in the Critical Period, 1783–1789* (New York, 1932), 5–29; *New-York Daily Gazette*, August 14, 1789; *Daily Advertiser*, December 2, 1789.

2. Petition of William Kerr and 45 Others Imprisoned for Debt in New York to the State Legislature, March 24, 1812, folder K, John W. Taylor Papers, NYHS; *Daily Advertiser*, December 5, 1798; *Gazette of the United States* (New York), October 6, 1790.

3. Marinus Willett to De Witt Clinton, March 11, 1790, reel 1, Clinton Papers; *Columbian*, September 6, October 3, 1810, February 14, 1811; *New-York Evening Post*, June 15, 1811; Presentment of Grand Jury of the Court of General Sessions, September 13, 1820, box 3165, City Clerk Documents.

4. SRDD, Petition to the State Legislature, December 12, 1788, in *Manual of the Corporation of the City of New York for 1869* (New York, 1869), 862–863; *Commercial Advertiser*, January 4, 1810; Julian Ursyn Niemcewicz, *Under Their Vine and Fig Tree: Travels through America in 1797–1799, 1805 with Some Further Account of Life in New Jersey*, trans. and ed. by Metchie J. E. Budka (*Collections* of the New Jersey Historical Society, XIV, 1965), 17; Petition of Humane Society to the State Legislature, n.d., reel 6, Clinton Papers; *New-York Evening Post*, March 15, 1806, August 18, 24, 1810, January 25, 1811; *Columbian*, August 13, 1810; *American Citizen*, September 28, 1810; *Shamrock* (New York), December 22, 1810. During the 1790's the New York pound was equivalent to $2.50 and a shilling to twelve and one-half cents.

5. Edwin T. Randall, "Imprisonment for Debt in America: Fact and Fiction," *Mississippi Valley Historical Review*, XXXIX (June 1952), 89–102. For descriptions of the New York City "liberties," see Gaol Limits, as Laid Down by Mangin, City Surveyor, July 1802, box 16, New York City Miscellaneous Manuscripts; *New-York Evening Post*, May 9, 1817.

6. *Independent Journal*, January 20, 1787; *A Sketch of the Origin and*

Progress of the Humane Society of the City of New-York (New York, 1814), 3; William Cock to James Duane, November 15, 1788, box 7, Duane Papers; *Daily Advertiser*, February 11, 1793, February 11, 1794, January 28, 1799.

7. *Ibid.*, January 30, 1788; *Sketch of the Humane Society*, 3.

8. *Daily Advertiser*, January 30, 1788, January 25, February 18, October 23, December 23, 1789, December 28, 1791, February 11, March 6, June 7, 1794; *Independent Journal*, October 23, September 10, 1788; *Commercial Advertiser*, November 20, 1798; *New-York Weekly Museum*, January 10, 1789, May 15, 1790.

9. *Daily Advertiser*, February 21, 1789, May 13, 1791, March 1, 1795, February 17, 1798, January 28, 1799; *New-York Evening Post*, January 9, 1802, January 8, 1803.

10. SRDD, Petition to the State Legislature, December 12, 1788, *Manual of the Corporation*, 862–863; Petition of Humane Society to the State Legislature, n.d., reel 6, Clinton Papers; *Laws*, 12th session, February 13, 1789, Chapter 24; *ibid.*, 14th session, March 21, 1791, Chapter 39; *ibid.*, 24th session, March 24, 1801, Chapter 66; *Sketch of the Humane Society*, 4–5.

11. Humane Society to De Witt Clinton, February 5, 1805, box 3155, City Clerk Documents; De Witt Clinton to Thomas Storm and Jacob Morton, February 14, 1805, reel 5, Clinton Papers; *MCC*, III, 684; *New-York Daily Gazette*, November 4, 1790; *Daily Advertiser*, September 1, October 20, 1790, January 1, 5, 15, 24, February 10, December 27, 28, 30, 1791, October 1, 3, 26, November 5, 1798, January 28, 1799; *Commercial Advertiser*, January 7, 1800; Samuel Miller, *Memoirs of the Rev. John Rodgers, D.D.* (New York, 1813), 337–338.

12. *New-York Evening Post*, January 8, 1803.

13. *Ibid.*, October 12, November 6, 1802, March 9, 1803; *Morning Chronicle* (New York), October 14, 1802; *Weekly Visitor* (New York), October 16, 1802; *Sketch of the Humane Society*, 6–7.

14. *New-York Evening Post*, August 27, November 16, 1803, February 5, April 11, 1805, March 15, 1806; *Daily Advertiser*, March 8, 1804; *Commercial Advertiser*, September 11, 1806, February 20, 1807; *MCC*, IV, 168, 178, 211, 240.

15. Humane Society, Reports of the Visiting Committee, 1805–1815, NYHS; *New-York Evening Post*, February 12, 1812.

16. *Laws*, 40th session, April 15, 1817, Chapter 260; *New-York Daily Advertiser*, December 6, 1824; *MCC*, XIV, 220; Royall, *Sketches*, 252.

17. *New-York Evening Post*, January 21, 1819, February 17, 1821, March 6, 1822.

18. *Commercial Advertiser*, February 20, 1807; *Sketch of the Humane Society*, 7; Elizabeth H. Thomson, "The Role of Physicians in the Humane Societies of the Eighteenth Century," *Bulletin of the History of Medicine*, XXXVII (1963), 43–51. The City Dispensary

initiated resuscitation operations in New York City in 1791. See *Daily Advertiser*, December 30, 1791, June 26, 1792.

19. David Hosack, *An Enquiry into the Causes of Suspended Animation from Drowning; with the Means of Restoring Life* (New York, 1792), 26–33.

20. *Directions for the Recovery of Persons Apparently Dead from Drowning*, 1806, broadside, NYHS; *New-York Evening Post*, December 6, 1806; *People's Friend* (New York), December 9, 1806; *Commercial Advertiser*, January 6, 1807; *Longworth's American Almanac, New-York Register, and City Directory, 1816–1817* (New York, 1816), 4–5; *Blunt's Stranger's Guide to the City of New-York* (New York, 1817), 297–298; Hosack, *An Enquiry*, iii–iv.

21. Ebenezer Burling to Humane Society [c. 1815], Society for the Suppression of Vice and Immorality Manuscripts, box 4, John Jay Papers, NYHS; *MCC*, vii, 345–346, viii, 379; Report of Committee on Applications to the Legislature, March 1, 1819, box 3176, City Clerk Documents.

22. *New-York Daily Advertiser*, June 18, 1819.

23. *A Report of a Committee of the Humane Society Appointed to Inquire into the Number of Tavern Licenses; the Manner of Granting Them; Their Effects upon the Community; and the Other Sources of Vice and Misery in This City* (New York, 1810). The report is also printed in the *Commercial Advertiser*, December 30, 1809. See *Public Advertiser*, January 19, 1810, for a public challenge to the accuracy of the Humane Society report.

24. *New-York Evening Post*, January 3, 12, 29, 1810; *MCC*, vi, 55, 91; Report of a Committee on the Petition of Several Charitable Societies, February 26, 1810, box 3174, City Clerk Documents; Petition of Committees of a Number of Charitable Societies and Institutions in the City of New-York to the State Legislature [c. 1810], box 4, Jay Papers.

25. *MCC*, iv, 261, 281, 729, vii, 770, ix, 439, 484, x, 663–664, xi, 460–461, xii, 168, 716, xvi, 672–673, xvii, 596; *Commercial Advertiser*, February 19, 1823; *New-York Daily Advertiser*, February 19, 1824; Humane Society Petitions to Common Council, January 18, 1808 (box 3180), January 20, 1817 (box 3181), January 5, 1818 (box 3176), February 16, 1818 (box 3176), December 2, 1819 (box 3176), January 26, 1824 (box 3152), City Clerk Documents.

26. De Witt Clinton to John Rodgers, April 26, 1805, reel 5, Clinton Papers; De Witt Clinton to Humane Society, February 11, 1809, *ibid.*; Petition of Humane Society to State Legislature, n.d. (draft copy in Clinton's handwriting), reel 6, *ibid.*; *Daily Advertiser*, October 3, 1798; *Commercial Advertiser*, February 21, 1817, January 24, 25, 1822; Felix Pascalis to Common Council, November 14, 1808, box 3180, City Clerk Documents.

27. For editorial endorsements of the Humane Society, see *Weekly Visitor*, October 16, 1802; *New-York Evening Post*, February 5,

1805; *Commercial Advertiser,* January 20, 1808; *New-York Magazine,* I (July 1814), 138; *New-York Daily Advertiser,* January 21, 1819. For a sampling of the reform literature, see *Time-Piece* (New York), December 13, 18, 25, 1797; *Columbian,* July 31, August 6, 13, 23, September 7, 10, 15, 19, October 3, 16, 20, 31, December 18, 1810, January 3, 12, 14, 24, 1811; *New-York Evening Post,* August 15, October 8, 12, 1810, February 28, March 1, 3, 4, 5, 8, 15, 18, 19, 20, 22, 25, 1817; *Public Advertiser,* September 26, 28, October 2, 4, 6, 8, 9, 17, 18, 19, 1810; *Commercial Advertiser,* March 13, 14, 18, 19, 21, 25, 1817.

28. *Forlorn Hope* (New York), March 24, 31, May 3, 10, 17, 24, August 30, September 13, 1800. The publication of *Forlorn Hope* was soon followed by the appearance of a second newspaper, *Prisoner of Hope* (New York), edited and published by William Sing between May 3 and August 23, 1800. Ostensibly published in the interest of imprisoned debtors, *Prisoner of Hope* was devoted to general news and hoped to profit from the patronage of humanitarian New Yorkers. See Clarence S. Brigham, *History and Bibliography of American Newspapers, 1690–1820* (2 vols., Worcester, Mass., 1947), I, 633, 681.

29. Humane Society members were listed each year in the New York City directories and in the annual reports of the organization.

30. *New-York Evening Post,* January 23, 1828, January 22, 1829, January 4, 25, 27, February 25, 26, 1831; *Laws,* 54th session, April 26, 1831, Chapter 300; *New-York Gazette,* October 16, 1832; *Proceedings of the Board of Aldermen,* III (1832), 26, 264, 270, XIV (1838), 306, 309. See also Samuel Rezneck, "The Social History of an American Depression, 1837–1843," *American Historical Review,* XL (July 1935), 662–687.

31. Oscar Handlin, "The Social System," in Lloyd Rodwin, ed., *The Future Metropolis* (New York, 1961), 17–41; Oscar and Mary Handlin, *The Dimensions of Liberty* (Cambridge, Mass., 1961), 89–112; Philip M. Hauser, "Urbanization: An Overview," in Philip M. Hauser and Leo F. Schnore, eds., *The Study of Urbanization* (New York, 1965), 25; Stephan Thernstrom, *Poverty and Progress: Social Mobility in a Nineteenth Century City* (Cambridge, Mass., 1964), 168–170.

CHAPTER 9

1. *New-York Evening Post,* January 15, 17, 18, 22, February 19, 1805.
2. *Commercial Advertiser,* January 9, 24, 1809; *New-York Evening Post,* January 21, 1809; *American Citizen,* January 24, March 1, 1809; *MCC,* V, 413–414, 429–430.
3. *Mercantile Advertiser,* December 31, 1808; *Constitution of the Assistance Society, for Relieving and Advising Sick and Poor Persons*

in the City of New-York (New York, 1809); *New-York Evening Post,* February 6, 1809.

4. *Ibid.*, January 5, 1810.

5. *Commercial Advertiser,* January 8, December 30, 1813, February 1, 1814; *Columbian,* December 20, 1811.

6. *New-York Evening Post,* January 5, 1810; *Columbian,* December 20, 1811; *Commercial Advertiser,* December 9, 1814; *Constitution of the Assistance Society,* 13.

7. This occupational breakdown has been achieved by comparing the names of managers with the city directories, a task eased by the fact that Assistance Society annual reports listed not only names but addresses of managers.

8. *New-York Gazette,* December 21, 1812; *New-York Evening Post,* December 18, 21, 23, 1813; *Commercial Advertiser,* March 9, 1814. On later efforts, see Petition of John Murray, Jr., and Others on Subject of Fuel for the Poor, April 8, 1816, box 3181, City Clerk Documents.

9. *New-York Evening Post,* February 17, 18, March 1, 10, 1817.

10. *Daily Advertiser,* September 1, October 20, 1790, January 1, 24, December 30, 1791.

11. *Ibid.*, December 30, 1791, June 26, 1792; *New-York Evening Post,* January 28, February 1, 1802, April 27, 1805, November 30, 1807, January 29, 1811, January 26, 1825; *New-York Gazette,* December 28, 1807.

12. David Hosack to De Witt Clinton, January 8, 1810, box 3174, City Clerk Documents; *MCC,* IV, 23, VI, 51, 348, VII, 406–407, VIII, 407–408, IX, 538–540; *New-York Evening Post,* January 3, 1816.

13. Samuel Bard, *A Discourse Upon the Duties of a Physician, with Some Sentiments, on the Usefulness and Necessity of a Public Hospital* (New York, 1769), 15; Isaac Collins, *An Account of the New-York Hospital* (New York, 1811), 3–15.

14. *Laws,* 11th session, March 1, 1788, Chapter 48; *ibid.*, 15th session, April 11, 1792, Chapter 67; *ibid.*, 18th session, March 31, 1795, Chapter 37; *ibid.*, 19th session, April 11, 1796, Chapter 57; *ibid.*, 24th session, March 20, 1801, Chapter 26; *ibid.*, 28th session, March 2, 1805, Chapter 21; *ibid.*, 29th session, March 14, 1806, Chapter 44; *ibid.*, 33rd session, March 23, 1810, Chapter 88.

15. Collins, *Account of the New-York Hospital,* 5–6, 29–55; François Alexandre Frédéric, duc de la Rochefoucauld Liancourt, *Travels Through the United States of North America* (2 vols., London, 1799), II, 460; Royall, *Sketches,* 245–246.

16. *New-York Evening Post,* July 12, 1802, August 10, 1808, March 22, 1816, May 30, 1821, March 24, 1825; *New-York Daily Advertiser,* March 23, 1821; *Commercial Advertiser,* November 20, 1823; *MCC,* V, 216; *Laws,* 39th session, April 17, 1816, Chapter 203; Thomas Eddy, *Hints for Introducing an Improved Mode of Treating the Insane in the Asylum* (New York, 1815).

17. *New-York Evening Post*, December 11, 1816, January 21, 1817, August 24, 1821, January 14, 1822, August 15, 1823, February 16, 1824; *Commercial Advertiser*, July 29, 1818.

18. Joanna Bethune, *The Power of Faith: Exemplified in the Life and Writings of the Late Mrs. Isabella Graham of New-York* (New York, 1816), 46–54; SRPW, *Constitution* . . . (New York, 1799); SRPW, Minute Books, 1797–1932, entries for December 13, 1802, February 13, 1804, April 23, 1805, November 8, 1809; *New-York Evening Post*, January 19, 1803, May 8, 1805.

19. SRPW, Minute Books, 1797–1932, entries for February 1, 1808, November 21, 1822; *MCC*, III, 732, IV, 124, VIII, 359–360; *Laws*, 26th session, April 3, 1803, Chapter 68; *New-York Evening Post*, December 5, 1821.

20. SRPW, *Constitution*; SRPW, Minute Books, 1797–1932, entries for January 20, 1803, February 3, March 30, 1812, March 27, 1813, January 6, 1817, November 3, 1823.

21. *Mercantile Advertiser*, March 15, 1806; *New-York Evening Post*, July 31, 1810, February 22, July 5, 1814, February 7, September 7, 1815, December 2, 1816, November 13, December 1, 1819; *Commercial Advertiser*, May 13, December 11, 1811, January 19, 1826. For more specific information on these charities, see Raymond A. Mohl, "Poverty, Public Relief, and Private Charity in New York City, 1784–1825" (unpublished Ph.D. dissertation, New York University, 1967), 242–256.

22. SRPW, Minute Books, 1797–1932, entry for March 1, 1816.

23. *Christian Herald*, XI (October 16, 1824), 632.

24. See Mohl, "Poverty, Public Relief, and Private Charity," 266–268.

25. *Commercial Advertiser*, December 2, 1800; *New-York Evening Post*, December 1, 1801, December 1, 1802; Petition of the French Benevolent Society, February 25, 1811, box 3149, City Clerk Documents. See also Erna Risch, "Immigrant Aid Societies before 1820," *Pennsylvania Magazine of History and Biography*, LX (January 1936), 15–33.

26. *Commercial Advertiser*, January 4, 1799; *Mercantile Advertiser*, January 3, 1813; *New-York Evening Post*, March 3, 1820, January 12, 1826.

27. La Rochefoucauld Liancourt, *Travels*, II, 461; *Laws*, 30th session, February 27, 1807, Chapter 23; *Mercantile Advertiser*, December 6, 1808.

28. For Protestant denominations, see Theodore Fiske Savage, *The Presbyterian Church in New York City* (New York, 1949), 48, and Floyd Appleton, *Church Philanthropy in New York* (New York, 1906), which deals with Episcopal charity, mainly after 1825. On the Quakers, see John Cox, Jr., *Quakerism in the City of New York, 1657–1930* (New York, 1930), 42–43 and New York Meeting for Sufferings, Minutes, 1758–1796, 1796–1821, Haviland Records Room, Society of Friends, New York City. On Catholics, see *New-*

York Evening Post, June 12, 1816, February 14, 18, 1817; Sister Marie de Lourdes Walsh, *The Sisters of Charity in New York, 1809–1959* (3 vols., New York, 1960), I, 29, 40, 48–50. On the Jews, see Hyman B. Grinstein, *The Rise of the Jewish Community of New York, 1654–1860* (Philadelphia, 1945), 104, 131–155.

29. Dwight, *Travels,* III, 440.

30. EMSYM, *Proceedings of the First Anniversary . . .* (New York, 1817), 12; Report of Auxiliary Societies Committee, November 18, 1819, Managers Minutes, American Bible Society Manuscripts, ABS; *Commercial Advertiser,* December 30, 1813, June 6, 1819.

CHAPTER 10

1. *Daily Advertiser,* January 30, 1788; *New-York Evening Post,* January 5, 1810; *Commercial Advertiser,* March 19, 1814; James Milnor, *The Widow and Her Mites* (New York, 1819), 9.

2. John Rodgers, Sermon for the Presbyterian Charity School, November 6, 1791, Manuscript Sermons, 1775–1806, John Rodgers Papers, NYHS; *Forlorn Hope,* May 10, 1800; John B. Romeyn, *The Good Samaritan* (New York, 1810), 8; Milnor, *The Widow and Her Mites,* 11; *New-York Gazette,* December 9, 1815.

3. *Commercial Advertiser,* December 30, 1813; Romeyn, *Good Samaritan,* 10; John McVickar, *An Address, Delivered before the Auxiliary New-York Bible and Common Prayer Book Society* (New York, 1818), 5.

4. *New-York Evening Post,* January 28, 1805; *Commercial Advertiser,* January 22, 1805; De Witt Clinton, *An Address, Delivered before Holland Lodge, December 24, 1793* (New York, 1859), 15.

5. *Gazette of the United States,* December 16, 1789; *Mercantile Advertiser,* October 15, 1802; *Weekly Visitor,* March 3, 1804; *Columbian,* August 6, 1810; *Commercial Advertiser,* February 17, 1814; McVickar, *Address before Auxiliary,* 5; Gardiner Spring, *A Sermon, Preached April 21, 1811, for the Benefit of a Society of Ladies, Instituted for the Relief of Poor Widows with Small Children* (New York, 1811), 18; Clinton, *Address before Holland Lodge,* 15. See also De Witt Clinton, *An Oration, On Benevolence, Delivered before the Society of Black Friars, in the City of New-York, At Their Anniversary Festival, On the 10th November, 1794* (New York, 1795).

6. *New-York Daily Gazette,* January 4, 1791; *New-York Evening Post,* January 15, 1805, January 5, 1810; *Commercial Advertiser,* January 9, 1809; John Stanford, *Annual Report, 1827, to the Honourable the Mayor & Common Council of the City of New-York, on the Subject of Religious Services Performed at the Alms-House, Penitentiary, New Hospital, Debtors' Prison and Bridewell* (New York, 1828), 3–4.

7. SRPW, Minute Books, 1797–1932, entry for November 27, 1823;

New-York Evening Post, November 14, 1816, November 29, 1822; Philip M. Whelpley, *A Sermon, Delivered on the 4th of February, 1816, for the Benefit of a Society of Ladies, Instituted for the Relief of Poor Widows with Small Children* (New York, 1816), 15.

8. *New-York Evening Post*, March 12, 1817; SRPW, Minute Books, 1797–1932, entry for November 21, 1822; *Assembly Journal*, 47th session (1824), II, Appendix B, 44; SPP, *Report on Pauperism*, 6.

9. SRPW, Minute Books, 1797–1932, entry for April 1800; *Assembly Journal*, 47th session (1824), II, Appendix B, 44; *MCC*, XII, 158; John H. Rice, *Charity at Home: A Sermon, Preached for the Benefit of the United Domestic Missionary Society* (New York, 1824), 15; John H. Hobart, *The Claims of the Orphan* (New York, 1820), 7.

10. *Daily Advertiser*, December 15, 1789; *Commercial Advertiser*, November 1, 1798; *MCC*, IX, 361; *New-York Evening Post*, February 26, 1817.

11. Lincoln, ed., *Messages from the Governors*, II, 914–915; *Assembly Journal*, 47th session (1824), II, Appendix B, 38–45.

12. *Mercantile Advertiser*, December 24, 1807.

13. *New-York Daily Advertiser*, February 19, 1824; *Christian Herald*, IV (November 29, 1817), 145; William O. Bourne, *History of the Public School Society of the City of New York* (New York, 1870), 90; Stafford, *New Missionary Field*, 42; Samuel Ackerly to Stephen Allen, June 4, 1827, Allen Papers; *New-York Evening Post*, March 3, 1817; *MCC*, IX, 236, 324, 361.

14. SRPW, Minute Books, 1797–1932, entry for November 16, 1815; *Commercial Advertiser*, January 18, 1805, December 11, 1811, January 8, December 30, 1813, March 9, 1814; *American Citizen*, May 13, 1800; New-York Asylum for Lying-in Women, Minutes of the Visiting Committee, 1823–1831, entries for April 5, October 21, 1824; *MCC*, IX, 61–62; Milnor, *The Widow and Her Mites*, 21; *New-York Evening Post*, March 15, 1806, January 22, 1829.

15. *Mercantile Advertiser*, January 17, 1811; *Commercial Advertiser*, February 1, 1814.

16. *New-York Daily Advertiser*, May 8, 1822; *Commercial Advertiser*, December 11, 1811; *New-York Evening Post*, July 5, 1814; Shamrock Society of New-York, *Emigration to America. Hints to Emigrants from Europe, Who Intend to Make a Permanent Residence in the United States* (New York, 1817), 13; *Christian Herald*, IX (May 18, 1822), 21; James Hardie, *The History of the Tread-Mill* (New York, 1824), 27; *New-York Magazine*, I (July 1814), 176–177.

17. SRPW, Minute Books, 1797–1932, entry for November 18, 1813; *Morning Chronicle*, October 14, 1802; Felix Pascalis to Common Council, November 14, 1808, box 3180, City Clerk Documents; *New-York Evening Post*, October 27, 1815; *Commercial Advertiser*, February 1, 1813.

CHAPTER 11

1. John Griscom, *A Discourse on the Importance of Character and Education in the United States* (New York, 1823), 7.
2. Two important interpretive studies on moral stewardship in the early nineteenth century are Clifford S. Griffin, *Their Brothers' Keepers: Moral Stewardship in the United States, 1800–1865* (New Brunswick, N. J., 1960), and Charles I. Foster, *An Errand of Mercy: The Evangelical United Front, 1790–1837* (Chapel Hill, N. C., 1960).
3. *New-York Weekly Journal*, February 14, 1737; *Gazette of the United States*, August 1, December 16, 1789; *MCC*, III, 337–338; *Commercial Advertiser*, March 16, 1805, May 17, 1817; *Assembly Journal*, 47th session (1824), II, Appendix B, 135.
4. Rodgers, Sermon for the Presbyterian Charity School, November 6, 1791, Rodgers Papers; Lincoln, ed., *Messages from the Governors*, II, 512, 528; Philip Lindsley to John Griscom, September, 17, 1823, John Griscom Correspondence, NYPL.
5. *Independent Journal*, December 8, 1784; *Daily Advertiser*, December 11, 1789, December 28, 1802; *New-York Daily Gazette*, October 8, 1790; *Greenleaf's New York Journal*, December 30, 1796; *Commercial Advertiser*, December 1, 1801, December 11, 1802, January 27, 1825; *New-York Evening Post*, December 26, 1803, December 20, 1809; *MCC*, II, 404, 628–629, VI, 565–566; *Laws*, 24th session, April 8, 1801, Chapter 189; Congregation of Sheareth Israel to De Witt Clinton, April 23, 1811, reel 2, Clinton Papers.
6. Kenneth Roberts and Anna M. Roberts, trans. and eds., *Moreau de St. Méry's American Journey, 1793–1798* (Garden City, N. Y., 1947), 152; *Daily Advertiser*, December 11, 1789, November 16, 1796; *New-York Weekly Museum*, November 13, 1790; *New-York Evening Post*, December 16, 1806; *Commercial Advertiser*, October 23, 1817; *Laws*, 18th session, April 9, 1795, Chapter 75; *ibid.*, 36th session, March 12, 1813, Chapter 42. The newspapers of November and December of each year are full of notices of charity sermons for the church schools.
7. Rodgers, Sermon for the Presbyterian Charity School, November 6, 1791, Rodgers Papers; *Independent Journal*, December 8, 1784; *American Minerva* (New York), October 10, 1794; *New-York Evening Post*, November 30, 1804, November 28, 1806, November 30, 1809.
8. *Daily Advertiser*, November 20, 1786, October 27, 1789, May 10, 1793; *Minerva*, November 15, 1796; *New-York Evening Post*, December 30, 1809; *Assembly Journal*, 47th session (1824), II, Appendix A, 24.
9. *MCC*, VII, 462, XIII, 244, 714; Petition of, Trustees of the African Free School, January 14, 1813, box 3181, City Clerk Documents;

Remonstrance of Inhabitants against the Petition of the African Free School, March 8, 1813, *ibid.*

10. Charles C. Andrews, *The History of the New-York African Free Schools* (New York, 1830), 47, 69–72, 111–112; *Commercial Advertiser*, February 14, 1806.

11. *Laws*, 18th session, April 9, 1795, Chapter 75; *ibid.*, 20th session, March 10, 1797, Chapter 34; *MCC*, II, 281, 296, 404, 628–629.

12. *Laws*, 24th session, April 8, 1801, Chapter 189; *MCC*, III, 12. The City Clerk Documents contain the annual school reports to the common council.

13. *New-York Evening Post*, March 6, 1812; John W. Pratt, *Religion, Politics, and Diversity: The Church-State Theme in New York History* (Ithaca, N.Y., 1967), 162–165.

14. *Laws*, 35th session, June 19, 1812, Chapter 242; *ibid.*, 36th session, March 12, 1813, Chapter 52; *ibid.*, 47th session, November 19, 1824, Chapter 276; *MCC*, VII, 775–776; *Commercial Advertiser*, January 27, 1825.

15. *Laws*, 28th session, April 9, 1805, Chapter 108; *New-York Evening Post*, May 7, 1805; Bourne, *Public School Society*, 3.

16. *MCC*, IV, 342, 357–358, 363, V, 76, 245, 649–650; John Murray, Jr., to Common Council, February 2, 1807, Wynant Van Zandt, Jr., Papers, NYPL; Free School Society to Common Council, July 18, 1808, box 3180, City Clerk Documents; *Laws*, 30th session, February 27, 1807, Chapter 20; *ibid.*, 34th session, March 30, 1811, Chapter 84; John Murray, Jr., to De Witt Clinton, March 12, 1808, reel 2, Clinton Papers; Divie Bethune to De Witt Clinton, February 26, 1812, *ibid.*; Thomas Eddy to De Witt Clinton, March 3, 1818, November 19, 1820, reel 3, *ibid.*

17. *Commercial Advertiser*, May 10, 1814, June 12, 1822, February 5, 1824; *New-York Evening Post*, December 3, 1825; *MCC*, XIII, 203–205.

18. *Laws*, 40th session, April 5, 1817, Chapter 145; *ibid.*, 45th session, February 8, 1822, Chapter 24; *ibid.*, 48th session, November 19, 1824, Chapter 276; *MCC*, XII, 630, 635, 680, 715, XIV, 498–499, 506, 521, 821–825, XV, 56–58; De Witt Clinton Diary, 1802–1828, entry for November 5, 1823; De Witt Clinton to Isaac Collins, December 23, 1823, reel 5, Clinton Papers; Stephen Allen to John Morss, February 29, 1824, Allen Papers; *Commercial Advertiser*, January 27, 1825; *New-York Evening Post*, May 5, November 14, 1825.

19. Petition of the Free School Society, December 1822, box 3165, City Clerk Documents; Bourne, *Public School Society*, 7, 15–16.

20. *Ibid.*, 36–39, 636–655; *Commercial Advertiser*, May 6, 1813, May 10, 1814; John F. Reigart, *The Lancasterian System of Instruction in the Schools of New York City* (New York, 1916), 65–85.

21. *Ibid.*, 10, 77–85.

22. *Commercial Advertiser*, February 7, August 7, 1816, October 20,

1820; *New-York Evening Post*, February 23, 26, 27, 1816; *Christian Herald*, x (November 1, 1823), 370; Edwin Wilbur Rice, *The Sunday School Movement, 1780–1917, and the American Sunday School Union, 1817–1917* (Philadelphia, 1917), 55–60.

23. *Commercial Advertiser*, March 21, May 8, July 30, 1816; *The Ninth Report of the New-York Female Union Society for the Promotion of Sabbath Schools* (New York, 1825), 23.

24. *Christian Herald*, i (August 3, 1816), 303, vii (November 4, 1820), 413, ix (May 18, 1822), 25, (February 1, 1823), 561, x (May 17, 1823), 15; *The Evangelical Guardian and Review* (New York), i (February 1818), 452.

25. *Christian Herald*, i (August 17, 1816), 322; *The American Sunday School Teachers' Magazine, and Journal of Education* (New York), i (March 1824), 100, (April 1824), 139, (May 1824), 176; RTS, *An Alphabet of Lessons for Children* (New York, n.d.), 4.

26. *Evangelical Guardian*, i (February 1818), 452, 458; *Commercial Advertiser*, May 8, 1816, February 9, 1818; SSUS, *First Report* . . . (New York, 1817), 18; John H. Hobart, *The Beneficial Effects of Sunday Schools Considered; In An Address* (New York, 1818), 28; James Milnor, *Address Delivered before the Superintendents, Teachers, and Pupils, of the Sunday Schools Attached to St. George's Church* (New York, 1817), 6; YMBS, *Second Annual Report* . . . (New York, 1826), 5; *Sunday School Teachers' Magazine*, I (January 1824), 60.

27. *Regulations of the Economical School* (New York, 1810); HSS, *First Annual Report* . . . (New York, 1825); *New-York Evening Post*, July 31, December 13, 1810, March 3, 1820; *Commercial Advertiser*, November 15, 1820; Bourne, *Public School Society*, 652–664.

28. William W. Campbell, *The Life and Writings of De Witt Clinton* (New York, 1849), 332; FSS, *Twentieth Annual Report* . . . (New York, 1825), 8; Bourne, *Public School Society*, xx.

CHAPTER 12

1. Perry Miller, *The Life of the Mind in America: From the Revolution to the Civil War* (New York, 1965), 57.

2. Ely, *Visits of Mercy*, i, xvi.

3. Stafford, *New Missionary Field*, 22; *Christian Herald*, xi (July 17, 1824), 427; RTS, *Sixth Annual Report* . . . (New York, 1818), 55; RTS, *Eighth Annual Report* . . . (New York, 1820), 67; McVickar, *Address before Auxiliary*, 21.

4. John Stanford, *A Discourse on Opening the New Building in the House of Refuge, New York, Established for the Reformation of Juvenile Offenders*, December 25, 1825, box 2, Stanford Manuscripts; Stafford, *New Missionary Field*, 49; FMS, *Second Annual Report* . . . (New York, 1818), 5; Oliver W. Elsbree, *The Rise*

of the Missionary Spirit in America, 1790–1815 (Williamsport, Pa., 1928), 150.

5. Stafford, *New Missionary Field*, 41, 44; Rice, *Charity at Home*, 15; NYBS, *First Report* . . . (New York, 1820), 10.

6. Charles I. Foster, "The Urban Missionary Movement, 1814–1837," *Pennsylvania Magazine of History and Biography*, LXXXV (January 1951), 49; Ralph E. Pumphrey, "Compassion and Protection: Dual Motivations in Social Welfare," *Social Service Review*, XXXIII (March 1959), 21–29.

7. *MCC*, I, 169, VIII, 93; *Commercial Advertiser*, December 14, 1813.

8. *New-York Evening Post*, November 12, 1810; Ezra Stiles Ely, *A Sermon for the Rich to Buy, That They May Benefit Themselves and the Poor* (New York, 1810), 24.

9. *Commercial Advertiser*, December 14, 1813, December 13, 1820; John R. Murray to Common Council, February 8, 1813, box 3181, City Clerk Documents; Charles G. Sommers, *Memoir of the Rev. John Stanford, D.D.* (New York, 1835), 111–112, 314.

10. *Commercial Advertiser*, December 14, 1813, December 13, 1820; SSGP, *Second Report* . . . (New York, 1815); John Stanford, Annual Report for 1822 to the Trustees of the Society for Preaching the Gospel among the Poor, Stanford Manuscripts; John Stanford, Diary, 1816–1831, *ibid.*; John Stanford, List of Sermons Preached, 1814–1830, box 2, *ibid.*

11. Report of Committee of Charity on Petition of the Trustees of the African Church, December 8, 1817, box 3175, City Clerk Documents; John Edwards to Common Council, January 26, 1824, box 3152, *ibid.; MCC*, XIII, 511.

12. *Commercial Advertiser*, March 1, 1809, May 16, 1816; *New-York Evening Post*, March 8, November 27, December 21, 1809; David J. Fant, *The Bible in New York: The Romance of Scripture Distribution in a World Metropolis from 1809 to 1948* (New York, 1948), 4–12.

13. *Commercial Advertiser*, May 16, 1816; ABCPB, *First Annual Report* . . . (New York, 1817), 7.

14. FABS, *Sixth Annual Report* . . . (New York, 1822), 26.

15. *Commercial Advertiser*, February 16, 1820; Fant, *Bible in New York*, 12.

16. *Christian Herald*, VIII (February 2, 1822), 569; MBS, *First Report* . . . (New York, 1817), 5–6; NYBS, *Seventh Report* . . . (New York, 1816), 7; FABS, *Eighth Annual Report* . . . (New York, 1824), 4; FABS, *Constitution and By-Laws* . . . (New York, 1816), 7.

17. FABS, *Eighth Annual Report*, 7, 13.

18. NYBS, *First Report* . . . (New York, 1820), 9, 10, 16; RTS, *Ninth Annual Report* . . . (New York, 1821), 10.

19. MBS, *Third Annual Report* . . . (New York, 1819), 8; FABS, *Tenth Annual Report* . . . (New York, 1826), 10, 14; *Christian*

Herald, IX (April 5, 1823), 690; ABS, Minutes of the Standing Committee, I (April 21, 1817), American Bible Society Manuscripts, ABS; FABS, *Sixth Annual Report,* 10; FABS, *Eleventh Annual Report* . . . (New York, 1827), 13; NYBS, *First Report,* 14.

20. NYBS, *First Report,* 10; M. Bruen, *A Discourse, Delivered at the Anniversary of the New-York Female Auxiliary Bible Society* (New York, 1823), 12; MBS, *Second Annual Report* . . . (New York, 1818), 8. See also *Christian Herald,* IX (August 3, 1822), 180.

21. ABCPB, *Fourth Annual Report* . . . (New York, 1820), 7; Elias Boudinot's Last Speech, May 10, 1821, Elias Boudinot Transcripts, 202, ABS; *Christian Herald,* IX (May 18, 1822), 18–19; MBS, *Constitution* . . . (New York, 1817), 5.

22. RTS, *Thirteenth Annual Report* . . . (New York, 1825), 5, 38–40.

23. RTS, First Annual Report . . . 1813, unpaged manuscript, New York City Mission Society; RTS, *Third Annual Report* . . . (New York, 1815), 10; RTS, *Fourth Annual Report* . . . (New York, 1816), 18; RTS, *Ninth Annual Report,* 21; RTS, *Twelfth Annual Report* . . . (New York, 1824), 5.

24. RTS, *A Caution Against Our Common Enemy* (New York, 1814), 3; RTS, *An Address, By Several Ministers in New-York, to Their Christian Fellow-citizens, Dissuading Them from Attending Theatrical Representations* (New York, 1812), 1, 5; RTS, *A Dialogue Between Two Seamen after a Storm* (New York, 1820), 5–7; RTS, *Alphabet of Lessons.*

25. RTS, *The Happy Cottagers* (New York, n.d.), 15; RTS, *The Dairyman's Daughter* (New York, n.d.), 4; RTS, *Pastoral Visits, and a Serious Address to Children and Youth* (New York, 1816), 1–2; RTS, *The Happy Man: or, The Life of William Kelly* (New York, n.d.), 6–8, 15.

26. RTS, *Tenth Annual Report* . . . (New York, 1822), 18–19; RTS, *Fifth Annual Report* . . . (New York, 1817), 45, 47; RTS, *Pastoral Visits,* 1; RTS, *Thirteenth Annual Report,* 9–12.

27. *An Account of the Benevolent Christian Society in the City of New-York* (New York, 1815); MCC, VIII, 90–91, 93–94.

28. YMMS, *First Annual Report* . . . (New York, 1817), 3; YMMS, *History of the Young Men's Missionary Society of New-York, Containing a Correct Account of the Recent Controversy Respecting Hopkinsian Doctrines* (New York, 1817), 8–11; Gardiner Spring, *A Brief View of the Facts, Which Gave Rise to the New-York Evangelical Missionary Society of Young Men* (New York, 1817), 4–16.

29. *Christian Herald,* VIII (August 4, 1821), 183–184; YMMS, *Third Annual Report* . . . (New York, 1818), 16–18.

30. EMSYM, *Proceedings of the First Anniversary,* 4–5; EMSYM, *Second Annual Report* . . . (New York, 1818), 45–46, 60; EMSYM, *Fifth Annual Report* . . . (New York, 1821), 14–15.

31. *Christian Herald,* VI (June 5, 1819), 122, (January 29, 1820), 569,

x (July 19, 1823), 154, (September 6, 1823), 252, xi (March 20, 1824), 186; Stafford, *New Missionary Field*, 34.

32. Alexander McClelland, *Plea for a Standing Ministry* (New York, 1818), 35–37; EMSYM, *Proceedings of the First Anniversary*, 27, 31; *Christian Herald*, viii (August 4, 1821), 185, (January 19, 1822), 540, x (July 5, 1823), 123, xi (January 17, 1824), 61, (April 3, 1824), 210.

33. Stafford, *New Missionary Field*, 16, 22, 29.

34. De Witt Clinton to Ward Stafford, December 17, 1817, reel 5, Clinton Papers; *Proceedings of a Convention of Delegates for the Formation of a Domestic Missionary Society* (New York, 1822), 1–3; UDMS, *Second Report* . . . (New York, 1824), 5–8; AHMS, *Constitution* . . . (New York, 1826).

35. *Commercial Advertiser*, July 15, 1815; Gardiner Spring, *An Appeal to the Citizens of New-York, in Behalf of the Christian Sabbath* (New York, 1823), 16.

CHAPTER 13

1. *The Letters and Papers of Cadwallader Colden* (New-York Historical Society *Collections*, lxviii, 1935), ix, 278; Bridenbaugh, *Cities in Revolt*, 358.

2. Othniel A. Pendleton, Jr., "Temperance and the Evangelical Churches," *Journal of the Presbyterian Historical Society*, xxv (March 1947), 15; John M. Duncan, *Travels through Part of the United States and Canada in 1818 and 1819* (2 vols., New York, 1823), ii, 322; Adam Hodgson, *Letters from North America, Written during a Tour in the United States and Canada* (2 vols., London, 1824), ii, 249; Basil Hall, *Travels in North America, in the Years 1827 and 1828* (3 vols., Edinburgh, 1829), ii, 84; Barck, ed., *Letters from John Pintard*, ii, 8.

3. *Daily Advertiser*, February 10, 1789; Humane Society, *Report on Tavern Licenses*, 6; *Christian Herald*, ix (July 20, 1822), 150, 151; SPP, *Documents Relative to Savings Banks, Intemperance, and Lotteries* (New York, 1819), 19.

4. Philadelphus, *The Moral Plague of Civil Society; or, the Pernicious Effects of the Love of Money on the Morals of Mankind: Exemplified in the Encouragement Given to the Use of Ardent Spirits in the United States, with the Proper Remedy for the Cure of This National Evil* (Philadelphia, 1821), 2–3, 15; Lyman Beecher, *Six Sermons on the Nature, Occasions, Signs, Evils, and Remedy of Intemperance* (Boston, 1827), 62; Charles Beecher, ed., *Autobiography, Correspondence, etc., of Lyman Beecher, D.D.* (2 vols., New York, 1864), i, 245.

5. Humane Society, *Report on Tavern Licenses*, 5, 8–9; [Anonymous], *Considerations on the Customary Use of Spirituous Liquors, by a Philanthropist* (Burlington, N. J., 1811), 10; Thomas Herttell, *An*

Exposé of the Causes of Intemperate Drinking, and the Means By Which It May Be Obviated (New York, 1819), 5; Alexander Gunn, *A Sermon, on the Prevailing Vice of Intemperate Drinking* (New York, 1813), 9, 13, 15.

6. Benjamin Rush, *An Inquiry into the Effects of Ardent Spirits upon the Human Body and Mind* (New York, 1811), 5–6; *Daily Advertiser*, June 25, 1789; John Stanford, *An Introductory Discourse, Delivered to the Lunatics in the Asylum, City of New-York* (New York, 1821), 4; *Forlorn Hope*, May 24, 1800; *Christian Herald*, IX (September 7, 1822), 248 (September 21, 1822), 264; *Commercial Advertiser*, August 2, 1820; Humane Society, *Report on Tavern Licenses*, 9; NYTS, *First Annual Report* . . . (New York, 1830), appendix, 2–3.

7. Humane Society, *Report on Tavern Licenses*, 7; MCC, VII, 73; *New-York Evening Post*, March 12, 1817; *Assembly Journal*, 47th session (1824), I, 387; NYTS, *First Annual Report*, 29.

8. L. H. Butterfield, ed., *Letters of Benjamin Rush* (2 vols., Princeton, N. J., 1951), I, 462; Nathaniel S. Prime, *The Pernicious Effects of Intemperance in the Use of Ardent Spirits, and the Remedy for that Evil; A Sermon* (Brooklyn, 1812), 4; [Anonymous], *Considerations on Spirituous Liquors*, 3; Philadelphus, *Moral Plague of Civil Society*, 5.

9. Beecher, *Six Sermons*, 54.

10. *New-York Evening Post*, November 17, 1809; MCC, IX, 236.

11. Humane Society, *Report on Tavern Licenses*, 6; SPP, *Documents Relative to Savings Banks, Intemperance, and Lotteries*, 18–19.

12. Herttell, *Exposé of Causes of Intemperate Drinking*, 7; *New-York Evening Post*, March 5, 1816; Humane Society, *Report on Tavern Licenses*, 8; Hardie, *History of the Tread-Mill*, 55; Gunn, *Sermon on Intemperate Drinking*, 9.

13. *Ibid.*, 14; *Christian Herald*, V (March 6, 1819), 718–719; SPP, Rough Minutes, 1819–1823, entry for December 5, 1821, NYHS.

14. MCC, VI, 788, 793, XIII, 301; Samuel Miller and Thomas Eddy to Common Council, December 23, 1811, box 3149, City Clerk Documents; Cadwallader D. Colden to Charles G. Haines, December 1, 1819, in SPP, *Second Annual Report*, 53; Stephen Allen to John Morss, February 18, 1823, Letterbook, 1821–1849, Allen Papers.

15. MCC, X, 298–300, XII, 198–200.

16. *Ibid.*, 162; *Commercial Advertiser*, April 3, 1817; Philadelphus, *Moral Plague of Civil Society*, 6.

17. [Anonymous], *Considerations on Spirituous Liquors*, 3; Philadelphus, *Moral Plague of Civil Society*, 6; Herttell, *Exposé of Causes of Intemperate Drinking*, 16–18; Beecher, *Six Sermons*, 73; John James Bound, *The Means of Curing and Preventing Intemperance* (New York, 1820), 38.

18. Joseph R. Gusfield, *Symbolic Crusade: Status Politics and the American Temperance Movement* (Urbana, Ill., 1963), 5.

CHAPTER 14

1. *Daily Advertiser*, March 12, 1789, February 16, 1790. See also Harold Syrett, ed., *The Papers of Alexander Hamilton* (15 vols. to date, New York, 1961–1969), x, 251–253, and New York Manufacturing Society, Constitution and Minutes, 1789–1792, NYHS.

2. *MCC*, VII, 763–764; *New-York Evening Post*, July 5, 1814, October 27, 1815, November 29, 1819; *Plan of the Society for the Promotion of Industry; with the First Report of the Board of Managers* (New York, 1816), 2; George W. Bethune, *Memoirs of Mrs. Joanna Bethune* (New York, 1863), 122.

3. *Time-Piece*, December 25, 1797; *Mercantile Advertiser*, December 31, 1807, March 30, 1809; *Commercial Advertiser*, November 28, 30, December 8, 1809; *New-York Evening Post*, February 26, 1817; Marinus Willett to De Witt Clinton, February 3, 1818, reel 3, Clinton Papers; Presentment of Grand Jury of the Court of General Sessions, August 18, 1820, box 3165, City Clerk Documents.

4. *MCC*, VII, 661, VIII, 384, XI, 694–696; Richard Furman to Stephen Allen, December 11, 1821, box 3149, City Clerk Documents.

5. *MCC*, XII, 158; Minutes of the Commisisoners of the Alms House, 1808–1829, entry for July 27, 1822; *Report of Special Committee on Pauperism, May 31, 1830* (n.p., n.d.), 9–10.

6. Stafford, *New Missionary Field*, 42; *Commercial Advertiser*, December 15, 1815.

7. On the influence of Bentham, see Edward Livingston to Jeremy Bentham, August 10, 1829, July 1, 1830, in John Bowring, ed., *The Works of Jeremy Bentham* (11 vols., Edinburgh, 1843), XI, 23, 51.

8. Robert R. Livingston to Edward Livingston, August 23, 1801, box 32, Robert R. Livingston Papers, NYHS.

9. Edward Livingston to James Warner, January 1, 1803, in *New-York Evening Post*, February 24, 1803.

10. Minutes of the General Society of Mechanics and Tradesmen of the City of New York, entry for January 4, 1803, typescript at offices of the society, 20 West 44th Street, New York City.

11. Mechanics Society Minutes, entries for January 5, February 2, 1803. The draft committee consisted of Jacob Sherred, John Mills, Peter H. Wendover, Philip I. Arcularius, and Cornelius Cryger.

12. Mechanics Society to Edward Livingston, February 2, 1803, in *New-York Evening Post*, February 24, 1803.

13. *Daily Advertiser*, January 19, 1803.

14. Mechanics Society Minutes, entry for February 2, 1803.

15. *Mercantile Advertiser*, February 25, 1803.

16. *Assembly Journal*, 26th session (1803), 96–109; *New-York Evening Post*, March 30, 1803.

17. *MCC*, III, 206, 209, 210–211, 213.

18. *Daily Advertiser*, March 5, 1803; *Commercial Advertiser*, March 5, 1803.

19. *Assembly Journal*, 26th session (1803), 178, 218.

20. *New-York Evening Post*, March 15, 21, 1803; *Daily Advertiser*, March 19, 1803; *American Citizen*, March 30, 1803.

21. *New-York Evening Post*, March 10, 19, 1803; *American Citizen*, March 18, 1803.

22. *New-York Evening Post*, March 21, 25, 29, 1803.

23. *Ibid.*, March 25, 26, 1803; *Daily Advertiser*, March 19, 1803.

24. *New-York Evening Post*, March 19, 25, 29, April 25, 1803.

25. *American Citizen*, March 26, April 11, 12, 23, 26, 1803; *Morning Chronicle*, April 27, 1803.

26. *New-York Evening Post*, April 29, 1803; *American Citizen*, April 30, 1803. Complete returns for New York City, Richmond, Brooklyn, Queens, Suffolk, and Westchester gave Broome 3,679 votes and Benson 2,918. Republicans triumphed throughout the state, taking eighty-three assembly seats to seventeen for the Federalists. See *American Citizen*, June 6, 1803, and Jabez D. Hammond, *The History of Political Parties in the State of New-York* (2 vols., Cooperstown, N. Y., 1847), I, 194–195.

27. Staughton Lynd and Alfred Young, "After Carl Becker: The Mechanics and New York City Politics, 1774–1801," *Labor History*, V (Fall 1964), 224; David Hackett Fischer, *The Revolution of American Conservatism: The Federalist Party in the Era of Jeffersonian Democracy* (New York, 1965), 150.

28. Livingston resigned as mayor because of embezzlement of customhouse receipts by a subordinate in the federal attorney's office, for which Livingston accepted full responsibility. He moved to New Orleans and began a new career in public service, serving as Louisiana legislator, United States representative, United States senator, secretary of state, and minister to France. Significantly, he never lost interest in humanitarian schemes, and the same plan to provide work relief to the poor was embodied in his famous Louisiana Code of the 1820's. See National Prison Association, *The Complete Works of Edward Livingston on Criminal Jurisprudence* (2 vols., New York, 1873), I, 528–537, 566–567; Eugene Smith, "Edward Livingston and the Louisiana Codes," *Columbia Law Review*, II (January 1902), 24–36.

CHAPTER 15

1. *Columbian*, February 20, 1817; Barck, ed., *Letters from John Pintard*, I, 97–98; Lincoln, ed., *Messages from the Governors*, II, 914–915; Thomas Eddy to De Witt Clinton, February 15, 1817, reel 3, Clinton Papers.

2. *New-York Evening Post*, March 12, 1817; *MCC*, IX, 360–362; *Commercial Advertiser*, August 16, 19, 20, 22, 25, 26, 27, 1817. The

Philadelphia organization suggested, among other things, careful investigation of all relief recipients, better education and apprenticeship training, public employment of the poor, and temperance reform.

3. SPP, *Report on Pauperism*, 2; John H. Griscom, *Memoir of John Griscom, LL.D.* (New York, 1859), 157–158; Barck, ed., *Letters from John Pintard*, I, 97.

4. *New-York Evening Post*, March 9, 10, 1818; Thomas Eddy to John Griscom, July 8, 1818, in Samuel L. Knapp, *The Life of Thomas Eddy* (New York, 1834), 284; SPP, *Report on Pauperism*, 3–4, 19. Of the eighty-nine individuals who served as managers of the SPP during its six years of existence, sixty-nine are identifiable. They came almost exclusively from the middle-class business and professional strata and included thirty-two merchants, eleven attorneys, eight physicians, six clergymen, five politicians, five mechanics, two teachers, and one editor.

5. *Ibid.*, 4–9.

6. *Ibid.*, 13–16; *New-York Evening Post*, February 24, March 12, 1818.

7. SPP, *Report on Pauperism*, 12; *Sunday School Teachers' Magazine*, I (September 1824), 310. See also SPP, Visitor's Book, n.d., NYHS. This record book, apparently the only one extant, covered a four-block area bounded by Broadway on the east, Chapel Street on the west, Leonard Street on the south, and White Street on the north—a district of three hundred whites and sixty-three blacks, most of the latter domestic servants or slaves. Visitors recommended five children to Sunday schools and rounded up five new teachers.

8. SPP, *First Annual Report* . . . (New York, 1818), 4–5; SPP, *Second Annual Report*, 5; *New-York Daily Advertiser*, February 15, 1820.

9. SPP, *Second Annual Report*, 6–11; SPP, *Documents Relative to Savings Banks, Intemperance, and Lotteries*, 17; *Commercial Advertiser*, December 15, 1818.

10. SPP, *Report to the Managers of the Society for the Prevention of Pauperism in New-York: by Their Committee on Idleness and Sources of Employment* (New York, 1819), 10–12; SPP, *Fifth Report* . . . (New York, 1821), 29–31; *New-York Evening Post*, April 18, 1820.

11. SPP, *Second Annual Report*, 13; SPP, *Fourth Annual Report* . . . (New York, 1821), 31; *Commercial Advertiser*, January 12, 13, 1819.

12. SPP, *Second Annual Report*, 17–36; SPP, *Documents Relative to Savings Banks, Intemperance, and Lotteries*, 21–26; SPP, *Report on the Penitentiary System in the United States* (New York, 1822).

13. SPP, *Fifth Report*, 8, 21, 24, 27; *Commercial Advertiser*, February 14, 1823.

14. Barck, ed., *Letters from John Pintard*, II, 356.

15. John Pintard, Remarks on a Plan for forming a Savings Association, December 11, 1809, box 11, John Pintard Papers, NYHS; *New-York Gazette,* November 29, 1816; *New-York Evening Post,* December 2, 1816; *Commercial Advertiser,* December 5, 1818.

16. *Ibid.,* June 26, 1819.

17. *Ibid.,* July 1, 6, 1819, February 15, 1820; *New-York Daily Advertiser,* March 7, 1821; *MCC,* x, 752–753.

18. *New-York Evening Post,* February 21, 1821.

19. *Ibid.,* May 7, 1821; *Commercial Advertiser,* June 1, 1821; SPP, *Fifth Report,* 38; SPP, Rough Minutes, 1819–1823, February 7, 21, March 21, 1821. Despite this failure, New York's philanthropists remained undaunted, for John Pintard reported in 1827 that a new fuel fund had been formed, one he hoped would benefit from past errors. Barck, ed., *Letters from John Pintard,* II, 356.

20. *Ibid.,* I, 104. See SPP, Rough Minutes, 1819–1823, for the variety of SPP concerns and activities.

21. *Ibid.,* January 12, March 1, 1820, December 5, 1821; SPP, *Second Annual Report,* 13–14, 83–91; SPP, *Plain Directions on Domestic Economy* (New York, 1821).

22. John Murray, Jr., to John Griscom, February 13, 1819, Griscom Correspondence; Cadwallader D. Colden to Charles G. Haines, December 1, 24, 1819, in SPP, *Second Annual Report,* 58–79.

23. John Pintard, Diary, 1798–1799, entry for January 17, 1799, box 8, Pintard Papers; John Griscom, *A Year in Europe, in 1818 and 1819* (2 vols., New York, 1824), I, 94, II, 262, 314; Knapp, *Life of Eddy,* 178–281.

24. Patrick Colquhoun, *A New and Appropriate System of Education for the Labouring People* (London, 1806), 78; Patrick Colquhoun, *A Treatise on Indigence* (London, 1806), 7–9, 11, 248–281. Colquhoun's ideas on poverty and indigence were regurgitated word for word in SPP, *Report on Idleness and Sources of Employment,* 4–5.

25. *New-York Evening Post,* December 24, 1802, February 16, May 10, 1803; Patrick Colquhoun to Thomas Eddy, February 19, 1803, July 26, 1808, April 19, June 14, 1816, February 20, 1818, in Knapp, *Life of Eddy,* 196–198, 220, 249, 257–258, 272.

26. SPP, Rough Minutes, 1819–1823, January 23, 1822.

27. *Christian Herald,* VII (March 3, 1821), 656; *New-York Evening Post,* August 22, 1821.

28. *Ibid.,* August 25, 30, 1821; *Commercial Advertiser,* December 19, 1821; SPP, *Fifth Report,* 5–6.

29. John Stanford, A Discourse on Opening the New Building in the House of Refuge, New York, Established for the Reformation of Juvenile Offenders, December 25, 1825, box 2, Stanford Manuscripts.

30. SPP, *Sixth Annual Report* . . . (New York, 1823), 4–12; Griscom, *Memoir of John Griscom,* 166–216.

31. SPP, *Report of a Committee Appointed by the Society for the Prevention of Pauperism, in the City of New-York, on the Expediency of Erecting an Institution for the Reformation of Juvenile Delinquents* (New York, 1824), 2, 24, 63; *Commercial Advertiser,* December 24, 1823. Detailed information about the London Philanthropic Society's asylum was sent to Griscom by one of its managers. See Peter Bedford to John Griscom, February 24, 1824, Griscom Correspondence.

32. *Commercial Advertiser,* November 23, 1825; N. C. Hart to Stephen Allen, December 17, 1834, Allen Papers.

33. James Pillans to John Griscom, October 27, 1821, Griscom Correspondence; John Griscom to John Pintard, August 17, 1821, June 8, 1826, boxes 7 and 8, Pintard Papers; John Griscom, *Monitorial Instruction: An Address Pronounced at the Opening of the New-York High-School* (New York, 1825), 192, 196–197, 213, 216.

34. SPP, *Documents Relative to Savings Banks, Intemperance, and Lotteries,* 21.

CHAPTER 16

1. Merle Curti, "Tradition and Innovation in American Philanthropy," *Proceedings of the American Philosophical Society,* 105 (April 1961), 146.

2. Knapp, *Life of Eddy,* 39.

3. *Commercial Advertiser,* August 16, 26, 1817; William E. Channing, *The Ministry for the Poor: A Discourse Delivered before the Benevolent Fraternity of Churches in Boston, on Their First Anniversary, April 9, 1835* (Boston, 1835), 3. See also Benjamin M. and Sylvia K. Selekman, "Mathew Carey," *Harvard Business Review,* XIX (Spring 1941), 326–341; Joseph McColgan, *Joseph Tuckerman: Pioneer in American Social Work* (Washington, 1940); and Blanche D. Coll, "The Baltimore Society for the Prevention of Pauperism, 1820–1822," *American Historical Review,* LVI (October 1955), 77–87.

4. Jacob A. Riis, *How the Other Half Lives* (paperback ed., New York, 1957), 35, 186. For surveys of the AICP, the COS, and the professionalization of social welfare, see Robert H. Bremner, *From the Depths: The Discovery of Poverty in the United States* (New York, 1956) and Roy Lubove, *The Professional Altruist: The Emergence of Social Work as a Career, 1880–1930* (Cambridge, Mass., 1965).

Index